GW01375178

CARNIVAL IN TEL AVIV

PURIM AND THE CELEBRATION
OF URBAN ZIONISM

HIZKY SHOHAM

Israel: Society, Culture, and History

Series Editor:
Yaacov Yadgar, Political Studies, Bar-Ilan University

Editorial Board:
Alan Dowty, Political Science and Middle Eastern Studies, University of Notre Dame
Tamar Katriel, Communication Ethnography, University of Haifa
Avi Sagi, Hermeneutics, Cultural Studies, and Philosophy, Bar-Ilan University
Allan Silver, Sociology, Columbia University
Anthony D. Smith, Nationalism and Ethnicity, London School of Economics
Yael Zerubavel, Jewish Studies and History, Rutgers University

ACADEMIC
STUDIES
PRESS

CARNIVAL IN TEL AVIV

PURIM AND THE CELEBRATION
OF URBAN ZIONISM

HIZKY SHOHAM

BOSTON / 2014

Library of Congress Cataloging-in-Publication Data:
A catalog record for this title is available from the Library of Congress.

Copyright © 2014 Academic Studies Press
All rights reserved

ISBN 978-1-118113-51-1 (hardback)
ISBN 978-1-618113-84-9 (paperback)
ISBN 978-1-618113-62-7 (electronic)

On the cover: "Purim in Tel-Aviv," by Ludwig Blum (1934).
Reproduced by permission of Ludwig Blum estate.

Cover design by Ivan Grave

Published by Academic Studies Press in 2014
28 Montfern Avenue
Brighton, MA 02135, USA
press@academicstudiespress.com
www.academicstudiespress.com

Paula E. Hyman (1946-2011), In Memoriam

Table of Contents

Acknowledgments ... vii
Introduction ... ix

Chapter 1. "All of you to Tel Aviv on Purim": A Local-National Festival ... 1
Chapter 2. "Travelling to Esther": A Civil-Religious and Pilgrimage Event ... 37
Chapter 3. "A Little Bit of Tradition" ... 63
Chapter 4. The Civilized-Carnivalesque Body ... 90
Chapter 5. "Mordechai is Riding a Horse": Political Performance ... 112
Chapter 6. "Our Only Romantic Festival": Hebrew Queen Esther ... 138
Chapter 7. Another New Jew: Urban Zionist Ideology ... 163

References ... 188
Bibliography ... 189
Index ... 219

Acknowledgments

Before acknowledging a number of scholars, colleagues and mentors, I would like to express my gratefulness to my family. Amalia, my best friend on earth, and my children Yehonatan, Noga, Ayelet and Tamar, are all sources of incessant pride and endless fun—two major constituents of the Tel Aviv Purim carnival, as the reader shall see hereafter. I would also like to thank my parents-in-law, Haim and Ester Levanon, for introducing me to the secrets of Purim; and to my parents, Yitzhak and Yonina Florsheim, who taught me that a good question is worth so much more than any answer.

Thanks are due to all the librarians, archivists and workers of the Central Zionist Archives, the poster collection at the national library, the Steven Spielberg Jewish Film Archives and the journal collection at Bar-Ilan University—where the primary sources were collected. I am particularly grateful to Ziona Raz, Nellie Verzerevsky and Rivka Pershel-Gershon from the Tel Aviv Municipal Archive.

In the long line of teachers and mentors whom I have met throughout the years, Adi Ophir, Anat Helman, Derek Penslar, Israel Bartal, Anita Shapira, Margalit Shilo, Arie Saposnik, Jeffrey Alexander, Philip Smith, Elli Stern, Janet Rabinowitch, and Dan Ben-Amos influenced this work majorly. I would also like to thank Yaacov Yadgar for his encouragement. Most of all, I would like to express my deep gratitude to my PhD advisors, Avi Sagi and Jacques Ehrenfreund, for their inspirational and dedicated guidance during the PhD, and for their continuous support afterwards. Avi Sagi, in particular, assisted in overcoming several obstacles to the publication of this book. Special thanks are due to my friends Yair Lipshitz, Avishalom Westreich, Shai Secunda, Micha Perry, Orit Rozin and Nissim Leon, along with my uncle Amotz Asa-el—just for being there.

This book was written over more than a decade, during which I was fortunate to have three academic homes. I was both a student and a lecturer in the Interdisciplinary Program for Hermeneutics and Cultural Studies at Bar-Ilan University. Led by—again—Avi Sagi, this unique program proved to be a most protective and fertile habitat for growing new ideas. My fellows and mentors in the Shalom Hartman Institute in Jerusalem never ceased to provoke new ways of thinking about Jewish cultures. And finally, I am indebted to the program for Judaic Studies at Yale University. I would like to specifically acknowledge Steven Fraade for his never-ending support, and Renee Reed, who always cared for everyone and everything. Most of all, however, I am grateful to Paula Hyman (1946–2011) for her immense encouragement regarding this particular project and so much else. Paula was a passionate scholar, an involved public intellectual, and a dedicated and generous mentor. She was a tough person, but well knew how to laugh. *Carnival in Tel Aviv* is dedicated to her memory.

Introduction

In 1935, in the Purim section of his daily newspaper, Uri Keisari (1901–1979), one of the most notable journalists in British mandate Palestine, described a Tel Aviv street conversation about the carnival. His interlocutor recalled memories from the first Purim celebrations fifteen years earlier, in 1920: "I remember the first year… I came [to Tel Aviv] from Haifa with my friends… each of us had a suitcase… and in each suitcase there was a special garment, a costume." However, a few hours before the ball in "Eden" theater, shocking news was heard: there was an attack on Tel-Hai, an isolated settlement in the upper Galilee, and six Jewish pioneers were killed, including their commander, the Jewish war-hero and Zionist leader Yosef Trumpeldor (1880–1920). The balls were cancelled. Keisari's interlocutor said that since then he could not celebrate Purim anymore "on this very day of Trumpeldor's death." Furthermore, the man criticized the fancy and grandiose Purim celebrations which overshadowed the heritage of Tel-Hai. Keisari asked him: "Don't you think that the popular tradition of the pilgrimage to Tel-Hai is enough?" and the man responded:

> What vanity! A few hundred youngsters break with Purim joy and make the journey to the site. But the masses, do you hear me? The "masses," the people, I'm telling you, they stick with the joy, the merriment of Ahasuerus, Esther and Mordechai! And the pilgrimage does not begin until the festivities are over, right after all four traditional balls, and the youngsters are then making the pilgrimage with scraped knees, broken bodies and tired souls.

Keisari added that "He spoke no more, I stopped asking, and both of us felt that it is not that good to die for the homeland."[1]

---

[1] Uri Keisari, "Keitzad hayim etzlenu: Divrey tuga misaviv le-yud dalet ba'adar…" [How Do We Live: Howlings around the Fourteenth of Adar], *Doar-Hayom* 19.2.1935. Ellipsis in original.

In 1935, the invented tradition of Tel-Hai was already well-established in the cultural life of Jewish Palestine in the British Mandate period (commonly referred to as the *Yishuv*). The name and heritage of Trumpeldor were embraced by Zionists across the political spectrum. Numerous stories, poems, and plays were written about the heroes of Tel-Hai, and an annual ritual emerged on the eleventh of *Adar* (three days before the fourteenth of *Adar*, the day of Purim) to commemorate the bloody incident: a challenging journey to the historical site in the upper Galilee, conducted by Zionist youth movements. The story about the hero who said on his deathbed "it is good to die for our country" (rather than "homeland" as in Keisari's text) had already become an essential part of Zionist political ritual and myth.[2]

Keisari's text directly targeted Purim celebrations. Unlike the Tel-Hai tradition, about which there was a consensus, the Purim celebrations were highly controversial, and were condemned by many as hedonist, escapist, and anti-nationalist. The nationalist criticism of the Tel Aviv Purim carnival deviated from the merely anti-hedonist criticism, since the supporters of the carnival contended that in addition to its economic value, it had educational and cultural value—which particularly aggravated the opponents: How could such a hedonist festival teach self-sacrifice? How could such a capitalist festival encourage the youth to serve the nation? And how could such an exilic festival, which celebrated the rescue of the Jews by court-romanticism, teach Jews the value of self responsibility and self defense?

The incidental proximity between the two invented traditions in the Hebrew calendar led Keisari to create a rhetoric conflict. Historically, Trumpeldor died three days before Purim, and no Purim ball was cancelled in 1920, although a few were postponed (only the carnival procession was cancelled).[3] Interestingly, Keisari conflated the two traditions not only on the calendar but also chronologically, by retrospectively determining an identical point of genesis for both: the Purim day of 1920. These mnemonic proximities sharpened the inevitable confrontation in content between the two different ways of constructing nationalist identity: on the one hand, self-sacrifice for the

---

[2] Goldstein & Shavit 1981; Liebman & Don-Yehiya 1983: 44–48; Zerubavel 1995: 41–43.

[3] "Hed yafo" [Feedback from Jaffa], *Doar-Hayom* 8.3.1920; "Birushalayim" [In Jerusalem], *Ha'aretz* 15.3.1920; *Hapo'el Hatza'ir* 21–22, 12.3.1920, p. 24.

Nation by frontier pioneers; on the other, a hedonist mass-celebration in the main urban center of Jewish Palestine.

Keisari's rhetorical point was that the tradition of Purim was born in sin. It was not a wrong interpretation of a true nationalist holiday, but an essentially anti-nationalist one. As Keisari himself put it bluntly, in another column addressed to the female public: "[Haman] at least knew to die on the gallows. Sometimes it is better to die on the gallows than to fall on the bed. Too bad that good old Mordechai didn't teach Esther this!"[4] A gender distinction between the two holidays was implied here as well: the Tel-Hai tradition was considered masculine, as it commemorated the heroism of "the new Jew," whereas the Purim tradition was depicted as women's business, and hence despised and exilic.

Disappointingly, the masses without a doubt preferred Purim over Tel-Hai. Probably many Purim celebrators, if asked, would agree with Keisari that in principal, "the death of Trumpeldor is much more important than the grace of Ahasuerus to Esther."[5] However, when it came to the Yishuv's public culture, Purim was felt much more strongly than the Tel-Hai tradition in the streets, media, and public life. Whereas Purim was celebrated by the masses on its original day in the calendar, the Tel-Hai Memorial Day was observed by a minority, only a few days after Purim and more than a week after its original day on the calendar, the eleventh of *Adar*.

The Tel Aviv Purim carnival expressed a substantively unfamiliar Zionist ideology: pro-urban, bourgeois, and capitalist. Although this ideology did not advocate for Puritanism and self-sacrifice, but mundane joy, it did propose that this happiness may be achieved within the context of a national framework. Hence, despite critics who viewed the carnival as anti-nationalist, *it did, in fact, express nationalist ideology*. Since the ideology of Urban Zionism didn't have any ideologues, it was neglected as a subject of scholarly study. However, the public event of Purim celebrations in Tel Aviv revealed not only its existence, but also its grip on Yishuv society. These celebrations will be interpreted here as key events through which we can understand Zionism as a mass movement which created an urban culture typical of the industrial age.

---

[4] Uri Keisari, "Ester, Akhashverosh, Haman, Mordekhai et Kompani..." [Esther, Ahasuerus, Haman, Mordechai, and co.], *Doar-Hayom* 22.3.1932.

[5] Keisari, supra note 1.

Urban Zionism

The link between urbanization and modern nationalism, which so troubled Keisari along with many others in the Zionist cultural and political elites, would not seem odd to students of comparative nationalism. In contemporary scholarship, this link is mainly associated with the theory of Ernst Gellner, who analyzed the rise of modern nationalism in the high-modern context of processes of urbanization and industrialization, which necessitated the development of a capitalist division of labor and a mobilizing education system with cultural unity over a defined territory.[6] In the case of Zionism, processes of urbanization and industrialization in late nineteenth- and twentieth-century Palestine and the links between those processes and the Zionist colonization are already well-recognized in economic and geographical literature. Indeed, based on standard measures of patterns of population, economic development, and socio-economic stratification, the Zionist project was in fact—from its outset—an eminently capitalist enterprise of urbanization.[7] However, regarding Zionist ideologies, myths, public rituals, and symbols, the Zionist pro-agriculturalist ethos is too often taken by scholars as a reliable description of the life-experience of Jewish immigrants to Palestine. An illuminating example may be found in the following analysis of Zionism by Gellner himself:

> Normally the nationalist process is inversely related to its verbiage, talking of peasants and making townsmen. Here [in the case of Zionism] it was really necessary to make a few surrogate peasants. [...] The manufacture of such [...] peasants from an urban background could not conceivably be an easy matter, and the surrogate peasant-soldiers were in fact formed by a species of a secular monastic order. This needed an ideology, and by a historic accident the suitable mixture of socialism and populism was indeed available and pervasive in the intellectual milieu in which the order did its recruiting.[8]

---

[6] Gellner 1983. Gellner was not the first, though, to connect the rise of modern nationalism to industrialization. See: Smith 1971.

[7] In a nutshell: Efrat 1984; Katz 1986; Kark 1990; Kellerman 1993; Metzer 1998: 8–9, 215; Troen 2003.

[8] Gellner 1983: 107. The leaps in the quoted text are my own.

Since Gellner's theory linked modern nationalism to the advance of industrialization and urbanization, the Zionist case seemed troubling. From the perspective of his best knowledge of this case, the alleged transformation of the European Jewish middle class into warriors and peasants in Palestine seemed to go against the current. Yet, he does not specify what made the Zionist verbiage essentially different from any other nationalist movements' talk, as this "mixture of socialism and populism" is far from unfamiliar in other types of nationalism, particularly in interwar Europe.[9]

The power of the Zionist pioneers' ethos to determine the image of Zionism for generations and to mislead many prominent scholars in addition to Gellner was derived from antisemitic stereotypes which specifically linked the Jews to European urbanization. The alleged anomie, alienation, and corruption of the industrial revolution were attributed to "typical" Jewish qualities such as detachment from the soil and lack of patriotism.[10] Regardless of their truth, many Zionist writers and activists accepted these stereotypes and desired to "invert the pyramid"; that is, to transform the typical Jewish middle-class city dweller of Central and Eastern Europe into "a new Jew": attached to his land, rooted, and "productive."[11] This internalized stereotype created a powerful anti-urban ethos for Zionism and the Yishuv. From an ideological perspective, rural "productive" life was glorified, and there was constant criticism of urban *"luft-gescheft"* (a derogatory Yiddish designation for "non-productive" livelihoods such as commerce).

Nonetheless, Zionism was a mass movement, and as such was suited to Gellner's theory more than he thought: just like the other types of nationalism, Zionism, from its outset, had been "talking of peasants and making townsmen." Indeed, the anti-urban doctrines had their influence, as the Zionist institutions assigned for settlement did not establish new cities in Palestine throughout the British period (1917–1948).[12] However, the consequence was not the agriculturalization of Palestine or of the Jews: the masses preferred to settle in cities, albeit not in mixed cities, and thus had one main option, namely Tel Aviv. This caused the

---

[9] Hobsbawm 1992: 123–130.

[10] Pulzer 1964: 65–73; Wistrich 1989: chapter 7; Kieval 1999.

[11] Zerubavel 1995: 20–28; Shapira 1997b; Eisenstadt 1998.

[12] Cohen 1977.

city's unparalleled rapid growth, from a population of 2,000 people in 1920, to around 160,000 in 1939, and 248,000 in 1948—which constituted more than a third of the entire Jewish population of Palestine.[13] Hence, this city was the sole center of Urban Zionism.

Since the "masses" were recognized as actually being composed of an urban middle-class which might have been suspicious regarding the socialist-agriculturalist ethos, a recent common scholarly opinion is that this ethos should be analyzed as a recruiting ethos, whose intention was to unify the Jewish society in Palestine, but not to genuinely turn townsmen into peasants. Moreover, the hegemonic Labor Movement itself is recently analyzed as more of a nationalist middle-class movement than a truly socialist one.[14] While there are many good explanations as to how the socialist-agricultural ethos achieved its dominance in the Zionist middle class on the narrow political level of the Labor Movement hegemony over Zionist institutions, the cultural analysis is still missing.[15] It is generally agreed that the key seems to lie with the "secular monastic order" mentioned by Gellner. This was a small group of pioneers who were very ideologically committed to the nationalist project and, in a complicated way, socialists. Some members—such as David Ben-Gurion and Berel Katzenelson—gained considerable power within Zionist institutions during the 1920s and the 1930s and had a major influence over its politics, image, myths, and symbols. Hence, Gellner's source was an acceptable narrative that actually represented the ideology of a very small elite of pioneers. This story constituted the period of "the second immigration" (*ha'aliya hashniya*, between 1903 or 1904 and 1914) as a formative period for the entire Zionist culture and society, and the mythical pioneers were considered the embodiment of the Zionist ideology, since the scholarship on ideology focused on those "monastic" elites.[16]

The pioneers' myths still dominate public opinion and the image of early Zionism: pioneers, *Kibbutzim*, warrior-peasants. The Palestine of early Zionism is too often imagined as a rural space in which sons (and sometimes daughters) of Eastern European Jewish city-dwellers

---

[13] Gertz 1947: 46; Shavit & Bigger 2001: 93; Shavit & Bigger 2007: 22.
[14] Sternhel 1998; Shapira 1996.
[15] For example: Shapiro 1976; Horowitz & Lissak 1978.
[16] See: Alroey 2004: 16–34; Shoham 2013a.

worked hard to become laborers and farmers.[17] This book attempts to defy traditional focus on Zionist elites in the scholarship on the history of Zionism, and instead aims to consider Zionism as a mass movement, focusing on the question: *What was the ideology of Zionism when considered as a mass movement, rather than a monastic movement?*[18]

Methodologically, phrasing the question this way is intended to elicit a more nuanced analysis of the relationship between ideas, society and space. It suggests studying ideology as performed in the public, sphere, rather than in mere programmatic texts.[19] In other words, it suggests focusing on the ethnographic dimensions of nationalism, instead of the narrow political ones.[20] Indeed, the study of Zionist ideology too often ignored the social dimension of ideas, which were treated as words floating in a vacuum.[21] Hence it was convenient for many to focus on the "monastic" movement, which produced a huge amount of ideological texts. These traditional political and intellectual histories treated Urban Zionism as a marginal movement on the ideological level. On one hand, it was assumed that its domination over Jewish economics and geography in Palestine was never converted to political power, let alone cultural domination.[22] In the cultural realm, it was assumed that the Zionist middle class did not make any significant contributions to Zionist myths, ethos, values, or ideology—an assumption that caused the overlooking of the Purim carnival in scholarship about Zionist public culture.[23] On the other hand, Urban Zionism itself was too often portrayed as untruthful to Zionism, as a hedonist "bubble" (as Tel Aviv is often referred to in contemporary Israel) which "subverted" the dominant socialist-agriculturalist ethos,

---

[17] Zakim 2004: 10–11.

[18] For recent discussions of Zionism as a mass-movement see: Halamish 2006; Razi 2009.

[19] Geertz 1973: 193–233; Larrain 1979: 13–16; Williams 1982: 26–30; Williams 1983: 153–157; Ricoeur 1991: 125–143.

[20] Anderson 1983; Chaterjee 1993; Brubaker 1996.

[21] See criticism: Swirsky 1979.

[22] Drory 1987; Drory 1990.

[23] See in particular: Liebman & Don-Yiheya 1983: 29. More about Zionist middle class (not necessarily urban): Giladi 1973; Ben-Porat 1999; Shamir 2000; Karlinsky 2005.

or at least as motivated by "selfish" economic motives alone and lacking interest in collectivist-nationalist activity.[24]

As we shall see hereafter, Urban Zionism was far from the margins, but its ideology had no ideologues. Whereas organized Zionist movements, in particular socialist Zionism, had talented spokespersons who lectured, promoted, and wrote explicit ideological manifestos, Urban Zionism had at most industrialists and administrators, such as Meir Dizengoff (1861–1936), Tel Aviv's chair and mayor from 1910 to 1936 (with but a few gaps).[25] To unearth this ideology, the research should first of all brush the history of Zionism against the traditional doctrinal bias, which treated programmatic and doctrinal texts as if they represent "Zionism" and ignored their complicated interplay with reality. The Tel Aviv Purim celebrations revealed not only that there was such a thing as Urban Zionism, but also affirmed its deep grip on the mainstream Yishuv society and the Zionist project.

It is therefore suggested that Zionism be thought of according to Gellner's theory — without embracing this theory as an all-encompassing explanation, or denying, for example, the significance of the ethnic component in Zionism as emphasized by Gellner's scholarly opponent, the sociologist Anthony Smith.[26] The focus on Urban Zionism strives to go beyond explicit doctrines, in order to understand Zionism as a mass movement rather than the tale (and tail) of the avant-garde "monastic orders."

Culture, Public Culture

In order to correct the anti-urban bias and portray a more balanced picture of Zionist ideology, this book relies on the broad anthropological definition of the concept of "culture." Generally, the recent shift to the concept of "culture" in academic discourse represents an attempt

---

[24] Drory 1983; Alroey 2003. More about Urban Zionism: Carmi & Rosenfeld 1971; Katz 1986; Shavit 2003; Troen 2003: 89–159; and of course: Helman 2007; Helman 2010.

[25] See also: Frenkel, Shenhav & Herzog 2000; Troen 2003: 89–100.

[26] See Smith's criticism of Gellner: Smith 1971: 138–150; Smith 1991. For discussions about their suitability to the case of Zionism see: Shimoni 1995: 4–21; Ben-Israel 1996.

to get beyond the old understanding of the concept as "the best that has been thought and said" and change it to refer to collective meanings and feelings, embedded in various social practices.[27]

One new focus of scholarly attention is *public culture*. It is based on the concept of public sphere, defined by the political theoretician Jürgen Habermas as the mediating sphere between state and society. The public sphere is the aggregate of social and cultural sites in which society appears as an entity that can never be fully dominated by politics, on one hand, but that is directed toward common political action, on the other—such as the modern concept of "public opinion."[28] The sociologist Jeffrey Alexander criticized and altered Habermas's conception of culture, broadly defined as the common myths, symbols, and values, which produce *meanings* with which the public sphere is created and its boundaries maintained.[29] The modern public sphere is comprised of various institutions such as law, politics (voting and other political activities), the world of letters (especially newspapers), and the market, including cultural institutions such as cafés, theaters, books—and festivals.

Historically, the bourgeois public sphere had arisen in the high modern era, accompanied by the rise of the concept of "society" and modern nationalism.[30] When national movements constitute their public sphere, a specific place emerges simultaneously as the physical center of the new public sphere and as its symbolic one: the capital city—not necessarily the official capital city.[31] For the Jewish sector in British Mandate Palestine, it was Tel Aviv that functioned as the center not only for the market, the world of Hebrew letters, and Zionist politics (housing the central offices of most Zionist parties and institutions) —but also its symbolic center, as this book strives to demonstrate (particularly in chapter two). As was recently shown

---

[27] On different meanings of "culture" see, in a nutshell: Hall 1980; Williams 1983: 87–93; Agnew 1986: xii; Brightman 1995; Alexander & Smith 1998; Sewell 1999. On the cultural turn in general see: Chartier 1988; Hunt 1989; Bonnel & Hunt 1999.

[28] Habermas 1989.

[29] Alexander 2006: 16.

[30] On the concept of society see: Arendt 1958: chapter 2; Elias 1978; Williams 1983: 45–48. On bourgeoisie and nationalism see, in particular: Mosse 1985.

[31] Anderson 1983: 53–57.

by historian Anat Helman, literary scholar Barbara Mann, and geographer Maoz Azaryahu, the "Jewishness" of the city's space was twofold: first, the municipality was understood as an "experiment" in Jewish sovereignty. To no less a degree, it was broadly spoken of as the only Jewish public sphere in the world.[32]

This book will attempt to go further and make cautious generalizations regarding ideological connections between Zionism and urbanism, industrialism and capitalism, with implications that extend beyond the local boundaries of Tel Aviv. Hereafter I will exploit the public event of Purim celebrations in Tel Aviv as a case study of Zionist public culture, and a canvas on which the ideological world of Urban Zionism was depicted.[33]

Methodologically, the book is what Bernard Cohn designates an "anthropological history." According to Cohn, historians should take from anthropology the idea of culture as the entire creation of human thought, while anthropologists should take from historians the idea that culture is dynamic and changing over time.[34] On one hand, the book relies broadly on primary sources and attempts to reconstruct the historical event "as it happened," that is, to provide a chronographic account. On the other hand, the questions asked and the models used are sociologically-anthropologically oriented.[35] As early as several decades ago "French cultural history" had notably integrated the broad anthropological definition of "culture" into historical archival research. Within this school, these were the *micro-historians*, who studied one village, one (unfamiliar) person, or one event in order to draw broader conclusions about the studied society. Specifically, my study follows the path of the distinguished monograph *Carnival in Romans* by the historian Emmanuel Le Roy Ladurie, an entire book dedicated to one carnival, held over several weeks in the French town of Romans in 1580.[36]

---

[32] Mann 2006; Azaryahu 2007a: 33–92; Helman 2008. See also: 2005.

[33] Methodologically, this implies the use of performance theory. See: Turner 1982a; Turner 1987: 21–32; Schechner 1985; Schechner 1988; Alexander 2004.

[34] Cohn 1987: 42. Thanks to Nissim Leon.

[35] On the mutual nearing of history and social sciences see, for example: Elias 1978: 221–263; Darnton 1984; Chartier 1988: 95–111; Geertz 1990; Burke 1992.

[36] Le Roy Ladurie 1979. See other row-models for micro-history: LeRoy Ladurie 1978; Davis 1983; Ginzburg 1992.

Indeed, sociologists and anthropologists since Durkheim consider a public event as constituting the *cultural public sphere*, and hence a convenient case-study for the work of ideologies, since it explicates ideas and communicates them to mass society.[37] Recent scholarship on public festivals tends to emphasize their social, economic, and political contexts on a local, national, or global level, while not losing sight of their inner cultural contents on all these levels. A festival creates what Simmel calls "a festive sociability," that is, a special bond between its participants, which is created during the event and for its sake, but has implications beyond its boundaries.[38] A holiday belongs to the spheres of consumption, family, education system, and the state, along with "tradition" (see chapter three), and therefore links the private sphere and personal life with the public sphere and the general society. Common practices such as abstaining from working for one day, buying a particular good in mass quantities, or imposing particular temporary limitations on public behavior make the holiday a social glue. Moreover, the shared experience of time may determine the separateness of a social group and its distinct identity, particularly when it uses a different calendar.[39] However, the holidays have a dynamic dimension, because they quickly adapt or react to transformations in the economic, political, social, and cultural conditions, allowing the historian to cautiously use them as an efficient historical indication for studying these processes.[40] As we shall see, the Purim carnival did create this festive sociability and played a major role in the constitution of the Jewish public sphere in Mandate Palestine.

It should be mentioned that the "cultural turn" was broadly applied to Judaic studies. Instead continuing to emphasize the study of Jewish religion and "high" texts, Judaic studies are recently more engaged with social sciences in order to go beyond the representative "tradition" or "Judaism" toward Jewish "culture," or rather,

---

[37] Durkheim [1912] 2008: 322–323; Handelman 1990; Douglas 1982: 72; McGuigan 2011.

[38] Sassatelli 2011: 13–15. This idea is akin to what the anthropologist Victor Turner named "*Communitas*" (see below, chapter two).

[39] Zerubavel 2003.

[40] Joselit 1994; Pleck 2000.

"cultures."[41] Jewish cultures throughout the ages and across the globe are increasingly recognized as multi-vocal. The depiction often portrayed in scholarship is of multiple cultural options, hybrid identities constructed in middle areas between Jews and non-Jews, and between different Jewish sub-groups and cultures.[42]

When it came to the study of Zionism, however, the cultural turn proves difficult to adopt. Aside from ideological and sociological aspects beyond our scope here, it was the concept of "ideology" that fulfilled the same veiling function for Zionism that "religion" did for pre-modern Judaism: everyone knew that Zionism was "ideological," in the same way in which everyone used to know that Judaism was "religious." While the existence of tense inner disputes in Zionism was never doubted, Zionism as a "surname" was portrayed as one-dimensional.

Nevertheless, Hebrew (pre-statehood) and Israeli public culture became an object of study in the early 1980s in various disciplines, with a growing tendency to broaden the scholarly perspectives on the history of Zionism. Some of these studies illuminated various symbolic aspects of the public culture in the face of the previous narrow political or intellectual histories, which yielded the conventional agriculturalist image as accepted by Gellner.[43] In due course, recent scholarship has given much attention to the various origins of Zionist public culture, while breaking it down into various components: food, clothing, language, architecture, urban planning, popular religion, music, and other elements—and the various, hybrid, and sometimes contradictory meanings generated within the nationalist cultural framework.[44] In this growing body of literature, there are extensive discussions about the complex relationship between the New Hebrew culture

---

[41] Shmueli 1990. See also: Biale 1994; Marcus 1996: 3; Biale 2002; Rosman 2007: 131–135.

[42] See: Rosman 2007: 82–110. See examples: Shternshis 2006; Veidlinger 2009; Berman 2009; and more.

[43] For example: Even-Zohar 1981; Liebman & Don-Yehiya 1983; Harshav 1993; Zerubavel 1995; Bernstein 1998a; Alroey 2004; Zakim 2006; Razi 2009; Mann 2010; Rozin 2011.

[44] For example: Ben-Artzi 1996; Nitzan-Shiftan 1996; Shavit 1996; Raz 1998; Almog 2000; Yassif 2002; Helman 2003; Penslar 2003; Berkowitz 2004 (the entire collection); Bilu 2004.

and tangent cultures in time and space: pre- or non-Zionist Jewish, local Arabic, and the many cultures of the various countries of origin of Jewish immigrants to Palestine. Of particular interest for us here is a recent series of innovative studies by the historian Anat Helman about Urban Zionist culture in the interwar era and its complicated relationship with capitalist consumer culture.[45]

Following Helman, my book utilizes the Tel Aviv Purim carnival as a case study to illuminate one of the hybrid zones of Zionist festive culture and capitalist leisure culture, which are scarcely explored in historical literature, except for Helman's studies. Although only a tiny number of Jewish immigrants came to Palestine from Western Europe and North America, the assumed cultural dominance of these regions on a global scale created a huge impact on Zionist public culture. Cultures are shaped not only by their origins, but also by their aspirations. As was recently revealed by the new cultural and social history of Zionism, in the Zionist case those were mostly western. In particular, Zionism shared with the Anglo-American culture a frontier myth and a self-assigned civilizing mission.[46]

Purim: Appropriating a Pre-modern Festival

One of the most widely discussed questions in the literature about modern urban festivals is the question of originality: to what extent can a festival that has been reproduced from abroad for economic and political purposes construct a unique local identity?[47] In the case of the Tel Aviv Purim carnival, there was no simple answer. The carnival was initially established as an imitation of contemporaneous Mediterranean urban celebrations, mainly for economic purposes—indeed, the festival was generally ignored by scholars of Zionist myths, public rituals, and civil religion due to its commercial character.[48] However, besides its economic benefit, the Tel Aviv Purim

---

[45] Helman 2010; Helman 2007 (and many articles which will be quoted in passim). See also: Halperin 2011.
[46] See: Troen 1999; Hirsch 2008.
[47] Sassatelli 2011.
[48] Shavit & Sitton (2004: 84–105) were the only ones to discuss Purim celebrations as part of Zionist culture. See also, supra note 22.

carnival appropriated the pre-modern Jewish and European winter communal celebrations in a complex hermeneutical process.

The opening point of the appropriation of Purim into the Zionist calendar was not the best. Purim was always considered exceptional in the Jewish calendar, due to its anarchic, "non-Jewish" (involving drunkenness, intentional desecrations, and other acts), or even anti-religious character (for example, the omission of God's name from the Book of Esther).[49] During the era of the Enlightenment, the traditional anarchic festival came under massive attack. Jewish reformers, leaders, and intellectuals condemned what they saw as its violent and uncivilized practices, which encouraged hatred and sometimes even led to bloodshed between Jews and their neighbors. This criticism caused a gradual—but consistent—decline in the traditional wild Purim celebrations.[50]

In addition to the enlightened criticism on Purim, Zionists were troubled by its "exilic" features— such as the saving of Jewish people by court intrigues rather than heroism. From the "new Jewish man" point of view, Purim was seen as an anti-heroic, Diasporic, and feminine festival, in which the Jews were saved thanks to women's business.[51] As early as 1913, some Zionist leaders suggested turning Purim into a special day of fundraising for the Jewish National Fund (JNF). Yaacov Rabinowitz (1875–1948), an influential Labor Movement writer, objected, and defined Purim as "a spiritual yellow stain" in Jewish history. Eliezer Ben-Yehuda (1858–1922), known as the "reviver" of the Hebrew language and the author of the first Hebrew dictionary, expressed a similar opinion a few years earlier (though he changed his mind, as we shall see below).[52] Purim was seen by many Zionist ideologues as unrespectable. Nevertheless, in a complicated way which will be described in this study, Purim became a central day on the Zionist calendar, due to the adherence of Urban Zionism to the idea of folklorism.

The link between Jewish nationalism and folklorism is still underemphasized in scholarship, in which the hostility of a few major intellectual figures towards Jewish folklore and "the negation of exile"

---

[49] Haris 1977; Hanegbi 1998; Polish 1999; Belkin 2002.

[50] Abrahams 1912: 266–272; Joselit 1994: 219–263; Belkin 2002: epilogue; Horowitz 2006; Har'el 2004.

[51] On "the new Jew," see: Zerubavel 1995: 20–28; Shapira 1997b; Eisenstadt 1998.

[52] Yaakov Rabinowitz, *Hapo'el Hatza'ir* 12.3.1913, 7; Dotan 1999: note 22.

was taken as characteristic of what the historian Yaakov Shavit calls "formal folk culture."[53] This oppositional attitude was in fact far from dominant. Among the many indicators of other views were the popularity of Yom-Tov Lewinsky's folklorist anthologies, *The Book of Festivals* (in nine volumes) and the *Encyclopedia for Lore and Tradition*;[54] the popularity of the folkloric play *Hadibuk*;[55] the vitality of folklorism in the development of Hebrew music and dance;[56] the intellectual interest aroused by the *"Yeda-am"* [a Hebrew neologism for "folklore"] society in the 1930s; and the fact that the organization known today as the Israeli Historical Society was established in 1928 as the Palestine Society for History and Ethnography. One of its first endeavors was a detailed questionnaire about Purim customs in Jewish Diaspora communities; its findings were published in the third volume of their academic journal, *Tzion* [Zion].[57] Zionist cultural entrepreneurs came of age in Central and Eastern Europe in a cultural atmosphere that glorified "the people" and viewed folklore as a source of vitality.[58] Most modern nationalist movements made extensive use of folklore, and Zionism was no exception.[59] Precisely because of its anarchic and "uncivilized" character, historical Purim was considered the most "folkish" festival in the Hebrew calendar. The tension between continuity and rupture which is considered by many scholars to be "the bedrock of Zionist discourse"[60] will stand in the focus of the ethnographic analysis of this book.

The Structure of the Book

The book is structured in line with its ethnographic emphasis. Chapters one and two present a thick description of the carnival. Chapter one

---

[53] See: Shavit 1996; Shavit & Sitton 2004: 25–28; Raz-Karkotzkin 1993.
[54] Lewinsky 1955; Lewinsky 1970. See: Schrire 2011.
[55] See, for example: Werses 1986; Kaynar 1998; Zer-Zion 2005.
[56] See: Roginsky 2007.
[57] "She'elon le-Purim (lepirsum)" [Purim Questionnaire (for publication)], *Doar-Hayom* 6.3.1928; *Tzion* 1/3, 1930, 33–48.
[58] See: Oinas 1978; Schrire 2011.
[59] See: Wilson 1976; Herzfeld 1982; Handler 1988; Bendix 1997.
[60] Penslar 2007: 3. See also: Roshwald 2004; Saposnik 2008: 9–16.

details the institutionalization of the carnival from its early development in the form of community balls and small neighborhood processions prior to World War I, through the 1935 event, which drew a quarter of a million participants, until the account of the procession's sudden cancellation in 1936 due to a lack of funding. Chapter two begins the ethnographic scene-setting by analyzing the carnival as a pilgrimage site for the entire Jewish sector of Palestine. The analysis uncovers the symbolic-ideological importance of Tel Aviv's urban space far beyond its local boundaries on a national scale.

Each of the remaining chapters analyzes one concrete cultural motif from the celebrations in order to reveal implicit ideological elements of Urban Zionism by broadening the interpretational frame to other Jewish cultures, as well as contemporaneous non-Jewish ones. Chapter three begins by analyzing the conceptual role of "tradition" in the discourse about "invented tradition." The discursive analysis examines the relationship between the invented tradition and the great tradition of Jewish Purim, to suggest a different perspective on the problem of continuity and rupture in the new Hebrew culture. Chapter four discusses the gap between the discursive carnivalesque character of the festival—commonly described as wild and anarchic—and its civilized and orderly character in reality. The role of the carnivalesque discourse, rather than subverting the social order, was to portray urban space as a "Jewish" space. Chapters five and six employ inter-textual perspective to analyze the appearance of the biblical figures of Esther, Haman, Mordechai, and the horse, and to trace the rich "meaning-network" of these characters. Chapter five explicates Zionist political views toward non-Jews implicit in the appearance of the two men and the horse. Chapter six reveals the sexo-political implications implicit in the Hebrew Queen Esther pageants and the politicization of the bourgeois priority of the objectifying male gaze in the public sphere. Finally, chapter seven offers a thorough depiction of urban-Zionist ideology on the basis of the preceding chapters. It deploys its opinions with regard to tensions between the Land of Israel and exile; the role of the Jewish past in the new culture; the "spatialization" of Jewish life; the role of cultural engineering; and the ideological significance of capitalism, leisure, and fun in nation-building.

Urban Zionism did not have ideologues, but Purim celebrations, which were the largest public event in British Palestine, open a window to its ideological world.

CHAPTER 1

"ALL OF YOU TO TEL AVIV ON PURIM":
A LOCAL-NATIONAL FESTIVAL

This chapter will describe the rise and fall of the carnival from beginning to end, with a focus on its institutional aspects, as the necessary background for the ethnographic explorations of the following chapters.

Anthropological and historical literature about modern nationalism and its public rituals customarily focuses on free outdoor events such as processions, public ceremonies, or street performances. This literature mostly ignores events with admission fees, such as balls or fairs, which superficially seem unrelated to the construction of national identities.[1] However, the study of urban festivals no longer considers their economic functions as "contaminating" their cultural authenticity, but as conflating with their cultural functions.[2] Indeed, paid events, such as the "people's fair" in interwar New York, constructed identities and produced various meanings, even if their initial motives were commercial.[3]

The Tel Aviv Purim carnival combined free outdoor events with indoor events that required admission fees. The street procession was always the carnival's core event, except for the years when the procession did not take place—before 1913 or 1914, in 1920 due to the Tel-Hai incident mentioned above, and in 1930, after the violent conflicts of the summer of 1929. In fact, for contemporaries, the word "carnival" (and its Hebrew neologism, "*Adloyada*") referred commonly to the costume procession, rather than to the entire event. The cultural impact of the balls, attended by two or three thousand people at most,

---

[1] See the following collections, dedicated mostly to outdoors events: Moore & Myerhoff 1977; Hobsbawm & Ranger 1983; Kideckel 1983; Kirshenblatt-Gimblett & McNamara 1985.

[2] McGuigan 2011.

[3] See: Susman 1984: 211–215.

was different from the impact of the procession, whose crowd reached six-digit numbers in the mid-1930s. Nevertheless, despite the differences between the two categories, both were part of the same cultural site, which integrated capitalist mass entertainment with nationalist ideology. This chapter will therefore describe the carnival as a "field of cultural production" with different agents, areas, discourses, and practices.[4]

The Purim carnival made its debut in the *Yishuv*'s public culture in 1908 with the first costume ball in Jaffa, and was an ongoing event until the cancellation of the procession in 1936 due to budgetary and administrative limitations. The micro-history of the carnival reveals several stages of institutionalization, defined by the four motives that guided the planning of such public events: 1) Fundraising (or making money); 2) Entertainment and/or education; 3) National identity construction (or ideological recruitment); and 4) Bolstering the fledgling economy. As we shall see, both the balls and the street-carnival began as fundraisers. The second and third motives followed shortly thereafter, but the fourth came into play only toward the late 1920s. The identity of the organizers and their motives suggest the following sub-periodization for the celebration:

1. The 1910s: communal events.
2. 1920–1924: *Kapai* (Palestine's Workers' Fund).
3. 1925–1928/9: JNF (Jewish National Fund).
4. 1928–1935: Tel Aviv municipality.
5. 1936: cancellation.

Within this sub-periodization, we may discern two main periods, with 1928 as a watershed. The first period was characterized by difficulties of institutionalization, a low level of organization, and a focus on fundraising as the main goal of the celebrations. The second period, by contrast, was characterized by a high level of institutionalization with expenses that resulted in a deficit for the public fund. During this peak period, Tel Aviv viewed itself as the world center of Purim celebrations.

---

[4] Bourdieu 1993: 29–73.

The Ottoman Period: Communal Events

As I mentioned in the introduction, as the nineteenth century drew to a close with the ongoing bourgeoisification of the Jews, there were only dim residues of traditional Purim celebrations in Europe.[5] The festival was adapted to bourgeois ways of life and re-interpreted "in a refined way" by the "Purim Association of New York" (1861–1902), which organized fancy charity dress balls to accrue donations of considerable sums of money for city hospitals and Jewish institutions. This model quickly spread throughout North America.[6]

Toward the turn of the century, this festive form declined in North America, but it was adopted and developed in Jaffa in the late Ottoman era, during the years before World War I.[7] It was in a Zionist cultural context that Jewish intellectuals and cultural entrepreneurs embarked on a more rigorous celebration of Purim, contended with its content and practices, and suggested new interpretations. It began with Purim balls of the *Hapo'el Hatza'ir* ["The Young Laborer"] Club in Jaffa in 1908, and later on, in 1913 or 1914, began the street carnival in Tel Aviv, then a Jewish suburb north of Jaffa.

The origins of these two cultural formats—ball and street carnival—may not be traced to Jewish tradition. In the late 1800s, charity balls were a widespread venue of leisure and pastime for the middle classes across Europe and the Americas. These balls were mostly organized in a communal venue, in clubs tied to a particular social class, profession, or similar affiliatio, and aspired to be an educational venue for culture and progress. In provincial towns as well as metropolises across the world, this cultural venue was vigorously adopted by non-profit organizations as a fundraiser.[8]

The regional socio-economic circumstances that led to the adaptation of the new Purim balls in Ottoman Palestine were enabled by its urbanization. In that context, a limited sphere of modern leisure—that

---

[5] See introduction, p. xxii

[6] Goodman 1949: 371–373 (quote from 371); Goodman 1950.

[7] Joselit 1994: 219–263.

[8] On American "Middletown" see the classical field research: Lynd & Lynd [1929] 1956: 281–288. On the Jewish workers' clubs in New York see: Michels 2005: 105–109. On East European Jewry see, for example: Shternshis 2006; Veidlinger 2009: 202–208.

is, leisure as a profitable field—began its formation and expansion. The balls were one of many events, alongside sports, music, dancing, public reading, and amateur theater, which began to emerge in Palestine in the 1900s, particularly (but not exclusively) in the Jewish sector.[9]

The initial motivation for organizing the first Purim ball was to raise money for the activity of the *Hapo'el Hatza'ir* club in Jaffa and specifically its Hebrew journal (which bore the same name). *Hapo'el Hatza'ir* was a newly founded (1906) social movement and political party which aspired to create a Jewish working class but disagreed with the Marxist and Yiddishist bias of its main rival labor party, *Po'aley Tzion*. Instead, it emphasized Narodnik-Tolstoyan values of return to the soil and self-productivization, as well as Hebrew literature. It newly founded journal, printed and published in Jaffa, functioned as the center of the minuscule Hebrew world of letters in Palestine.[10]

At its outset, the journal had no more than a few hundred subscribers, and hence was published only sporadically. The movement sought to expand its financial resources, and the local Jaffa club came up with the idea of organizing a Purim ball. Since the club members produced the balls voluntarily, the expenses of costumes, decoration, and other costs were relatively low. The balls were sold out, and in 1910 there was even a mass altercation over tickets, which was resolved only when it reached the Ottoman courts.[11] The events were highly profitable: in 1909, the income was more than 200 Frank, and it came to 600 Frank in 1910.[12] The profitability of the balls was also evident in the steep increase in ticket prices between 1908 and 1914.[13]

---

[9] Ram 1996: 120–121; Naor 2003: 81–88; and particularly: Lev Tov 2007. On the characteristics of modern leisure see: Rojek 1985; Turner 1982b.

[10] Shapira, Y. 1968; 292–293; Govrin 1985; Tzahor 1998: 234; Shavit 1998.

[11] *Hapo'el Hatza'ir* 15.3.1910 (no serial number), 15; *Hapo'el Hatza'ir* 12, 31.3.1911, 19.

[12] *Hapo'el Hatza'ir* Adar 1909 (no serial number and Gregorian date), 14; *Hapo'el Hatza'ir* 12, 31.3.1911, 19. See also: Lev Tov 2007: 122.

[13] The prices were 1.5–7 *Bishlik* (the Turkish currency) in 1909; and 1.5–11 (French) francs in 1914. Although it is hard to assess the exact increase, due to the complex mixed monetary system of late Ottoman Empire, this is in-

The first ball, in 1908, was advertised as "a new spectacle never seen in Palestine."[14] Unfortunately, it was not fully realized due to a bloody fight, which took place in town that very night, when an Arab youngster was stabbed by several Russian-Jewish youth because of a romantic dispute, causing the Turkish police to forcefully intervene and make many arrests. Retrospectively, some historians saw this event as the first nationalist bloodshed between Jews and Arabs since the beginning of Jewish immigration to Palestine (unlike previous incidents, which were merely local mayhem).[15] As for the Purim ball, contemporaneous sources disagree as to whether this fight took place soon after the event began, or toward its end, and whether or not the ball was cancelled.[16] In any case, the occasion was a financial success, despite the distress.

The idea of Purim costume balls had spread rapidly from Jaffa to Jerusalem, Haifa, and Jewish colonies such as Petah Tikva and Rehovot, as well as to other clubs, communities, and organizations in Jaffa itself. When the local *Hapo'el Hatza'ir* club in Jerusalem organized a Purim ball, it was defined as "the first one ever in our city."[17] According to Boaz Lev Tov, the historian of leisure culture in Ottoman Palestine, the balls of *Hapo'el Hatza'ir* were quickly transformed into the "highlights" of Jaffa's leisure events—even though there were several organizational fiascos.[18] The balls of *Hapo'el Hatza'ir* in Jaffa continued to function as the center of this new field of cultural production, whereas the other agents—including *"Betzal'el"* school in Jerusalem, *"Hamaccabi"* and *Tze'irey Hamizrakh* ["Oriental youth"—a Yemenite clubs, and others, functioned as a cultural periphery. Although at that stage, Jaffa was still smaller and less populated than Jerusalem, it had

---

crease reached by far the epochal inflation which did not exceed 1% during these five years (Gross 2000: 42–60).

[14] *Hapo'el Hatza'ir*, second *Adar*, 1908 (no serial number), 17.

[15] See somewhat exaggerated descriptions: Druyanov 1936: 81; Dinur 1955: 208–209; Lewinsky 1955: 279; Sheva 1977: 266–268. For balanced analyses see: Eliav 1974; Mandel 1976: 26–28; Shapira 1992: 104; Hazan 2002: 248–249.

[16] *Hapo'el Hatza'ir*, Adar b, 1908 (no serial number and gregorian date), 12–13. *Ha-olam* 14, 1.4.1908, 186–188.

[17] *Haheirut* 29.3.1910.

[18] Lev Tov 2007: 100.

already begun to establish itself as the cultural center of Palestine, particularly in the matter of cultural trends.[19]

The balls' programs were to a great extent similar in all of their venues, and were consistent with a *communal format*. Like the organizers, the performers were always amateur members of the community. The guiding principle was the eclectic use of various available cultural media. As in similar Eastern European events, for the most part there was a performance of a Yiddish play, usually (but not always) translated to Hebrew, such as plays by Y.L. Peretz, Sholem Aleichem, Yitzhak Katzenelson, and others. The plays were mostly related in some way to the *Purimspiel* tradition, vaudeville plays (carnivalesque farces), or adaptations of biblical episodes such as the Book of Esther. Sometimes there were folkloric performances describing Jewish Diaspora communities, such as those of Yemen or Eastern Europe, or satirical performances about the *Yishuv*. In addition, the program included speeches by local leaders or businessmen, with poetry and prose readings, the playing of classical music, pantomime (or "live pictures" as it was called), satirical monologues, costumes contest, gymnastic performances, fireworks (or "Bengalese fire" as it was called), confetti, music and dancing. These media had nothing in common except their cultural availability.[20]

These were communal events, in which everyone knew one another, and community members displayed their talents on stage and entertained the audience of fellow community members, with the purpose of collecting money for community institutions. Nationalist messages, if they appeared at all, were modest and indirect. Socialist messages were totally absent. The balls functioned as Zionist cultural sites not because of their messages, but because they constructed the identity of the community by presenting its "slice of life" onstage—as communal theatre is defined by anthropologist Victor Turner.[21] It emphasized the community character of the new leisure sphere, the

---

[19] See: Kark 1980: 24; Kark 1990: 146–155; Ram 1996: 203–210; Kellerman 1993: 122–136; Lev Tov 2007: 90–96.

[20] See balls programs, for example: announcements in Ze'evi 1988: 359, 360, 477, 478; *Hapo'el Hatza'ir* Sh'vat 1909 (no serial number and Gregorian date), 1; *Hapo'el Hatza'ir* Adar 1909 (no serial number and Gregorian date), 13–14; *Haheirut* 20.3.1912; *Haheirut* 25.3.1913; *Hapo'el Hatza'ir* 21, 16.3.1914, 16.

[21] See: Turner 1982a: 16; Turner quoted in: Bennett 1997: 105.

arenas of which were mostly semi-public spaces—cafés, hotels, ballrooms, libraries, schools, and ideological-political clubs, rather than the street. It thus exemplified the community character of Zionist activity in Ottoman Palestine.[22]

As we shall see, after World War I the center of leisure activity moved to the street and the market, and indicated the creation of a new Jewish public sphere. The communal element became secondary with the surprising and rapid growth of the urban space of interwar Tel Aviv, while the urban bourgeoisie dominated the leisure sphere that was once the province of the Labor Movement circles.

The Purim street carnival of 1914 may be seen, retrospectively, as offering a harbinger of the creation of outdoor Jewish public culture. It was the first organized carnival to be reported in the newspapers of the era, and the first of which we have corroborated evidence. It was reported that

> Last Saturday night, a costume procession was held outdoors in Tel Aviv. This was a sort of Hebrew "carnival" and an innovation which attracted masses of people to Tel Aviv's streets that night.

After describing the procession's route through the suburban streets, the writer added that

> This was but the formal part of the procession, [and] until a late night hour, individual and group costumes were seen loitering on the streets. Some utilized this opportunity to collect small sums of money from the crowd on behalf of the JNF. The lack of order, the crowding and the unruliness of the crowd, somewhat obscured the ambiance.

The procession was organized by Eisenstein, a teacher.[23]

The first carnival organizer was Avraham Eisenstein, later known as Avraham Aldema (1884–1963), for many years the art teacher

---

[22]   See: Saposnik 2008.

[23]   *Hapo'el Hatza'ir* 21, 16.3.1914, 16; A.M. Heiman, "Mikhtavim mi-yafo" [Letters from Jaffa], *Heheirut* 30.3.1914.

in "Herzlia" Hebrew school in Tel Aviv and a prominent figure in Purim balls, already known for his creative costumes.[24] Many years later, in his memoirs, he described an earlier Purim procession (which probably took place in 1913) as an educational event for which his students were required to dress as biblical figures to gain knowledge of the Oriental style then dominant at the Betzal'el Art School in Jerusalem.[25] Meir Dizengoff, then the chair of the Tel Aviv committee, liked the idea, and on behalf of the committee offered Aldema financial assistance for the next year.[26] We may assume that, for people such as Dizengoff, the educational rationale was what differentiated Aldema's procession from the Purim of 1911, for example, when "groups of costumed children and youngsters walked from house to house and sang."[27] Another clue to the organizers' motives is revealed in the report which stated that some of the amateur performers collected money for the JNF.

Like many other components of Zionist invented traditions, the Purim carnival was initiated by a teacher and his students.[28] Although this was a street event which later on evolved into a huge mass event, in 1914 it was celebrated within the suburban community of *Akhuzat-Bayit* and the "Herzlia" school located there.

Although it appeared that at this stage no one, including members of the JNF, thought about earning money from the carnival in an organized manner, this option had actually been widely discussed, and it was often recognized that the Purim festival could, by its nature, be made into a fundraiser. In 1912, several JNF activists suggested that Purim would be decreed as "a day of *Shalach-Monos* for the JNF" — reappropriating the traditional practice of sending food, drink, or gifts to friends, relatives, and neighbors on Purim. In that spirit, the JNF "prepared medals as prizes for children who would collect money

---

[24] *Hapo'el Hatza'ir* Adar 1909 (no serial number and Gregorian date), 13–14.

[25] Manor 2004.

[26] Aldema's memoirs were never published, but were quoted in: Aieh-Sapir 2003: 103. It seems that Lewinsky's description relies on this story. See: Lewinsky 1955: 281.

[27] "Be-Eretz-Israel" [In the Land of Israel], *Ha-olam* 29.3.1911 (no serial number), 18–19.

[28] The most notable example to invention of teachers was *Tu B'shvat*. See: Shavit & Sitton 2004: 48–49; Saposnik 2008: 61–62.

for the nation's fund."²⁹ Others suggested that the traditional "half *shekel*" (a customary annual charity given during the month of the Purim holiday) and the *Shalach-Monos* would be allocated throughout the Jewish world as a donation for the redemption of Jerusalem.³⁰ As a response to the suggested connection between the redemption of Jerusalem and Purim, the writer Yaakov Rabinowitz published a pungent article, already mentioned in passim above, in which he attacked the very idea of utilizing the exilic and despised festival of Purim for such a sublime purpose. From his perspective, there was a direct connection between Purim, a "spiritual yellow stain," and the *"schnorr"* (a Yiddish word which in that context referred to dishonorable begging) methods which were regularly used by Zionist institutions.³¹

Historically, Rabinowitz had a point: the traditional Purim celebrations included special charity activities, known as "Purim-money" (*ma'ot Purim*), which comprised a separate Jewish legal ("Halakhic") category for charitable giving. In the case of the standard commandment to give charity, the giver must confirm that the beggar is indeed a person in need of charity. But on Purim, no confirmations should be requested, and charity should be given to anyone who asks for it, in the spirit of the festive atmosphere.³²

Zionist fundraising had effectively used this *"schnorr* tradition." Despite the harsh criticism of Zionist *"schnorr"* culture, and the explicit Zionist contempt for living on charity in contrast to earning one's living, the charity turned into an important mechanism not only for fundraising, but for ideological recruitment as well. Initiated and promoted by "teachers for the JNF," the "blue box" became a domestic cult whose object was the JNF itself. Its praxis of worship was the donation.³³ In due course, the practical intersection of Purim and the JNF proved crucial for the institutionalization of the carnival and the

---

[29] *Ha-or*, 11th of Adar, year 30 [1912]; *He-heirut* 11.3.1912.

[30] These were Yehoshua Barzilay (1855–1918) and Menahem Ussishkin (1863–1941), who later became the president of the JNF (*Ha-heirut* 13.3.1913; *Ha-heirut* 16.3.1913). On the background of this initiative see: Shilo 1989: 105; Katz 1989.

[31] Ya'akov Rabinowitz, *Hapo'el Hatza'ir* 21.3.1913, 7.

[32] Maimonides, the laws of Megillah 2:16. See also BT Avoda Zara 17:2–18:1, Bava Metzi'a 78:2; Shulhan Arukh orakh-hayim 694.

[33] Bar-Gal 2003; Shavit & Sitton 2004: 48–52.

balls. As we shall see, it served not only as another way to fundraise and to propagate Zionist ideology, but as a way to re-interpret Purim to meet the moral and aesthetic standards of a "modern" culture.

The 1920s: Fundraising

The new British rule after World War I brought many changes to Palestine, among them a noteworthy acceleration in urbanization and industrialization processes. One unpredicted factor not planned by either Zionist institutions or the British government was the rapid growth of the urban area of northern Jaffa (the first plan for the urban development of Tel Aviv was commissioned as late as 1925).[34] The former suburb of Jaffa was very quickly transformed into a separate urban space with its own "sense of place" as a "Jewish city." After 1948, the young city eventually conquered and swallowed its mother-city.[35] Purim celebrations turned into "Tel Aviv's festival," and were a good indicator for the evolution of the Jewish urban public sphere.

The JNF was not the only institution to discover the power of Purim as a fundraiser. During Purim 1920, the Palestine Workers' Fund, known as *Kapai*, tried to organize a "flower festival," inspired by the "flower war" in Nice, France. The entire town was meant to be decorated with flowers, and the festival was to be accompanied by a costume procession and a costume ball. Unfortunately, the outdoor event was cancelled because of the Tel-Hai incident (the indoor events took place, though with some delay).[36] Although the idea of a flower festival was abandoned, *Kapai* continued to organize costume processions every year from 1921 to 1924. Continuing the tradition initiated before World War I, the procession was organized and led by Avraham Aldema. The role of the procession was to attract crowds from the hinterland to the city in order to solicit donations by selling stamps and ribbons in the street. In addition to the costume proces-

---

[34] See: Welter 2009.

[35] The literature on the growth of Tel Aviv is voluminous. See, in a nutshell: Shavit & Bigger 2001; LeVine 2005; Rotbard 2005; Shoham 2012.

[36] "Hed Yafo" (Feedback from Jaffa), *Doar-Hayom* 8.3.1920. See: Genihovsky 1994: 72.

sion, there were a few more centers for happenings, such as gymnastis performances in a sports field or bicycle parades on other streets.[37]

Since the personnel of *Kapai* focused on fundraising, they did not dedicate much thought to the content of the carnival. In order not to overspend, they accepted everyone who wanted to participate—businesses, private people, and institutions—and did not set standards for inclusion. They did not employ marshals and did not even bother to put into place barriers (such as ropes) to distinguish the procession from the crowd. As a result, the procession was not very regimented.

In the meantime, many organizations throughout the country continued to organize indoor Purim balls in keeping with the community model of the late Ottoman era. Before World War I, this format was particularly popular in the "new *Yishuv*"—that is, among the more "modern" segments of Jewish society. Later, Purim balls became widespread throughout the region, including in classical "old Yishuv" sites such as Tiberias and Safed (and later on even Beirut and Cairo). Purim balls were organized by "Talmud-Torah" schools (traditional religious schools with minimal secular studies), Sephardic communities, and also by youth clubs, schools, small peripheral and rural communities, and public institutions. These balls included some element of fundraising for a community institution.[38]

---

[37] "Hag ha-Purim beyafo: Tahaluhkat hamasekhot letovat kapay" (Purim festival in Jaffa: Costumes procession for *Kapai*), *Ha'aretz* 28.3.1928; "Lehag ha-Purim" (For Purim festival), *Ha'aretz* 26.2.1924; an announcement on *Kapai*'s costumes festival, posters collection in University and national library, file v1969/4 (Carmiel 1999: 230); from *Kapai* to Tel Aviv committee, 28.2.1921, TAMA 216–01.

[38] Examples of Purim balls were: "Maccabi" and the scouts of Zikhron-Ya'akov (*Ha'aretz* 10.3.1920); "Maccabi" in Jerusalem and school children in Rishon-Letzion (*Ha'aretz* 12.3.1920); boys of Sephardic Talmud-torah in Jerusalem (*Doar-Hayom* 8.3.1920); girls' school students in Jerusalem (*Doar-Hayom* 28.3.1921); Tiberian community (*Ha'aretz* 15.3.1920); orphans' home in Safed (*Doar-Hayom* 21.3.1922); a play "Ahasuerus" by amateurs from Persian ethnic group in Jerusalem ("Me-hayey yerushalayim" [Life in Jerusalem], *Ha'aretz* 7.3.1921); or amateurs theatre of pioneers with local maidens in Petah-Tiqwa (*Doar-Hayom* 31.3.1921). In Beirut and Cairo this format arrived a little later, only in the late 1920s. See: "Purim be-kahir" (Purim in Cairo), *Ha'aretz* 13.3.1928; "Beirut," *Doar-Hayom* 8.3.1931; "Beirut," *Doar-Hayom* 31.3.1932.

The communal format was now dominant in the "provinces"—whether geographic, institutional, or social—but not in Tel Aviv. Time did not stand still in this effervescent town and Tel Aviv introduced cultural innovations which always arrived at the periphery a few years later. Even before it acquired demographic centrality, Tel Aviv already functioned as a cultural capital and as the trend-setter for the entire Yishuv and even for non-Jewish Palestine.

One notable Tel Aviv entrepreneur who recognized the cultural and financial opportunity offered by Purim was Baruch Agadati (1895–1976), a painter, choreographer, dancer, film producer, and bohemian. He was an experimental artist and a Zionist ideologue who made major contributions to the development of Hebrew dance and cinema, and understood his enterprise as a contribution to the creation of Zionist festive culture.[39] Agadati spent much of his time abroad, where he learned new technologies for mass-entertainment and implemented them in his grandiose Purim balls. Agadati formed quite an intriguing business partnership with significant Zionist institutions, primarily the JNF, in order to organize the largest and fanciest Purim balls, which stood out as a unique mix of profitable capitalist mass-entertainment and Zionist ideology.

As early as 1921, Agadati organized a costume ball for 500 guests (by invitation only) at the "Eden" theater in Tel Aviv. The guests included writers, artists, local politicians, and business leaders, who paid the full ticket price to earn this privilege.[40] In a way, this celebrity event—the first of its kind in Tel Aviv—returned the balls' genre from the community event to the pre-modern aristocratic format. The guest list was a significant factor in branding Agadati's balls as the places where things happen.

Another element, which already appeared in the 1921 ball, was a costume procession that would parade through the crowd, influenced by the street-carnival that evolved at that time. Whereas at the community balls the audience was passive and sat quietly, here the audience was meant to be active and to engage with the performers,

---

[39] On his experiments in dancing see: Manor 1986; Eshel 1991. On his experiments on documentary and feature cinema see: Shnitzer 1994: 34, 63; Gross & Gross 1991: 12, 80–82, 135–160; Shoham 2011b.

[40] "Hag ha-Purim be-yafo" [Purim festival in Jaffa], *Ha'aretz* 28.3.1921.

so as to blur the distinction between the performers and the audience. The frontal theatrical format was abandoned, and instead the event was now a huge "happening" based on active amusements, akin to modern theme parks.

Agadati commissioned professional entertainers for his Purim ball, and some were even brought in from abroad. In 1922, he brought a circus with clowns, magicians, and acrobats from Beirut.[41] Unlike in the first year, from 1922 and onward everyone could buy tickets, and the ball was a fully commercial event. The balls became enormously successful, attended by thousands of people. Beginning in 1926, Agadati divided the balls' events and spread them over several evenings, so as to differentiate between the ordinary people (workers or members of the middle class) and the aristocrat celebrities.[42]

In the years that followed, two additional important innovations were imported by Agadati from North America: jazz music and dancing as the party's highlight, and beauty pageants (or "Hebrew Queen Esther"), only six years after their initiation in Atlantic City (see chapter six).

The amplified attention given here to Agadati and his balls is not intended to link the phenomenon to one man, significant as he may have been. In the terms of Bourdieu, Purim balls were formed as a cultural field, structured along patterns of production, distribution, and consumption of culture. These structures organized the patterns of taste and style which were disseminated in the field and created its unique stratification.[43] Agadati was located at the center of the field, but there were many additional actors there. The definition of Agadati as a main taste-maker in the field is *not* linked to the question of originality: did he create the cultural formats by himself or replicate others? There were a few obvious cases in which he imitated a cultural practice from another actor in the field. But it was only after Agadati put it into practice that it was used by other entrepreneurs and became conventional in the field. One such instance was the introduction of the food counter at Agadati's balls in 1925, after the owners of "Eden"

---

[41] *Ha'aretz* 22.2.1922.

[42] See: Carmiel 1999: 12–155.

[43] Bourdieu, supra note 4.

theatre did it in 1924.[44] His main cultural role was to obtain technologies of mass-entertainment from beyond the field, abroad, or the margins of the field—and then to replicate and disseminate them throughout the field. Agadati functioned here as a name, a brand, rather than as a real person, since every year "his" balls were actually organized by a large group of people (as we shall see) but were marketed under his name (much like Walt Disney). Agadati's name became a main agent in this field, which means that innovations that appeared at his balls became trendy, whereas other ideas could pass under the public radar. Agadati's name and its accompanying symbolic capital were crucial in the Purim balls' attainment of a structured and competitive economic field.

Agadati surprised his competitors almost every year with some cultural innovation, which almost immediately became common throughout the entire field. Beginning in the mid-1920s, most Purim balls across Palestine held a costume procession that paraded among the crowd and not on stage, and the balls' programs were focused on jazz and other trendy dance styles. A few years after the introduction of Hebrew Queen Esther into Agadati's balls in 1926, every ball, even the communal ones, elected its own "Queen Esther." After Agadati cancelled the pageant in 1930, it took two or three years until the custom disappeared from the other balls throughout the country. After Agadati retired from organizing balls in 1934 for unknown reasons, it was only two or three years before mass Purim balls were no longer organized.

Besides Agadati's, grandiose Purim balls were also organized by the workers' theatre group "*Ohel*" [tent] beginning in 1930, and in 1932–1933 "*Ohel*" was in partnership with Agadati. Other mass balls were organized by the satirical theatres "*Hakumkum*" [the water boiler] and "*Hamataté*" [the broom]. Somewhat more modest balls were organized in commercial institutions, such as hotels, cafés, and theatres.[45] There were also youth movements and sports associations—in par-

---

[44] "Megilat Purim bete'atron Eden" [The book of Purim in Eden theatre], *Ha'aretz* 19.3.1924; Carmiel 1999: 96–97.

[45] Such as: "Spector" hotel (Ze'evi 1988: 483) and "Palatin" hotel (*Doar-Hayom* 14.3.1927; "Tel-Aviv," *Doar-Hayom* 19.2.1931); café "Lorentz" in Jaffa or casino "galey-aviv" (Carmiel 1999: 168), "Eden" theatre (Ze'evi 1988: 481, 482; *Doar-Hayom* 2.3.1923; "Olelot Purim be-Tel-Aviv" [Purim stories in

ticular, the non-political ones such as the scouts and *"Hamaccabi"* — as well as *"Landsmanshaftn,"* the ethnic associations of Jews from Yemen, Hungary, Iran, Bukhara, and other regions, and political movements such as *"Beitar"* (oriented to the right-wing) and *"Hapo'el"* (oriented to the Labor Movement). Balls were also organized by schools, small communities, student associations, and other groups, such as the club of discharged soldiers, "Menorah."[46]

As for the guests, we have a few estimations and a bit of data. As mentioned before, there were about 500 people on the guest list for Agadati's ball in 1921. Since Tel Aviv's population amounted then to no more than 3,000 people (including children), many of the guests were probably from side out of the town, which was surely true of the "Arabs and Christians" who attended.[47] In 1926, the main ball was attended by about 2,500 people, while "thousands gathered near the gate [of the ballroom] to watch the costumes."[48] In 1929, when the Tel Aviv municipality assumed responsibility for the street carnival, it began to collect a tax of 10 *Mils* (that is, a *Grush*, 1/100 of Palestine pound) for each ball ticket. According to the Municipality's data, on that Purim, 10,664 tickets were sold to Agadati's four balls. Along with the other balls that year, held by *"Hamataté,"* the "Eden" and *"Ophir"* theatres, and the Yemenite club, the total number of Purim ball tickets sold was 19,116 (the entire population of the city was no more than 40,000). In 1932, the figures were similar.[49] These figures demonstrate that even when the special taxes are considered (including the JNF donation, to be discussed below), this was a highly profitable business.

[ ] Tel Aviv], *Ha'aretz* 6.3.1931) or "Ophir" theatre (internal memorandum, 3.4.1929, TAMA file 04–3218a). See: Carmiel 1999: 156–172.

[46] Such as: the students' association "el-al" ("Tel-Aviv," *Doar-Hayom* 19.2.1931); ball of World Association of Hebrew Youth (announcement by World Association of Hebrew Youth, *Ha'aretz* 7.3.1928); "Menorah" balls (announcement of "Menorah," *Doar-Hayom* 27.2.1931). On civil society and *"Landsmanshaftn"* in interwar Tel Aviv see: Helman 2006b.

[47] "Hag hapurim beyafo" (Purim festival in Jaffa), *Ha'aretz* 28.3.1921. For Tel Aviv's population see below, chapter two, table 1.

[48] *Ha'aretz* 1.3.1926.

[49] Municipal memorandum, 3.4.1929, TAMA file 04–3218a; *Doar-Hayom* 5.4.1929. In that year, the municipality's revenue from the balls were 150 Palestine pounds ("Tel Aviv," *Doar-Hayom* 3.4.1929).

The role of the balls as a site of national identity construction relies on much more than the numbers, though. It is probable, of course, that there were many individuals who had no personal interest in the balls. That said, the huge numbers of guests, the quantity and quality of elite figures in attendance, and above all the steady stream of nationalist discourse regarding the balls—all indicate their central cultural function. As we have seen, among those who did not attend, many crowded to watch the costumed guests entering the balls, and in any case these entrances were a major attraction of the carnival.[50] Many more read the juicy newspaper descriptions and the various publications, and imagined themselves as guests. There was no other cultural phenomenon of such scope in British Palestine, and in the pre-TV period, the balls attracted great attention (which was obviously exaggerated in relation to the actual events).

This capitalist-nationalist culture drew criticism motivated by a nationalist puritan ethos. Whereas mere capitalist culture could have been tolerated, it was the combination of nationalism and capitalism that irritated the critics. The writer A.Z. Rabinowitch (1854–1945), a prominent opponent, wrote that "Purim days are upcoming, and here and there, there are talks about preparations to masquerade and dancing balls which have multiplied and in recent years wore the deceptive cloak of alleged nationalism."[51] Many critics targeted what they viewed as escapism and hedonism, and labeled the bond with nationalism as hypocrisy on both sides.[52] Nevertheless, the vast rhetorical exchanges revealed that the balls were indeed understood by many to be a national culture.

Elsewhere I elaborate in detail the balls' program and the actual experience of visiting the event. Very generally, it may be said that the balls were designed to create a multi-sensory experience. Every single guest was struck by a flood of stimuli directed toward the five senses. The mass balls were intentionally designed to produce and amplify

---

[50] Supra note 47.

[51] A.Z. Rabinowitch, "Beveit yisrael ra'iti sha'aruriya (Hoshe'a vav)" [In the house if Israel I have seen indignity (Hosea 6)]," a proclamation from 12.1.1931, posters collection, national library of Jerusalem, file V1836/e.

[52] See, for example: H. Shorer, "Ivelet-Purim" [The foolishness of Purim], *Hapo'el Hatza'ir* 8 (19), 14.3.1930, 2–3; idem, "Hamasekha sheli" [My mask], *Hapo'el Hatza'ir* 22–23, 18.3.1932, 12.

what was perceived as an urban experience. In terms developed in performance theory, the balls demonstrated "restored behavior" of crowdedness, urban alienation and individual isolation.[53] For the average Tel Avivian (who mostly immigrated there from Eastern Europe or Yemen), this experience was familiar from the literature of western urbanism (Dickens, for example), rather than from everyday life, since Tel Aviv developed such urban characteristics only after the mid-1930s.[54]

Purim: The Festival of the JNF

This capitalist character of the field did not prevent Zionist institutions in general, and the JNF in particular, from engaging in intensive fundraising linked to Purim. Whereas the 1910-era initiatives mentioned above were carried out in a fragmented way, if at all, in the 1920s, the link between the JNF and Purim was formalized. In 1923, awareness of Purim's fundraising potential, realized in both *Kapai*'s carnival and the mass balls, led JNF activists to the decision made at their annual national conference: a "tax" of a half-*Grush* (1/100 of Egyptian pound) would be added to every Purim ball ticket. The amount was, at the time, about 5% of the ticket price.[55]

Unlike other Zionist funds, the JNF never limited itself to mere fundraising. Officially, its main task since its foundation in 1901 was to purchase and develop land in Palestine. However, the JNF was intensively involved in Zionist educational and cultural activity through its Department of Publicity, and its endeavors extended far beyond its immediate fundraising needs.[56] Among many other activities, they suggested new interpretations for the historical exilic Purim:

> [The Nation that desired to] atone for the spiritually alien elements which clung to the exile's festival, inserted its own qualities of soul and being, the foundation of active public joint:

---

[53] Schechner 1985: 35–40.

[54] Shoham 2013b: 111–135. On urban characteristics of Tel Aviv since the mid-1930s see: Razi 2009.

[55] *Ha'aretz* 24.1.1923. The Egyptian pound was the Palestinian currency until 1927.

[56] Bar-Gal 2003.

makhatzit hashekel [half the shekel] [...] *mishloach manot* [...] and gifts to the poor [...] even in the exile. And now that the public sensibility of the Nation is set free, it is only natural that the land of Israel will take the first place in this festival.[57]

In other words, the criticism of the exilic nature of the festival was harnessed by the Department of Publicity of the JNF in favor of their needs, re-interpreting the *"schnorr"* tradition as an example of a healthy public life which Jews had even in exile. As proved by historian Hagit Lavsky, criticism of the *schnorr* policy was based on aesthetics rather than ethics: it targeted individuals who lived on charity and exhibited humiliated mannerisms, but organized charities and donations in the national context were elevated.[58]

Accordingly, the personnel of this department thought about many new and creative ways to celebrate Purim and increase donations. The Department organized Purim balls with revenues donated to the fund. The balls took place first in Palestine in 1923, and beginning in 1925 throughout the Jewish world. The department advised local activists about educational costumes, and many ways to increase the income of these events beyond ticket sales, such as selling ribbons, flowers, and flags; selling rights to play ; and collecting "JNF Shalach-Manos" door-to-door.[59] Some suggested using traditional *Purimspielers* to collect money on Purim, "in which every Jew and Jewess [is] expected to send *Shalach-Monos* to their people, a check for Kakal [JNF]."[60] It was assumed that "Purim has the capacity for fundraising,"[61] and officially, Purim was one of the "four yearly projects" for JNF fundraising and actually became the main annual fundraiser.

Purim was so important to the JNF that, in 1925, the fourteenth Zionist Congress approved a JNF monopoly over other Zionist organizations in collecting donations on Purim day. From that time onward,

---

[57] "Purim" [no author], CZA, file KKL5/4917/1.

[58] Lavsky 2002. See also Shenhav 2004.

[59] A formal letter from JNF executive to activists in North America, 1927 (no date), CZA, file KKL5/2452; *Karnenu* Adar 1929, CZA file KKL5/2521.

[60] An announcement of Canadian Zionist organization, no date, CZA file KKL5/930.

[61] From the central office of the JNF to national offices, 28.12.1928, CZA file KKL5/930.

Chapter 1. "All of you to Tel Aviv on Purim": A Local-National Festival

no Zionist organization other than the JNF was permitted to fundraise on Purim day without permission from the local JNF office. This resolution was valid at least through 1936.[62]

Indeed, in many places in Palestine it was assured that "all ball organizers received permission from the JNF, and deducted some of their income, according to the agreement."[63] In Tel Aviv, however, the enforcement of this resolution was difficult, since it was the main location of established Purim celebrations which were not JNF initiatives. As early as Purim 1923, JNF ribbons were sold in the streets of Tel Aviv alongside *Kapai*'s ribbons.[64] In 1924, following the death of the Zionist leader Max Nordau (1849–1923), the JNF declared Purim to be "Nordau day," and collected money to establish a village in his name. Ribbons were sold, pairs of volunteers conducted door-to-door solicitation, balls were organized, and *Shalach-Monos* for the JNF were collected. However, *Kapai* insisted on organizing the carnival street-procession. The local Jaffa/Tel Aviv JNF office published a furious letter in the newspapers, in which *Kapai* was accused of disobeying the JNF's central office. Eventually they reached a compromise: JNF's ribbons were sold in the streets until 2 p.m., and after that only *Kapai*'s.[65] On Purim 1925, there was no more debate: the local office of the JNF in Tel Aviv, now backed by the aforementioned Zionist Congress resolution, took over the carnival and was the sole organizer of the procession until 1928.

As for the balls, the JNF needed a more sophisticated technique than collecting voluntary "taxes" as it did everywhere else. Many of the ball organizers in Tel Aviv, especially the many whose motivations were commercial rather than cultural, educational, or communal—would probably have refused to deduct this donation from their

---

[62] From F. Rosenblit, a member of Zionist executive in London, to Zionist associations, 13.2.1927, CZA file KKL5/2106; from Zionist organization to all Zionist federations and fractions towards Purim 1930, 21.2.1930, CZA file KKL5/3587/1; from central JNF office in Jerusalem to local offices, 30.1.1935, CZA KKL5/6312; a reminder about the prohibition to fundraise on Purim, *Doar-Hayom* 1.3.1936.

[63] This report concerned Jerusalem (*Ha'aretz* and *Doar-Hayom* 15.3.1927). See also: "Yerushalayim" (Jerusalem), *Ha'aretz* 28.2.1928.

[64] "Tel-Aviv," *Ha'aretz* 1.3.1923.

[65] A public letter from the JNF's national office, *Ha'aretz* 19.3.1924; "Yafo ve-Tel-Aviv" (Jaffa and Tel Aviv), *Doar-Hayom* 23.2.1924.

income. The local chamber of the JNF found an original solution: they entered into a concealed partnership with Baruch Agadati.

Beginning in 1923, all announcements and advertisements for Agadati's balls prominently declared that no less than 50% of the full income from the balls (and not just the net profits) would be donated to the JNF. Rather than a donation, it was business cooperation. For the public eye, the JNF was depicted as merely sharing the income, but actually, the JNF and Agadati organized the balls together and the costs were equally divided. The local apparatus of the JNF provided office services and advertisement, and also shared the expenses.[66] This cooperation continued until 1928.[67] After it was discontinued in 1929, the JNF indeed began, with partial success, to collect "taxes" from incomes of Purim balls in Tel Aviv, as was customary elsewhere.[68]

Since the organizers of the street-carnival and the main balls were now one and the same, the links between the two were tightened. Agadati named the main ball "the carnival ball," and was highly involved with the street-carnival as well. Hebrew Queen Esther was "the ball's queen" and at the same time "the procession's queen," and led the carnival procession in an open car.[69]

The connections between the balls and the carnival were not only organizational but also thematic. In 1925, the procession was officially dedicated to a special topic: the encouragement of Jewish industry and commerce ("*Totzeret Ha'aretz*"). In practical terms, this meant that every Jewish business was permitted to participate in the procession and advertise itself. Some businesses did so without even trying to add a light-hearted touch to amuse the crowd—which generated vociferous criticism regarding the carnival's commercialization.[70] The criticism caused the organizers to add a few original floats each

---

[66] See: *Ha'aretz* 8.3.1925; an announcement of local JNF office in Tel Aviv and Jaffa, *Doar-Hayom* 6.3.1928; *Ha'aretz* 1.2.1926.

[67] See two separate stories about the two different activities of JNF and Agadati: *Ha'aretz* 7.2.1929; *Ha'aretz* 3.3.1929.

[68] *Doar-Hayom* and *Ha'aretz* 22.3.1929.

[69] "Yafo ve-Tel-Aviv" (Jaffa and Tel Aviv), *Ha'aretz* 22.1.1926. See chapter five.

[70] Carmiel 1999: 241–242; "Hashavu'a ba-pe'ula lema'an Totzeret Ha'aretz" [This week's activity for Jewish products], *Doar-Hayom* 13.3.1935. For criticism on commercialization see, for example: editorial letter, *Ha'aretz* 8.3.1927.

year, which were somewhat more satirical, or at least promotional, to endorse Zionist agricultural ethos, highly promoted by the JNF publicity on every other day. Nonetheless, the commercial component continued to take the central place in the procession. As noted by historian Anat Helman, the carnival displayed a "celebration of economy," which was quite at odds with the Zionist puritan ethos.[71] The capitalist logic of the balls thus permeated the street carnival, and boosting the economy became a serious consideration in its favor beginning in the mid-1920s.

These links with the carnival helped Agadati's balls to acquire a growing reputation as much more than mere entertainment: they were considered original Hebrew culture, the genesis of a unique Hebrew tradition. "Hebrew Queen Esther" was but the most eminent example of this discourse (see chapter six). This reputation radiated to the entire field of Purim balls, to which the Hebrew-Zionist media dedicated many inches of widespread reports, stories, atmospheric descriptions, analyses, and cultural critiques, which sometimes related even to minor balls and discussed insignificant details. These celebrations were understood as one of the most important phenomena of the new Hebrew culture in Palestine. The announcement of a "50% donation" promoted the national value of the capitalist event.

In other words, Agadati was ahead of his competitors not only in the techniques of entertainment, but also in the commercial use of nationalist ideology. His competitors tried to catch up with him, but of course no one could afford to set aside half of their income to give to the JNF—for the most part, donations were no more than 15%, and more frequently around 5%, of the ticket price.[72] At one ball in Rehovot, it was announced that the JNF would receive 30% of the ball's income, alongside an apology for the exceptionally high prices

---

[71]   Helman 2006: 388–389. On the celebration of the economy see Abrahams 1982. On the puritan ethos see Almog 2000: 209–225. On the "totzeret ha'aretz" campaigns see: Shoham 2013c.

[72]   See an announcement on Purim balls in *migrash harusim* in Jerusalem, *Doar-Hayom* 2.3.1928; an announcement on a ball in "Bristol" café in Jerusalem, *Doar-Hayom* 7.3.1930; an announcement of "world association of Hebrew youth," *Doar-Hayom* 4.3.1927; supra note 55; and many more.

of the tickets.[73] The fact that the JNF made such a clever commercial use of nationalist ideology indicates that it played the big game by the capitalists' rules, and defeated them on their home field.

The concealment of the partnership by both partners implies that both were aware of a certain ideological inconsistency. Moreover, this misinformation served both sides. The balls drew heavy criticism for their hedonism, escapism, and inappropriateness for a nationalist project. With Hebrew Queen Esther, gender issues were added and the carnival was criticized as immodest (see chapter six). Had the attackers known that the JNF itself, and not a private entrepreneur, stood behind these controversial cultural events their attacks would have been devastating. Instead, Agadati, who was known as a bohemian and spent much of his time abroad, attracted such harsh criticism by younger artists, journalists, and critics that, in one instance, he sued the authors of a protest proclamation for defamation.[74] But this bohemian reputation helped to sell tickets. From his perspective, to defend himself against criticism, it was more convenient to point out the 50% donation to the JNF, rather than depict himself as the JNF's business partner.

Despite the concealed and contradictory intentions of the organizers, the final cultural product was a combination of nationalism and capitalism, or a capitalist nationalism. Willingly or not, the JNF was a central agent for the importation of capitalist mass culture and its assimilation into the New Hebrew culture, whereas the Tel Aviv Bohemians had a significant role in nation-building. To use Bourdieu's words, Zionism was commoditized and sold in "the market of symbolic goods."[75] At the same time, capitalist mass-culture was nationalized as an "authentic" national culture. Although each side depicted (and probably genuinely thought about) this cooperation as a tactical collaboration with an inevitably powerful force, nationalism and capitalism were entangled in terms of the content as well, as we shall see throughout this book.

---

[73] "Neshef hasiyum," [Final carnival ball], *Doar-Hayom* 6.3.1928; an announcement on the "final carnival ball," *Doar-Hayom* 9.3.1928.

[74] "Mana shel ha-trask" [Some lessons from the "trask"], posters collection in national and university library in Jerusalem, file v/1836e; Ze'evi 1988: 493. It should be mentioned that the JNF's part was not ignored in these posters. See also: Carmiel 1999: 105 and note 248; Helman 2007: 89–91.

[75] Bourdieu 1993: 112–141.

Unsurprisingly, this connection was well-understood by the Arab-Palestinian press, which closely surveyed Purim celebrations every year, and reported that "[they] organized balls, in which money was collected, to achieve political goals."[76] From the Arab perspective, the Zionist anti-urban rhetoric did not conceal the eminently urban features of the emerging Jewish public sphere in Palestine.

1928–1936: Peak Time

The few years of the JNF's responsibility for the street-carnival were characterized by a constant process of institutionalization. The numbers of out-of-town visitors had significantly increased each year, and Purim celebrations throughout the country (outside Tel Aviv) sharply declined (see chapter two). The JNF's activists were attentive to criticism and made attempts to improve the carnival. They organized mass public amusements before the procession, such as comic and real sports competitions, gym performances, or chess games in which people posed as the chess pieces. They added a few orchestras (such as the British Police Orchestra) to accompany the celebrations and provided public dancing.[77] In response to criticism about commercialization, they featured political-satirical floats that required considerable financial investment and added dances and a comic act at the procession's departure.[78] In response to criticism about inadequate artistic standards, they employed experts who were present in the office during the days before the carnival and provided guidance regarding parade floats.[79] But there was a catch: the constant requirement to

---

[76] From *Al-Jazira* newspaper, translated and appeared in: "Me-ha'itonut ha-arvit" [From Arab media], *Ha'aretz* 2.3.1926.

[77] "Yemey ha-Purim be-Tel-Aviv" [Purim days in Tel Aviv], *Doar-Hayom* 12.3.1925; "Yafo ve-Tel-Aviv" [Jaffa and Tel Aviv], *Ha'aretz* 9.2.1926; "Tel-Aviv ve-yafo" [Tel Aviv and Jaffa], *Ha'aretz* 18.3.1927; "Purim be-Tel-Aviv" [Purim in Tel Aviv], *Ha'aretz* 20.3.1927; "Hakarnaval be-Tel-Aviv" [The carnival in Tel Aviv], *Ha'aretz* 21.3.1927.

[78] "Purim be'eretz Israel: Be-Tel-Aviv" [Purim in Palestine: In Tel Aviv], *Doar-Hayom* 2.3.1926; "Purim be-Tel-Aviv," *Ha'aretz* 1.3.1926. For criticism of commercialization see supra note 70.

[79] "Tel-Aviv ve-yafo: Mikhtav galuy latoshavim me'et hava'ada hamesaderet" [Tel Aviv and Jaffa: An open letter to the residents from the organizing com-

"improve" the carnival also increased the expenditures, and in 1928, it turned out that the income from the sale of stamps and ribbons did not cover the costs. The carnival that had started out as a fundraiser had become a financial burden. Hence, a few weeks before Purim 1928, the JNF announced that it would not organize the carnival that year.

This announcement triggered a widespread and distressed public debate. An overwhelming majority of people—hundreds of residents who signed a petition, and journalists, intellectuals, artists, and officials—exerted substantial pressure in making the categorical demand to retain the carnival. The question was how and by whom.[80] The announcement by JNF's national office stated that

> The value of the carnival, in our opinion, lies in the creation of a folk character for the Purim festival, and the elevation of the public spirit. In due course, the carnival became a tradition, and is now attended by thousands of guests and tourists. One can assume that if it will be enriched and improved in content, it will turn into a real economic power by attracting tourists.[81]

While fundraising was not addressed, the other three aforementioned motives to organize public events appeared here: the development of national culture and its transformation into a tradition (a key concept here; see chapter three), mass entertainment (or "elevation of the public spirit"), and—this is the first time it was explicitly mentioned—the encouragement of economic activity by marketing the carnival as a tourist attraction. The fundraising component had lost its relevance, since at this stage, apparently, the carnival operated at a deficit.

The JNF appealed to various Zionist institutions, but the Tel Aviv municipality was the only one to take on the challenge and share the expenses and the organization costs with the JNF, while affirm-

---

mittee], *Ha'aretz* 13.3.1927. For criticism on disorder see: "Yemey ha-Purim be-Tel-Aviv" [Purim days in Tel Aviv], *Doar-Hayom* 12.3.1925.

[80] "Yafo ve-Tel-Aviv" [Jaffa and Tel Aviv], *Doar-Hayom* 20.2.1928; "Tel-Aviv ve-yafo" [Tel Aviv and Jaffa], *Ha'aretz* 17.2.1928.

[81] Y. Ben-Ya'akov and A. Kamini, from JNF national office, an editorial letter, *Ha'aretz* 14.2.1928. See also: "Parashat hayom: Purim benosakh eretz-Israel" [Daily affair: Purim in Palestine style], *Doar-Hayom* 4.3.1928.

ing their logic.[82] In 1929, the institutions co-organized and co-sponsored the carnival.[83] In 1930, the JNF shirked its responsibility and left it to the municipality alone. Although the carnival was eventually cancelled that year due to the violent conflict in the summer of 1929, the municipality was alone in making serious attempts to organize it.[84] From 1931 onward, the municipality carried this burden alone.[85]

The JNF renounced not only its role in conducting the Purim carnival, but also its role in the mass Purim balls. After 1928–1929, the JNF resorted to other fundraising techniques, such as a Purim bazaar (some 100,000 used items were sold), door-to-door solicitation, and other activities.[86]

Why did the municipality assume this responsibility? In addition to the reasons mentioned above, the self-image of the city as a sovereign entity seemed to have a crucial role. Toward the late 1920s, the city began to develop its mythical discourse as the "first Hebrew city," which was exemplified, in one instance, in the grandiose celebration of the twentieth anniversary of the city (previous significant dates, such as the fifteenth anniversary, were not given a single public mention).[87] Purim was already identified with the Zionist city, and became an eminent ideological expression of Urban Zionism.

The municipality introduced new standards of professionalization—bureaucratic, organizational, financial, and artistic—and the celebrations reached heights hitherto unknown in the festive culture of the young *Yishuv*. The committee, which was now comprised of city council members, artists from various fields, writers, and representatives of several Zionist institutions, was assembled by the beginning of winter. The carnival was expanded in time and space to almost three

---

[82] A plan of action by the Purim committee, 15.1.1929, TAMA 04–3218a.

[83] "Likrat hagigot Purim" [Towards Purim celebrations], *Doar-Hayom* 11.3.1929.

[84] From Dizengoff to Zionist Board/National Council/JNF/Keren Hayesod, 23.1.1930, TAMA 04–3218a, and CZA S30/2307; from the JNF to Tel Aviv municipality, TAMA 04–3218a; from Dizengoff to the JNF's Jerusalem office, 3.2.1930, TAMA 04–3218a.

[85] *Ha'aretz* 2.2.1931.

[86] *Doar-Hayom* and *Ha'aretz* 22.3.1929; from central JNF office in Jerusalem to local offices, 30.1.1935, CZA KKL5/6312.

[87] See: Azaryahu 2009; Shoham 2012.

days in larger areas of the city. However, during this process, the carnival evolved from an event that invited active audience participation into a well-organized event that left the audience in a passive role. In the concepts developed by Alexander, it was a transition from a "ritual," in which performers and audience take active part, into a "performance" by active performers in front of a passive audience.[88]

The most evident change was organizational: the municipality initiated the use of ropes, marshals, and even police horsemen to establish boundaries between the procession's route and the crowd. The committee began to put private individuals and groups under contracts which obligated the city to provide financial assistance, while the other party was obligated to participate in the procession, or pay a fee. The idea was to enhance the "artistic level" of the parade floats, and the committee helped with professional advice, materials, and equipment.[89] Only floats which demonstrated a "satisfying artistic level" were allowed to participate in the parade. Hence, despite the committee's attempts, public participation declined somewhat toward the mid-1930s.

The committee tried (with limited success) to encourage the public to decorate the city with greenery, flowers, photos of prominent Zionist figures, national or carnival flags, and colorful lighting. The municipality its part and constructed spectacular lighting with different images, such as a palace, a big tent, the burning bush (in the central synagogue), and others. After 1934, three illustrated gates were placed above the central Mugrabi square, painted by artist Nahum Guttmann (1898–1980), on biblical themes from the Book of Esther.[90] The committee also introduced new technologies, such as loudspeakers and radio (the first broadcasting station in Palestine was initiated in 1936).[91]

---

[88] Alexander 2004.

[89] A series of contracts between the committee and a few people, TAMA 04–3219b.

[90] "Hahakhanot le-Purim be-Tel-Aviv" [Preparations for Purim in Tel Aviv], *Doar-Hayom* 28.2.1934; "Likrat nishfey ha-Purim be-Tel-Aviv" [Towards Purim balls in Tel Aviv], and "Tel-Aviv," *Doar-Hayom* 17.3.1935. See pictures: Carmiel 1999: 233; Carmiel 2004: 202.

[91] "Miyedi'ot va'adat hahagigot" [From the celebrations committee], *Davar* 15.2.1934; *Davar* 1.3.1934; *Ha'aretz* 2.3.1934. On the radio in British Palestine, see Stanton 2013.

A significant change from 1928 onward was the prevention of the participation of floats which lacked a satirical or artistic motif in performance, whether made by commercial or non-profit organizations. Considerable sums of money were allocated as prizes for floats in the procession, and thus, as early as in 1928, "most of the procession's participants had a national-public or even political character."[92] Indeed, alongside the presentation of national values or educational institutions, there was growing number of controversial floats which described actual disputes between Labor Movement and right-wing Revisionist Zionists, religious and secular, farmers and workers, and others, as well as critiques of the British government. Among the educational floats, a special place was assigned to the Yemenite group *Tze'irey Hamizrakh* ("Oriental youth") whose members, even in the mid-1920s, were considered "authentic" performers of folk culture, which many described as the "highlight of the procession."[93] These floats left a deep mark on the collective consciousness, including that of those who were not present, but heard about the proletarian Tel Aviv group that won prizes and recognition on Purim and interpreted this recognition as "a sure sign of redemption" from their difficult socio-economic situation (see chapter four).[94] Other Jewish ethnic groups such as Caucasians and Egyptians conducted folkloric performances in the carnival as well.[95]

In 1931, the organizing committee began to give the streets special comic names from the Book of Esther, such as "speaker of his people's own language" ["*umedaber kilshon amo*"—Esther 1:22] for Ben-Yehuda Street (Ben-Yehuda was considered the "reviver of the Hebrew language"); or "and Haman restrained himself" [*vayit'apak Haman*—Esther 5:10] for *Magen-David* square, with reference to the public restrooms at the site.

---

[92] "Purim be-Tel-Aviv" [Purim in Tel Aviv], *Ha'aretz* 7.3.1928. See pictures: Carmiel 1999: 161, 200, 239; Carmiel 2004: 201.

[93] See: "Tel-Aviv: Yemey ha-Purim" [Tel Aviv: The days of Purim], *Davar* 1.3.1926; "Hakarnaval hapurimi be-Tel-Aviv" [Purim carnival in Tel Aviv], *Ha'aretz* 24.3.1932.

[94] Doniach 1933: 156–157. This author, who was based in North America at the time, apparently translated the words of the newspaper story (supra note 92) word by word. See also: "Mikhtavim lama'arekhet" [Editorial letters], *Ha'aretz* 9.3.1928.

[95] See, for example, Carmiel 1999: 244.

In 1932, the committee decided to introduce a new Hebrew word for carnival, and appointed a special committee of copywriters to come up with a neologism: *"Adloyada"* (see chapter four). This new name symbolized a general tendency to empower the carnival in all respects. The committee introduced opening and closing ceremonies, which included music, theatre, and dance performances, in addition to children's performances, which expanded the carnival to three days.[96] These, and additional street spectacles, were performed on "Esther's Palace," a new public stage built in Mugrabi square in anticipation of Purim every year beginning in 1932. This was a huge, three-story street theater, with three 30-meter-high figures of biblical King Ahasuerus, Mordechai, and Esther, built on top of the third story. The first floor could carry an orchestra of a few dozen musicians to accompany the shows (with as many as 60 people). The middle floor was used for the performances (as many as 16 people), with "oriental" gates (that is, gates with round boughs) in the background. The entire cost of this stage was 320 Palestine pounds.[97]

In addition, several orchestras were spread throughout the city and played waltzes, marches, and ethnic music to encourage public dancing. The public amusements included horse races (with Bedouin and English participants alongside Jewish clubs), dancers and choirs in the streets, and popular songs that were written for the occasion.[98]

In 1932, a generic and thematic change was introduced as well. Until then, the non-commercial floats touched mainly upon actual politics or displayed educational and cultural activities. Beginning in 1932, the committee decided to take responsibility for a central float. This float depicted a nationalist meta-narrative, from the bible to Zionism,

---

[96] "Hilulat hapurim maka galey hayim" [Purim joy is expanding], *Doar-Hayom* 22.3.1932.

[97] For additional photos of Esther's Palace, see Fisher 1984: 96; fragments 71-76 from Axelrod cinema news broadcast, Spielberg Jewish Film Archive, Hebrew University, Jerusalem, VT ax10; unidentified British film, Spielberg Jewish Film Archive, Hebrew University, Jerusalem, VT 00034; and a contract for the construction of this project, 25.2.1932, TAMA 04–3219c.

[98] "Tel-Aviv," *Doar-Hayom* 1.3.1932; "Tel-Aviv: Va'adat mif'aley Purim" [Tel Aviv: The committee for Purim projects], *Doar-Hayom* 11.3.1932; "Tel-Aviv," *Doar-Hayom* 13.3.1932; "Likrat hakarnaval" [Towards the carnival], *Doar-Hayom* 18.3.1932; "Seder hagigot hapurim be-Tel-Aviv" [Program of Purim celebrations in Tel Aviv], *Doar-Hayom* 22.3.1932.

with changing themes: "the *aliyot* [immigrations] to the Land of Israel" (1932), "poetry in Israel" (1933), "Israel's tribes past and present" (1934), and "from slavery to freedom" (1935). The first three themes were suggested by Haim N. Bialik (1873–1934), considered the era's "national poet." These floats cost hundreds of Palestine pounds.[99] The mundane language of satire and the display of Zionist achievements was transformed into a mythical language of Jewish meta-historical narratives. When a float of the biblical tribes with their flags paraded past, "masters of tradition in the crowd reminded their neighbors of the verses which determined each tribe's flag."[100] Another observer commented that these historical floats "display history as a holy of holies, and [display] the present as profane of profanes."[101] Floats displaying Zionist achievements, including those made by the JNF, the Hebrew University, the Hebrew Technion in Haifa, the "Zebulon" naval school, and others, did not disappear, however.[102] The carnival was so expanded that in 1934 the procession included more than 100 floats.

Toward the mid-1930s, another interesting development was the gradual disappearance of the political floats which gave expression to the internal political disputes of the *Yishuv*. After 1934, when relations between left- and right-wing factions in the *Yishuv* deteriorated after the unresolved murder of the Zionist-socialist politician Haim Arlosoroff (1899–1933), the committee made major efforts to close down these floats. Indeed, as early as 1931, controversial floats — that is, floats presented by one group to criticize another — were not common in the procession. Paradoxically, the carnival's last two years witnessed two political scandals.

The first was a massive fight between two youth groups, *Hapo'el* and *Beitar*, which occurred during Purim 1934. It began a few hours after the procession, when Labor Movement *Hapo'el* paraders passed near the Revisionist Zionist club and an altercation ensued — which was eventually stopped by British police, who made numerous arrests. As one would expect, in *Doar-Hayom*, the right-wing newspaper, the

---

[99] TAMA 04–3219c; Carmiel 1999: 246–249.

[100] *Davar* 2.3.1934.

[101] MT, *Ha'aretz* 4.3.1934.

[102] *Ha'aretz* 5.3.1931, 1; "Hakarnaval ha-purimi be-Tel-Aviv" [Purim carnival in Tel Aviv], *Ha'aretz* 24.3.1932; Carmiel 1999: 56; Carmiel 2004: 198–199.

Hapo'el youth were accused of initiating the fight, and in the Labor Movement newspapers *Davar* and *Hapo'el Hatza'ir*, the opposite stance was taken. Probably the most accurate and reliable description was provided by the "tabloid" *Iton Meyuhad*, which reported that "the mischievous youth of the political parties violate the festival's joy while defending their opinions with punches, bricks, and stick beatings."[103]

The second scandal took place right before the procession of 1935, following severe labor disputes in Petah-Tikva. Rosa Cohen (1890–1937), the city council member representing the Labor Party (and the mother of future Israeli Prime Minister Yitzhak Rabin), forbade the traditional procession of Petah-Tikva youth on horseback from the "Maccabi Absalom" Club, led by the settlement's heroic protector, Avraham Shapira (1870–1965). The argument delayed the entire procession for two hours, and eventually Shapira and his young fellows rode twenty minutes ahead of the procession. The Farmers' Association of Palestine [*hit'ahadut ha-ikarim*] protested to Mayor Dizengoff regarding "the humiliating and offensive attitude shown toward our fellow-riders, led by Avraham Shapira, by an official Tel Aviv municipality institution such as the committee for Purim celebrations—publicly, during the celebration."[104]

A public event can bring social tensions to the surface of public consciousness and contain them—and thus enables society to diffuse potential conflict.[105] The committee's close inspections disrupted the process of the alleviation of internal tensions, which then erupted in public life in different ways, much less pleasant than controversial parade floats.

These scandals, however, did not prevent many from seeing these years as the carnival's finest hour. The periphery was utterly abandoned during Purim, and no Purim celebrations were organized

---

[103] A.S. Yuris, "Purim shehushbat" [An interrupted Purim], *Hapo'el Hatza'ir* 9.3.1934, 12–13; *Davar* 2.3.1934; "Hitpartzut damim mashbita shuv simhat hahag be-Tel-Aviv" [Again, a bloody brawl ruins the festival's joy in Tel Aviv], *Doar-Hayom* 4.3.1934; *Iton Metuhad* 4.3.1934, 1; *Yediot Iriyat Tel-Aviv* 5 (1934), 197.

[104] "Tahalukhat ha-Adloyada be-Tel-Aviv" [The carnival procession in Tel Aviv], *Doar-Hayom* 21.3.1935; a letter of complaint from H. Ariav, chair of *hit'ahadut ha-ikarim*, to the Tel Aviv municipality, 10.4.1935, TAMA file 04–3222.

[105] See: Handelman 1990: 10–12.

beyond Tel Aviv—everyone travelled to the city, and none celebrated in their home communities. It was also an international event, which drew not only many tourists from abroad but also a notorious international pickpocket, who was caught during the carnival.[106] The public was requested not to bring children to the opening ceremony due to the anticipated crowds as early as 1933.[107] In 1934 and 1935, there were recurring reports of fainting and minor injuries as outcomes of excessive crowding or falls from heights, as well as thefts—which were unknown before 1932, when the municipal police and the "Red Star of David" (the Jewish first-aid organization) were idle during the carnival. Roofs and balconies were so overcrowded that in-house municipal correspondence revealed severe concerns about collapsing structures (with relief that the dangers were not realized).[108] Since the crowding and the noise diminished capacities to see and hear the show, the 1934 opening ceremony was abbreviated to more rapidly disperse the crowd.[109]

These were the years during which the entire *Yishuv* made the pilgrimage to Tel Aviv, and which imprinted the carnival in the Zionist/Israeli collective memory. In 1935, the new tradition seemed strong and stable. Hence, the news of the cancellation of the carnival which began to spread throughout the city in the winter of 1936 had the impact of a thunderstorm on a sunny day.

The Decline

The municipality's implementation of higher standards led to greater public expenses for materials, equipment and, wages for painters, writers, dancers, choreographers, actors, musicians, stage hands, contractors, marshals, and the director of the procession—Moshe Halevi (1895–1974), a notable director from the "*Ohel*" theatre. In addition, there were expenses for ads, publications, office work, and temporary

---

[106] *Palestine Post* 2.3.1934.

[107] "Tel-Aviv," *Doar-Hayom* 10.3.1933.

[108] CZA, photos collection, phkh 4144; Hanoch 1932: 29; *Yediot Iriyat Tel-Aviv* 5 (1935), 147–148; Carmiel 1999: 247–248; Carmiel 2004: 202; and more.

[109] *Palestine Post* 1.3.1934; *Ha'aretz* 1.3.1934; *Davar* 2.3.1934; a memorandum, a summary of Purim celebrations of 1934, 26.3.1934, TAMA 04–3220c.

policemen. The municipality was not always capable of meeting the cost, since the deficit was always deeper than anticipated.[110]

Unfortunately, the income did not come close to meeting the expenses. The institutionalization of the carnival in the 1920s decreased public participation, and despite open pleas from the municipality, no money was donated to cover the deficit. For unknown reasons, the carnival's financing was never included in the municipality's annual budget. Every winter, someone would remember that Purim was approaching, and then scramble to assemble an organizing committee. This committee immediately started seeking financing for the celebrations. There would be a patchwork of donations, special budgets and additional sources of income, and most years it somehow was held together—with particular credit to vigorous fundraising by Mayor Dizengoff, who personally took responsibility for a great deal of the carnival and in 1934 raised more than 1,000 Palestine pounds, which covered most of the deficit.[111]

In 1935, Dizengoff was severely ill, and the city's officials did not give much attention to the carnival, leaving it with a deficit of over 3,000 Palestine pounds.[112] In 1936, Dizengoff's illness, along with the embarrassing fact that the previous year's deficit was not yet covered, led to the decision to celebrate Dizengoff's seventy-fifth birthday on Purim day. Instead of the carnival committee, the city's secretary assembled a "committee for Purim and Dizengoff's Jubilee," which decided, "due to reasons of budget, [...] to cancel the procession for one year and instead, to focus on amusements and shows for three

---

[110] See: a program for Tel Aviv Purim celebrations, 15.1.1929, TAMA 04–3218a; Carmiel 1999: 233–234; an agreement between Moshe Halevi and the Tel Aviv municipality, 24.3.1932, TAMA 04–3219b; from Arye Lubin to Dizengoff, 27.3.1931, TAMA 04–3218b.

[111] Expense report [no date, from 1933], TAMA 04–3220b; expense report about Purim and internal memorandum about the carnival, 26.3.1934; from Dizengoff to the municipality management, 2.1.1935, TAMA 04–3220c; protocol of the meeting of the organizing committee, 10.2.1935, TAMA 04–3221c; from Moshe Halevi to the carnival committee, 22.3.1935, TAMA 03–3211d.

[112] The protocol of the meeting of the organizing committee, 10.2.1935, TAMA 04–3221c.

Chapter 1. "All of you to Tel Aviv on Purim": A Local-National Festival

nights and two days on the 'civic field.'"[113] The merchants' association protested the decision, but as Dizengoff himself reminded them in his pungent response, they had consistently refused to donate money to the carnival in previous years.[114]

In the public media announcement, the cancellation was explained by the municipality as the outcome of the "state of world Jewry and the limitations and edicts in Palestine."[115] The "Arab revolt" broke out a month later, after Passover, and was remembered by many as the real reason for the cessation of the carnival.[116] However, while the atmosphere in Purim of 1936 was already strained, the reasons for the cancellations were merely budgetary and administrative.[117] The carnival was temporarily cancelled only for the year of 1936, but as bureaucrats know too well, nothing is more permanent than a temporary decision. The next *Adloyada* procession in Tel Aviv was organized in 1955, in a different form and context.

This was part of a general process of the decline of all Purim celebrations, including the balls. Public interest in the balls had begun to weaken in the early 1930s. Fewer newspaper inches were dedicated to the balls, and, in general, they were treated as banal parties no different from everyday Tel Aviv parties. In 1934, Agadati retired from organizing the balls, and in 1935, as part of its desperate search for new sources of income, the carnival committee drastically raised the balls' "carnival taxes" and minimized the potential profit. Because there was no procession in 1936, and there were few out-of-town guests, the balls resulted in heavy losses for their organizers. In fact, very few

---

[113] An announcement on the assemblage of the committee, 29.1.1936; TAMA 04–3222; a memorandum by Moshe Halevi, program for Purim celebrations of 1936, TAMA 04–3222.

[114] From the Tel Aviv and Jaffa merchants' association to the municipality, 20.2.1936; from Palestine industrialists' association to the municipality, 2.3.1936; from Dizengoff to industrialists' association, 3.3.1936 — TAMA 04–3222.

[115] Protocol of the meeting of the city's directorate, 3.2.1936, TAMA 04–3222; "Bney Tel-Aviv asurim bahagiga: Rak hayeladim rasha'im lismoakh" [Tel Avivians are prohibited from joy: Only the children are permitted], *Doar-Hayom* 3.3.1936.

[116] For example: Shprut 1990.

[117] "Tel-Aviv," *Doar-Hayom* 8.3.1936.

of the locals came.[118] In 1937, there were still a few thousand guests at the balls, but the balls were not "news" for the media anymore, on national or even a local level, and the economic and security conditions prevalent since April 1936 did not help either.[119] Although Purim balls continued to exist—and actually remain in existence to this day—they are considered private parties with no national and intellectual interest. As early as 1935, when the carnival still existed, there were reports of a few dozen "private costume balls."[120] Eventually, these alone remained in the field.

The decline of Purim celebrations after the mid-1930s was emblematic of a general historical process of the decline of Tel Aviv as a site of Zionist identity construction. Several independent studies signify its watershed as 1936. According to Moshe Zimmerman, the historian of Hebrew cinema, Tel Aviv's presence in the Zionist imagination as a national site—in newspapers, literature, and cinema—was at its peak during periods of relative political quiet. During wartime, the Zionist consciousness was focused on the frontier: wars, illegal immigration (*ha'apala*), border skirmishes, and related events. Zionist culture could envision Tel Aviv as the indulging and warm home front, or—much more often—as the decadent rear, which pioneers could question the value of defending, but Tel Aviv was no more viewed as the place where the new society and state were built.[121] In 1936, when the "Arab revolt" broke out, there was a change in the Zionist policy regarding resource distribution. Zionist institutions decreased their involvement in leisure culture, and there was a related decrease of public interest in developing a new festive culture. Accordingly, 1936 signified a new stage in the combined history of Tel Aviv and Urban Zionism. Its rapid development persisted, and it continued to function as the Yishuv's commercial, cultural, and even political center. However, Tel Aviv almost disappeared from Zionist cinema, literature, and historiography.[122] The mythological discourse regarding the city as a unique place diminished during this period, and returned

---

[118] *Doar-Hayom* 10.3.1936.
[119] *Ha'aretz* 25.2.1937.
[120] *Ha'aretz* 17.3.1935.
[121] Zimmerman 2001a: 30–31.
[122] See ibid.; Yekuti'eli-Cohen 1990: 7, 99–110; Shenker 2005: 77.

only toward the end of the 1950s.[123] The rapid development of the city was not slowed in 1936, but the city's role as a site of Zionist identity construction dramatically dwindled.

As for Purim celebrations, it could be said that their decline was a result of the decline of several prominent figures, such as Dizengoff (who died in 1936), Agadati (who retired in 1934) and perhaps also Bialik (who died in 1934).[124] In addition, it was a result of new political circumstances and the transformations in leisure culture and economic priorities of the Yishuv caused by the Arab revolt. On a broader level, however, these determinants should be located within socio-cultural and political processes: without mass public events, the significance of the city as a national site of identity construction was diminished.

Conclusion

The definition of Purim as "Tel Aviv's festival" by contemporaneous and current observers had a solid foundation.[125] The city and the festival fed each other, and their rise and fall were combined.

The correlation between the city and the festival was recognized not only in Palestine but throughout the Jewish world. The Purim carnival and the balls, and the Hebrew Queen Esther in particular, were perceived as original Hebrew culture. A Purim ball in Warsaw, for example, bore the title "a night in Tel Aviv," and ticket-purchasers were promised that "it will resemble the traditional Purim balls in Tel Aviv. The halls will be lightened in white and azure."[126] "Queen Esther" pageants were held throughout the Jewish world.[127] An open letter of the JNF's executive in North America stated that

---

[123] Azaryahu 2007a: chapter 3.

[124] See, for example: Shprut 1990.

[125] For contemporaries' observations see, for example: Arieh-Sapir 1997: 177; Gaster 1953: 227. For retrospective assessments see: Shavit & Sitton 2004: 98; Helman 2007: 84–91.

[126] "Varsha" [Warsaw], *Doar-Hayom* 11.3.1931.

[127] "Ester hamalka ha-ostralit" [Australian Queen Esther—in Melbourne], *Ha'aretz* 5.3.1931; "Kabalat panim le-ester hamalka mi-New York" [A reception to New Yorker queen Esther], The posters collection, national library of Jerusalem, file V1969/3; two Yiddish invitations to Purim ball in Madison-

> Purim carnivals are not new. They were traditionally performed by our people since early times. Purim is a time of joy. In the large cities of Palestine, Purim carnivals are organized to benefit the JNF. We want to create this joy in our country as well, to benefit the JNF.[128]

Interestingly, even non-Jewish groups in Palestine began to organize costume balls, which incidentally or not, took place around Purim.[129]

In other words, Purim carnivals were understood as the unique contribution of Tel Aviv, as the only Jewish public sphere in the world, to the general Jewish culture. Purim carnivals were the first cultural practice produced in Palestine and disseminated to the diaspora, following Ahad-Ha'Am's vision of a Jewish cultural center in Palestine (although Ahad-Ha'Am himself would probably wrinkle his nose). The rise and fall of the carnival and the symbolic status of the city were combined, in a way that makes the chicken-and-egg question pointless.

The significance of the carnival beyond Tel Aviv's municipal jurisdiction will be analyzed in the next chapter.

---

square-garden, New York, 1930, and Chicago, 1934 (photos collections, Beit Ariela, Tel Aviv, file 1460); Brodsky 2004: chapter 3.

[128] An open letter of the JNF executive in America, no date, CZA KKL5/2452.

[129] See: "Yafo" [Jaffa], *Doar-Hayom* 23.2.1933 (a report about a carnival organized by the Christian workers association in Jaffa); Khalidi 1984: 158.

Chapter 2

"Travelling to Esther":
A Civil-Religious and Pilgrimage Event*

Pilgrimage and Tourism

Alongside its nationalist aspirations, the Purim carnival was first and foremost a tourist attraction for the residents of Palestine. Since British Mandate Palestine was not abundant with tourist events, its relative provinciality and somewhat kitschy character did not prevent the entire *Yishuv* from flocking to Tel Aviv to celebrate its festival.

In this chapter, I employ an anthropological perspective, which interprets this tourist event as an annual pilgrimage to Tel Aviv and thus reveals its ritualistic dimension, while elaborating on its ethnographic scene. Moreover, this chapter rediscovers the Purim carnival as the most powerful civil-religious event in Mandatory Palestine, both in terms of the number of participants and in symbolic terms, demonstrating both the penetration of capitalist culture into the life of the *Yishuv* and the emergence of Tel Aviv as the central Zionist public sphere. As we shall see, the carnival positioned Tel Aviv as the center of Jewish Palestine, not only in economic and cultural contexts but also in symbolic and civil-religious contexts. A visit to the carnival was understood as a journey to the emerging cultural capital of the *Yishuv*, and as an attempt to get a glimpse of its life. The Purim carnival thus both reflected and created the symbolic significance of the city not only for its residents but for the entire *Yishuv*.

Recent anthropological theory has drawn increasing attention to structural similarities between the pilgrim, who seeks the salvation of soul (and body), and the tourist, who seeks recreation of body

---

* Parts of this chapter appeared as a journal article in *Journal of Israeli History* 28.1 (2009): 1–20.

(and soul).[1] According to Turner's comprehensive theory, the element of a physical journey to another geographical place constitutes for both the tourist and the pilgrim a departure from their ordinary life to a distinctly "other" reality, thus deepening an assumed division between "ordinary" and "non-ordinary" life. Turner defined pilgrimage as a *liminal* phenomenon, characterized by an imagined release from social fetters and boundaries—village, class, and so on—while creating a sort of universal fraternity, which he called *Communitas*.[2] This liminality is also characteristic of tourist sites. Turner's model was criticized for neglecting social hierarchies and tensions, which *Communitas* does not conceal.[3] Nonetheless, his conceptualization may be appropriate to our analysis, since Turner considered the liminal phenomenon to be an element shared by both leisure and religious activities, particularly in the era of industrial capitalism.[4]

My discussion is based on the broader classical anthropological concept of religion, defined not by the presence of the divine or the supernatural, but rather by the structural division of profane and sacred.[5] This definition can include both solemn and playful activity, allowing the religious destination of the pilgrimage to be a solemn site, such as the tomb of a saint, a memorial monument, or a place of a historical divine revelation, or a playful site, such as a theme park or a large urban center. This structural perspective does not assume a necessary clash between fun and religiosity, and hence includes "secular ritual."[6]

As we shall see, the journey to Tel Aviv was, above all else, a journey from Palestine's cultural periphery to its evolving center, a search for national identity through an exceptional kind of *Communitas*. Tel Aviv was believed to embody a valued ideal, and hence, the Purim carnival was more a classical pilgrimage site than a typical tourist

---

[1] MacCannell 1975: 42–43; Cohen 1992; Morinis 1992: 4; Reader 1993.

[2] Turner 1969: 94–130; Turner 1974: 195–196; Turner & Turner 1978: 1–39. "Liminality" comes from the Latin word *limen* (threshold). *Communitas* comes from the catholic ritual.

[3] Morinis 1992: 9.

[4] Turner 1982b: 20–60.

[5] Durkheim 1915: 40–41. For the analogy between religion and leisure, see especially 381–383.

[6] Moore and Myerhoff 1977; Moore 1980.

site, since "The pilgrimage center can house a national identity, the identity of ethnic group, regional culture, or transnational religious group."[7] Purim celebrations functioned as a secular site to which the entire *Yishuv* made pilgrimage to "worship" the religion of nationalism, and the pilgrimage positioned Tel Aviv as the central shrine of that religion.

Mass Travel to Tel Aviv for Purim

Despite its leaders' aspirations, Mandatory Tel Aviv was not by any means a central tourist attraction. It lacked historical and religious sites, to say nothing of its unbearable climate during the summer months, by European and North American standards. Moreover, its main natural tourist resource, the seashore, was underdeveloped during most of the Mandate period due to inappropriate urban planning. Yet, Tel Aviv's leisure services—cinemas, theatres, cafés, restaurants, and the like—were more developed than in any other city in Palestine.[8]

Tel Aviv's main draw as a tourist attraction was its image as the "first Hebrew city" after 2,000 years of exile. Contemporaneous visitors—Jews and non-Jews alike—were deeply impressed by this unique historical phenomenon. This was a place where one could see in the streets "policemen, postmen, members of the municipal council, street sweepers, bus drivers, manual workers, teachers, builders— all without exception are Jews."[9] In other words, Tel Aviv was attractive to foreign visitors only by virtue of its being a normal western city, except that it was thoroughly Jewish in all of its social strata. This myth of "the first Hebrew city," powerful as it may have been, could not draw tourists for more than a few days. Hence, even Zionist tourist organizations invested their energies in new agricultural settlements or ancient religious sites.[10]

---

[7] Morinis 1992: 5.

[8] Efrat 1984: 56–64; Cohen-Hattab 2006: 53–61; Goldberg 2005: 38–40, 62–63, 90.

[9] *Yediot Iriyat Tel-Aviv* 1937–8, 117. Cited in Azaryahu 2007a: 73; See also Kahn 1936: 98–147; Mann 2006:142–144.

[10] Berkowitz 1997.

As a result, the Tel Aviv tourist industry of the 1920s and 1930s, until 1936, was mostly based upon "hallmark tourist events"—the Levant Fair, the Maccabia ("Jewish Olympic games"), and the Purim carnival.[11] In order to position Tel Aviv as Palestine's commercial, cultural, and leisure center, all three events were packaged together and marketed as the "spring events." As such, they attracted visitors in numbers from tens to hundreds of thousands; no more than 25,000 were tourists from abroad. In other words, the majority of the visitors to these events came from within the country. As the most "westernized" city in Palestine, Tel Aviv was more attractive to the country's residents, Jews, Arabs, and British, and thus became a center of domestic tourism. Whereas the other two "hallmark events" attracted some foreign visitors—businesspeople attended the Levant fair and athletes came to the Maccabia—the visitors to the Purim carnival were almost exclusively residents of Palestine, Jews and Arabs alike, who found it the best tourist attraction in the (quite provincial) region. However, each year, most of the crowd came from outside the city itself, as illustrated in Table 1.

The table clearly shows that as early as the *Kapai* period (1921–1924), the carnival attracted out-of-town visitors, who probably came, at this stage, from Jaffa and its hinterland. The JNF period witnessed a quantitative leap, and for the first time there were reports about shortages in food supplies in Tel Aviv during the carnival. In 1926, the Jerusalem newspaper *Doar-Hayom* reported on massive traffic to Tel Aviv before Purim, while for the first time, tickets to Agadati's balls were sold in Jerusalem in advance.[12] Until 1928, the numbers remained stable (probably due to the economic downturn during those years). Beginning in 1929, under the auspices of the municipality, the carnival drew a stable increase in the numbers of the visitors, which surpassed the growth rate of Tel Aviv's population. As noted in Chapter one, during the 1930s, the crowds became a real problem, which sometimes even disrupted the program.[13]

The mass pilgrimage to Tel Aviv for Purim is evident not only from the estimated figures reported in the Jewish press—num-

---

[11] Hall 1995; Goldberg 2005: 92–166, 223–224.
[12] "Yerushalayim yom yom: Neshef Agadati" [Everyday Jerusalem: Agadati's ball], *Doar-Hayom* 25.2.1926.
[13] See above, Chapter one, p. 31.

Chapter 2. "Travelling to Esther": A Civil-Religious and Pilgrimage Event

Table 1. Numbers of visitors to the Tel Aviv Purim carnival in relation to the Jewish population of Tel Aviv and Palestine.

Year	Estimated number of visitors*	Population of Tel Aviv**	Population of the Jewish sector in Palestine***
1923	10,000	16,554	89,660
1924	10,000	21,610	94,945
1925	10,000	34,200	121,725
1926	Thousands of guests, reports on shortages of food during the festival (no numerical evaluation)	38,000	149,500
1927	Tens of thousands	37,729	149,789
1928	30,000	38,239	151,656
1929	80,000? (according to *Davar* and *Do'ar ha-Yom*)	40,000	156,481
1930	[no procession]	42,000	164,796
1931	40,000–50,000	46,101	174,606
1932	50,000–70,000	52,240	192,137
1933	Tens of thousands (for the first time, reports on unpleasant overcrowding in the streets)	72,000–80,000	234,967
1934	100,000–150,000	86,000–100,000	282,975
1935	250,000	120,000	355,157

* Based on reports in the four main daily newspapers: *Doar-Hayom, Ha'aretz, Davar*, and *Palestine Post*.
** Based on *Yedi'ot Iriyat Tel-Aviv* 6–7 (1934): p. 295; Druyanov 1936: 340–41; Shavit and Bigger 2001: 93.
*** Based on Gertz 1947: 46.

bers which, of course, are likely to be exaggerated. The numbers are also evident from an examination of the transformations in the map of Purim celebrations throughout the country. During the first half of the 1920s, Tel Aviv's Purim carnival had already become the largest in the country, but local entrepreneurs in many culturally peripheral places such as Jerusalem, Haifa, and the agricultural settlements also organized successful Purim balls and processions. In 1927, however, local Jerusalem entrepreneurs tried to organize a carnival similar to Tel Aviv's. It failed, and the failure of the children's procession was explained as follows: "Ms. Sukenik who was supposed to supervise the procession—travelled to Tel Aviv and left everything in the hands of the other teachers, who were not ready for that."[14] During the 1920s, there was a spontaneous popular carnival celebrated annually on Jerusalem's main road, Jaffa Street, which suddenly lost its popularity and diminished in 1928–1929 (see chapter four).[15] In 1930, due to the cancellation of Tel Aviv's carnival (after the violent conflict of the preceding summer), the Jerusalem carnival once again became a very popular event.[16] However, in the following year it was much smaller, and in 1932 there was no sign of any Purim carnival in Jerusalem. The Jerusalem newspaper lamented the fact that the "foppish, mischievous, hedonist Tel Aviv has attracted all the children of Jerusalem."[17] It reported empty streets, and balls which lacked participants in dance and costume competitions. During the 1930s, there were fewer and fewer Purim balls in Jerusalem, while those who stubbornly persisted in organizing them incurred a financial loss. Jerusalemites traveled to Tel Aviv, as did residents of Haifa and most other Jewish communities.[18]

Meanwhile, transportation venues to Tel Aviv increased every Purim. All transportation services, whether offered by individuals or companies, charged exorbitant prices as Purim approached.[19] To compete, the railway services to Tel Aviv were also augmented during the Purim holiday season. Thousands of passengers from all over Palestine and other parts of the Middle East were transported to Tel Aviv in hundreds of train cars, which remained in Tel Aviv until the end of the carnival and then transported the travelers back home. In 1931, for example, 7,000 people came to Tel Aviv by train alone. Auto and bus transportation services were busy as well: in 1933, on the Hebrew date of the twelfth of Adar alone (three days before the carnival), the automobiles of the "*Hena*" company transported 2,200 people

---

[14] "Yerushalayim yom yom" [Jerusalem every day], *Doar-Hayom* 13.3.1927.
[15] "Yerushalyim" [Jerusalem], *Doar-Hayom* 9.3.1928; "Purim bi-Yerushalayim" [Purim in Jerusalem], *Doar-Hayom* 28.3.1929.
[16] "Purim bi-Yerushalayim" [Purim in Jerusalem], *Doar-Hayom* 17.3.1930.
[17] "Yerushalayim" [Jerusalem], *Doar-Hayom* 6.3.1931.
[18] "Purim bi-Yerushalayim" [Purim in Jerusalem], *Doar-Hayom* 24.3.1932.
[19] "Tel-Aviv," *Doar-Hayom* 25.2.1929.

from Jerusalem to Tel Aviv; and in 1934, on the day of Purim, a full bus arrived in Tel Aviv every three minutes.[20]

Perhaps the most telling illustration of the mass pilgrimage to Tel Aviv for Purim was the concern expressed by Mayor Dizengoff, in a confidential letter addressed to several senior Zionist officials, about holding the carnival in 1930, in the wake of the riots in the summer of 1929. Dizengoff feared that entire settlements would be left empty and unprotected when their residents departed for the carnival. Again, it is important to note that this letter was confidential.[21]

At the carnival's peak in the mid-1930s, the Tel Aviv municipality opened an information office, which directed visitors to rooms available for rent in the city. Many people stayed with friends, on mattresses they brought from home, or simply slept on the beach. All hotels and guesthouses were fully occupied, and many visitors were compelled to find lodgings with Jaffa's Arab population.[22]

No wonder that the main headline of *Doar-Hayom* one Purim was: "Purim 1934 in Tel Aviv: Cities, colonies and villages empty of their residents, all traveling to the *Adloyada*."[23] Indeed, the cessation of the Purim carnival in 1936–1937 was a key factor in the sharp decline in general tourism in the country (mostly due to security restrictions), both foreign and domestic, from that year onward.[24]

---

[20] *Doar-Hayom*, 4.3.1930; "Yerushalayim" [Jerusalem], *Doar-Hayom*, 3.3.1931; "Yom etmol be-Tel-Aviv ha-hogeget" [Yesterday in festive Tel Aviv], *Davar*, 27.3.1929; "Tel-Aviv," *Doar-Hayom* 6.3.1931; "Yerushalayim" [Jerusalem] *Doar-Hayom* 12.2.1933; *Palestine Post*, 2.3.1934.

[21] A confidential letter from Dizengoff to Zionist Board/National Committee/JNF/Keren Hayesod, 23.1.1930, TAMA 04–3218a, and CZA S30/2307.

[22] "Hagigot Purim" [Purim celebrations], *Ha'aretz* 12.3.1933; "Mah she-ani ro'eh ve-shome'a be-Tel Aviv" [What I see and hear in Tel Aviv], *Doar-Hayom* 25.2.1934; "Likrat Purim be-Tel-Aviv" [Towards Purim in Tel Aviv], *Doar-Hayom* 18.3.1929; Municipal Announcement no. 5, 22.2.1932, TAMA 04–3219a; "Meha-itonut ha-arvit" [From the Arab press], *Ha'aretz* 13.3.1933.

[23] *Doar-Hayom* 1.3.1934, p. 1.

[24] Cohen-Hattab 2006: 36; Cohen-Hattab discusses the data on railway passengers, but assumes that the main tourist center was Jerusalem (ibid., 49–51). As we saw here, Tel Aviv had a significant contribution to the increase in domestic tourism, particularly between the years 1932–1935. See also Goldberg 2005: 208.

Who were these "pilgrims"? If we review the figures in Table 1, it is unlikely that they were drawn only from certain sub-sectors within the *Yishuv*. We know that among the visitors there were many Arabs (not only from nearby Jaffa, but also from more distant Haifa, Jerusalem, and the Samaria region), ultra-Orthodox Jews, and, other groups that resided in Palestine, such as British soldiers and officials or German Templers. At the peak of the carnival there were also international non-Jewish tourists, southern desert Bedouins, and even some French soldiers from Syria. Although their participation was remarkable, the non-Jews were numerically insignificant. The absolute majority of the visitors were Jews. Even though many people probably stayed at home, due to restrictions of health, money, or individual interest, it is most likely that the vast majority of residents of every type of Jewish community and sub-sector traveled to Tel Aviv. Participation in these events crossed boundaries of profession, ethnic origin, religious and political affiliation, settlement sector, and even age.[25]

The similarity between the crowds flocking to Tel Aviv and participants in other mass pilgrimages did not go unnoticed by contemporaneous observers. In most cases, they remarked upon it with mild amusement. One report trumpeted: "Today as well, the trains kept bringing 'pilgrims' from all over the country."[26] Putting the word in quotation marks indicated a degree of embarrassment evoked by the term. This expression appeared repeatedly in many contemporaneous reports.[27] However, some took the analogy more seriously:

---

[25] "Ha-karnaval ha-purimi be-Tel-Aviv" [The Purim carnival in Tel Aviv], *Doar-Hayom* 24.3.1932; "Yom etmol be-Tel-Aviv ha-hogeget" [Yesterday in festive Tel Aviv], *Davar* 27.3.1929; "*Falastin* modi'a" [The newspaper *Falastin* announces], *Ha'aretz* 21.3.1935. Reports on the participation of Arabs in the carnival recurred every year, in the Arab press as well. See the photo in Carmiel 1999: 49. That Orthodox Jews also took part is indicated by a public statement by rabbis, forbidding travel to Tel Aviv at Purim (see announcement from the protest assembly in the Me'ah-She'arim Yeshiva, 26th of Tevet 1930, TAMA 04–3218a).

[26] "Purim be-Tel-Aviv" [Purim in Tel Aviv], *Ha'aretz* 6.3.1928.

[27] For example: "Al ha-perek: Purim be-Tel-Aviv ha-hogeget" [On the agenda: Purim in the celebrating Tel Aviv], *Ha'aretz* 28.3.1929; "Tel-Aviv ha-hogeget" [The celebrating Tel Aviv], *Doar-Hayom* 28.3.1929.

Tel Aviv became *Tel-Talpiot* during this week. All routes are leading to her, all trains and vehicles are coming to her. Tens of thousands are assembling in the streets, from Jerusalem, Haifa, and the colonies of Judea, the Jezreel Valley, and the Galilee. A huge national assemblage. A wonderful pilgrimage.[28]

The expression *"Tel-Talpiot"* was taken from the Midrash and Talmud, where it was used to denote post-destruction Jerusalem. For the ancient Jewish rabbis, the destroyed city of Jerusalem continued to function as a virtual spiritual center: real pilgrimage to the temple of Jerusalem was replaced by an imaginary pilgrimage. During prayer, Jews were instructed to turn their faces towards Jerusalem.[29] Now, in the Zionist era, the old tradition of pilgrimage was reestablished in reality—with Tel Aviv as a substitute for Jerusalem as the new cultural center of the Jewish world.

Tel Aviv's ritualistic trumping of Jerusalem was apparent also in the decision to conduct the main procession on the Hebrew date of the fifteenth of Adar, the day after Purim, known as *Shushan Purim*, when Jerusalem traditionally held its own separate Purim celebration (as did other ancient urban centers such as Jericho).[30] Purim was traditionally an urban festival. As early as the era of the Sages, its rituals would have been performed on market days, when villagers assembled in the local city. Subsequently, in the late Middle Ages, the Renaissance, and early modern times, Purim was celebrated mostly in urban centers, to which Jewish villagers from nearby areas flocked.[31] In Mandatory Palestine, that urban center was Tel Aviv.

---

[28] "Lamrot ha-matar: Purim mutzlakh be-Tel-Aviv" [Despite the downpour: A successful Purim in Tel Aviv], *Doar-Hayom* 5.3.1931.

[29] See *Shir ha-Shirim Rabbah* (commentary on Song of Songs) 4:4; BT *Berakhot* 30: 1.

[30] Public announcement to the press, 6.2.1933, TAMA 04–3220a; "Likrat Purim" [Towards Purim], *Davar* 12.3.1933.

[31] Mishnah Megillah 1:1; BT Megillah 2:1, and Rashi; Bar-Ilan 1987; Belkin 2002: 58.

The Journey

Within the experience of pilgrimage, the role of the journey is to change the pilgrims' ordinary time-space continuum as they make their way to a different place over a period of time. This change is seldom sudden. Rather, it comprises consecutive phases: the preparations of the pilgrims for their journey and a gradual disengagement from everyday life in preparation for the destined day. The pilgrim's arrival at the destination is also gradual, in both time and space.[32]

The main ethnographic-historiographic problem of analyzing the Purim carnival as a pilgrimage event is that most accounts of the carnival—including fictitious experiences of provincials, as described below—were written by Tel Aviv residents, who did not experience the journey to their city. Baruch Agadati, for example, announced that "the travelers to Tel Aviv for the festival are requested to get dressed in their costumes in their homes and to joyfully travel to Tel Aviv."[33] Agadati asked the pilgrims to immerse themselves in the atmosphere while still at home and during their journey, but it seems that only few, if any, fulfilled this request.

One exception was the Jerusalem satirist Yeshayahu Karniel, author of the satirical column "Azmavet" in the Jerusalem newspaper *Doar-Hayom* for more than a decade. During the Purim season, he often wrote his columns as a sort of a travelogue about the journey from Jerusalem to Tel Aviv. One of these columns opened with the following description:

> There are three kinds of celebrations in Palestine: the celebration of Rabbi Shimon [Bar Yohai] at Miron, the celebration of Rabbi Meir *ba'al ha-nes* [the miracle-worker] in Tiberias and the celebration of Rabbi Meir *bli nes* [miracle-less] in Tel Aviv.[34]

Karniel was well aware of the secular character of the celebration, and thus attributed its patronage to "Rabbi Meir [referring to Mayor Meir Dizengoff] *miracle-less*." Nevertheless, he emphasized the

---

[32] Turner 1974: 187.
[33] Announcement of Agadati's balls, *Ha'aretz* 4.3.1928.
[34] "Amar Azmavet" [Thus spoke Azmavet], *Doar-Hayom* 25.3.1932 (emphasis in original).

Chapter 2. "Travelling to Esther": A Civil-Religious and Pilgrimage Event

nature of the event as a pilgrimage. As he recounted, when he went to do his laundry in the Jerusalem neighborhood *Me'ah-She'arim*, he suddenly saw a huge convoy of Bukharan "Jews and Jewesses, old and young, tall and stout women in colorful clothing, walking like those who had gone out of Egypt, or as if they, God forbid, were running away from an earthquake." These people were loaded down with luggage, including food, carpets and mattresses. They sat on their pillows in the street, "for hours in the heat of the day, waiting for the large cars that would take them to Tel Aviv."

Karniel's story accords with Turner's description of the first stage of pilgrimage—the departure from ordinary life. These Bukharan Jews told Karniel that they were "traveling to [Queen] Esther." The protracted wait in the street for the cars enabled the pilgrims to gradually depart from their everyday lives and to immerse themselves in the appropriate mood.

According to Karniel's story, on the following day he found another sort of departure from everyday life—at Jerusalem's railway station:

> Two troops have assembled at the Jerusalem railway station. Our cousins are traveling to prostrate themselves upon the prophet's tomb in Mecca, while our brethren of Israel run hither and thither, urgent and pushing, just like Ahashtranim [Biblical Persian: fast riders (Esther 8:10)], with bundles of every size and shape in their hands and on their shoulders. Women, encumbered with pillows and mattresses, with wailing infants, all jostle and elbow each other, as they perilously hoist themselves up the ladder to the third-class compartments, so as to fight for places on the train, while there is great commotion all around.

Nevertheless, even here, many were forced to wait in the street due to the shortage of train tickets:

> And every time I pass near the office of "Mahir" [the transportation company], I see young and old, men and women in the line, beseechingly gazing at the faces of the clerk who is holding the telephone, and of his wife, while asking the clerk to at least save them a place for *tomorrow*, as if traveling were an act of grace on their part. Three maidens, with bare arms and chests, evening, Tel Aviv, wear bands on their lapels, and have already

been sitting on their bags in the street for two hours, awaiting their turn...³⁵

These episodes refer explicitly to the classic travel story "Shem and Japheth on the Train" by the noted Yiddish writer Mendele Moykher-Sforim, from whose works Karniel took many expressions word for word. As a satirist, however, Karniel also borrowed Mendele's ironic eye, mocking the Jews' provincial herd instinct (characteristic of pilgrims and tourists alike), which, as shown here, had not changed much during the transfer from Mendele's "Kisalon" ("fooltown") to Jerusalem.³⁶

Moreover, Karniel drew the reader's attention to the similarity between the journey to Tel Aviv and the pilgrimage to Mecca. Both had a family character, both involved a huge amount of portable belongings, and both shared the anxious determination to arrive at the shrine on time. Indeed, non-satirical descriptions of panic during the journey to Tel Aviv were repeated in other accounts as well, such as a "woman, with a baby in her arms, [who] was fighting valiantly to take her place in the automobile in order to see the carnival." Or: "They were in such haste to get on the cars, that babies were passed through the windows."³⁷ Passengers prepared themselves for travel, not only in terms of logistics, but also thematically—such as wearing appropriate festive clothing (décolletages) and JNF bands, or other carnival symbols. Unlike Mecca, Tel Aviv was a holy site only during the festival days, so that anyone not there at the right time would not experience the "spiritual uplifting."

---

[35] "Miba'ad la-masveh (Shi'urim be-histaklut)" [From behind the veil (Lessons in looking)], *Doar-Hayom* 9.3.1928. The somewhat non-fluent translation was true to the original Hebrew.

[36] Moykher-Sforim 1991: 377–378. For the modern trait of deriding the tourist's herd instinct, see MacCannell 1975: 9–10. I would like to thank Barbara Mann for drawing my attention to the remarkable resemblance between Karniel's column and Mendele's story.

[37] "Miba'ad la-masveh (Shi'urim be-histaklut)" [From behind the veil (Lessons in looking)], *Doar-Hayom* 9.3.1928; "Yerushalayim" [Jerusalem], *Doar-Hayom* 12.3.1933.

The journey itself is always an important component of the pilgrimage experience. One youth group came from Haifa on foot.[38] Most visitors arrived by train or automated transportation, and overcrowding was the most notable feature of the journey. According to Karniel, again echoing Mendele, in most cars "one must sit so crowded that men and women share their legs while they are jammed together like herrings in a barrel."[39] The experience of overcrowding on the way to the festive central location would serve as preparation for the mass crowding at the event itself.[40]

In the city itself, there were diverse distinctions of sacred time and space. The focus of the celebrations and the pilgrims' interest was the procession, which attracted the greatest number of spectators. Those unable to stay in the city for more than a few hours arrived just for the procession. Hours before, the audience gathered in the streets to take up the best positions for viewing the procession. Sports competitions, humorous competitions, and special shows for children were held before the procession, which traditionally took place at 2 p. m. The same cultural mechanism of gradual distinction operated on the spatial level: the street was expropriated from ordinary public life in order to "sanctify" it for the procession.[41]

The journey home is an opportunity for pilgrims to share their new experiences and process their meaning for the everyday life to which they return. Karniel described a train encounter with a young man on his way back to Jerusalem. Comparing Tel Aviv with Jerusalem, the man contended that in Jerusalem, despite its virtues, he was "in the Arab's, the Englishman's, the gentiles' domain, but on this joyful day I come to Tel Aviv because this is my home … [there] I dwell within my people!"[42] The trip had given this man fresh food for thought regarding his everyday life in Jerusalem.

The experience of the visit extends to the return home. During their journey back to Haifa, young men and women filled a whole train

---

[38] "Yom etmol be-Tel-Aviv ha-hogeget" [Yesterday in festive Tel Aviv], *Davar* 27.3.1929.

[39] "Amar Azmavet" (supra note 34).

[40] Morinis 1992: 15.

[41] On the sacralization of tourist sites, see MacCannell 1975: 43–48.

[42] "Amar Azmavet," *Doar-Hayom* 17.3.1933.

carriage, dancing and singing all the way. One youngster auctioned an orange to the public to benefit the JNF. Continuing the carnival atmosphere, the orange was sold for 620 mil (0.62 Palestine pound).[43]

On their return to the provinces, pilgrims gained the special reputation of those who "were there," which enabled them to share their newly acquired spiritual assets with the unfortunate people who stayed at home.[44] The returnees from Tel Aviv organized additional Purim celebrations in the periphery. Thus, for example, under the headline "A Delayed Purim," the Jerusalem newspaper reported that "most Jerusalemites who traveled to the Tel Aviv carnival came back yesterday," with youngsters wearing Purim costumes as they walked, sang, or danced along Jerusalem's Jaffa Street.[45] That same year, the Jerusalem carnival was held only on the Hebrew date of the eighteenth of Adar, when the celebrators returned from Tel Aviv and wanted to carry on the festivities in their own city. In the 1930s, at the carnival's peak, significant Purim balls were organized on the periphery (for example, in Petah-Tikvah, Rehovot, and Rishon Letzion) —only a few days after Purim, when the celebrators had returned from Tel Aviv. At some stage, the temporal extension of the festival was named "the Purim dancing season," especially in the peripherie, and some called it "Purim *Isru-hag*."[46] It took a few days for everyone (including the youngsters) to return to everyday life and for the intense memory of the city's Purim merriment to gradually fade.

The journey to Tel Aviv and back, therefore, bore the essential characteristics of a pilgrimage. The pilgrims left behind their everyday lives, anticipating a grandiose event. As in classic pilgrimages, they traveled in groups, crowding together in cars, trains, and automobiles.[47] They began arriving in the city a few days before the car-

---

[43] "Haifa," *Doar-Hayom* 10.3.1931.

[44] Barber 1991: 151.

[45] "Yerushalayim: Purim she-nidhah" [Jerusalem: A delayed Purim], *Doar-Hayom* 8.3.1931.

[46] "Petah-Tikvah," *Doar-Hayom* 27.2.1934; "Tel-Aviv ve-Yafo: Isru-hag shel Purim" [Tel Aviv and Jaffa: Purim *Isru-hag*], *Ha'aretz* 11.3.1928. "Isru-hag" (lit.: the day after a festival; see Psalms 118:27) is the "additional" day after each of the three biblical pilgrim festivals (Passover, Pentecost and Tabernacles).

[47] See: Morinis 1992: 15.

nival, while the city itself was being decorated in preparation for the big day. In time and space, the preparations took place in concentric circles, gradually reaching the core of the festival: the carnival procession, held between 2 and 4 p. m. on the Hebrew date of the fifteenth of Adar along Tel Aviv's Hayam, Ben-Yehuda, Allenby, and Herzl streets. On the evenings before and after, there were opening and closing ceremonies, but these were attended by no more than half of those who had watched the procession. The procession was the core event of the pilgrimage.

The Destination

So far, we have shed light on the function of the journey in terms of a pilgrimage. What happens when the pilgrims arrive at the center? According to Turner, the celebrations at the holy site include three necessary ingredients: solemnity, amusement, and commerce.[48] These three elements were all very much in evidence at the Tel Aviv Purim carnival:

Solemnity: the solemn spirit of the carnival was apparent, first and foremost, in the municipality's almost obsessive maintenance of public order, which seemed inconsistent with the mythic carnivalesque abandon but was in fact characteristic of the Zionist *civilizing process* (see chapter four). Moreover, popular songs, theatre, dance, and musical street-shows disseminated the nationalist futurist spirit, which was essentially quite serious. Above all, this spirit was evident in the lavish historical floats, which were features of the parade from 1932 onward. The themes—"the *aliyot* [immigrations] to the Land of Israel," "the poetry of Israel," "Israelite tribes ever after," and "from slavery to freedom"—had clear contemporaneous implications. These overblown floats endowed Jewish history with an aura of sacredness. From this perspective, the physical configuration of a procession was the most appropriate format for exhibiting history: spatially distant from its audience, the procession creates a cultic aura, inducing mystification linked to its performance.[49] These floats and the multitude

---

[48] Turner 1974: 187, 221.
[49] Kirshenblatt-Gimblett & McNamara 1985.

of similar projects, not particularly humorous by nature, were mostly designed to present Jewish sovereignty over urban space.

Amusement: Despite the presence of solemn national ideology, amusement and entertainment played a key role in the carnival. To begin with, the celebrations' explicit aim, as declared by Mayor Dizengoff in his annual opening speech at the festival, was to offer an opportunity for an annual recreation from "our national work."[50] Amusement was indeed the organizing principle of most carnival events other than the procession. In addition to sports or humorous competitions, the carnival featured spectacular lighting and street decorations. The procession itself included entertaining elements, such as the throwing of confetti on the parade.[51] Some floats were indeed slightly comical, particularly those with elements of political satire—whether directed outward (criticizing British policy) or inward (reflecting the political disputes of the *Yishuv*). Unlike other pilgrimage sites, here the aspect of amusement was apparent and explicit. That there should be such a huge gathering just to watch a procession indicates the lack of more entertaining spectacles for Palestine's provincial residents.

Commerce: this element was no less conspicuous than the former two. At first, the carnival was the main source of revenue for several economic sectors, among them owners of restaurants, kiosks, hotels and small boarding houses; not to mention the porters, shoe-shiners, drink sellers, carters, and anyone else employed in the transportation services. None hesitated to charge much steeper prices during the Purim season than during the rest of the year. The municipality did its best to counter the phenomenon, even threatening to prepare a "black list" of businesses that charges exaggerated prices—with no results. To prevent profiteering, the municipality even appealed to the residents, asking them to host visitors for free, but this appeal was met with indifference and even scorn. These complaints were repeated every year, so powerfully as to evoke the antisemitic stereotype of the

---

[50] Meir Dizengoff, "Birkat he-hag" [The festival greeting], *Ha'aretz* 18.3.1935; English version in TAMA 04–3222.

[51] For a full program for the Purim carnival of 1934, and an outline for the Purim carnival of 1935, see TAMA 04–3221a. For the confetti, see for example: "Ha-karnaval be-Tel-Aviv" [Tel Aviv carnival], *Davar* 28.3.1928.

lucre-craving Jew.[52] The most extreme critic was the writer Avigdor Hame'iri (1890–1970), who spoke of the "incurable peddler," and welcomed the cessation of the carnival in 1936 for that reason alone.[53] The clearest evidence of the profits made during the Purim carnival was the fact that after its cancellation, the first and most overwhelming protest to reach the municipality came from the Tel Aviv and Jaffa merchants' organization.[54]

However, commercial prosperity was not the concern of the merchants alone; it was powerfully felt in the street as well. During the carnival, the municipality allowed merchants to display their stock outside their stores, on the streets, and to extend their business hours until ten at night.[55] Illegal peddlers, many of them Arabs, walked through the streets, offering food, drink, or costume accessories.[56] Strolling about the Tel Aviv streets during Purim would have been an intensive shopping experience, as visitors incessantly confronted the temptation to buy, in addition to massive fundraising by the JNF and other national institutions.[57] In short, the sight of money changing hands was an integral aspect of the carnival experience.

The market experience was also revealed on the symbolic level. Under the guise of "promoting *Totzeret Ha'aretz*" (Jewish products), the procession always included many commercial floats.[58] Despite the criticism, and the general consensus that "the commercial ad requires

---

[52] *Iton Meyuhad* 18.2.1934; Uri Keisari, "Keitzad hayim etzlenu" [How we live], *Doar-Hayom* 25.3.1935; *Yedi'ot Iriyat Tel-Aviv* 5 (1935): 138.

[53] Avigdor Hame'iri, "Tagranei Purim" [Purim hucksters], *Doar-Hayom* 12.3.1931; idem, "Al mot la-karnaval" [On the death of the carnival], *Ha'aretz* 8.3.1936.

[54] From the Tel Aviv and Jaffa merchants' organization to the municipality, 20.2.1936; and from the Palestine industrialists' association to the municipality, 2.3.1936; from Dizengoff to industrialists' association, 3.3.1936, TMA 04–3222.

[55] Carnival Committee advertisement, *Doar-Hayom* 6.3.1928; "Tel-Aviv ve-Yafo" [Tel Aviv and Jaffa], *Ha'aretz* 2.3.1928; "Likhvod Purim" [In honor of Purim], *Doar-Hayom* 21.3.1929.

[56] From A. Yemini to Tel Aviv municipality, received on 9.3.1936, TMA 04–3222.

[57] "Amar azmavet" [Thus spoke azmavet], *Doar-Hayom* 25.3.1932.

[58] Chapter one, supra note 70.

much caution," economic activity and its performance were a major part of the event.[59]

Following Abrahams, Helman has interpreted the Tel Aviv Purim carnival as "celebrating the economy": every year it depicted and celebrated the abundant agricultural, industrial, and commercial products of the *Yishuv*. Economic activity, therefore, not only took place "backstage," but was also acted and performed "on stage," in the carnival procession itself.[60] This reflection of the centrality of commercial activity in the new Zionist society indicated the development of a typical capitalist consumer society, tied with nationalist ideology.[61]

In fact, the three elements of solemnity, amusement, and commerce were intertwined in every aspect of the carnival, in the *Adloyada* procession and the official and unofficial surrounding activities. According to Helman, these three elements were a permanent feature of Tel Aviv's everyday life, which integrated amusement and entertainment, hectic commercial activity and solemn futurist Zionist ideology. But beyond everyday life, this discourse was intensified by the prevailing image of Tel Aviv as the new Jewish place of fun and sun, commerce and leisure, a city of freedom in contrast to the darkness of Exile. For Tel Aviv's permanent residents, the Purim carnival was a festive reflection of their ordinary life, somewhat intensified. For non-residents, however, the Purim carnival provided an annual opportunity to share this experience. Due to its singularity, the one-day Jewish urbanity they experienced was more of a ritual than a true mundane experience.

A children's play, originally written as promotion for the carnival, well illustrates this imaginative dimension. The play takes place in a small village and portrays the panic that characterized the collective travel to the carnival. It describes how all community activity, agricultural cycles, and other important cultural-ideological values were swept away in favor of the urgent need to travel to Tel Aviv. The play opens as follows:

---

[59] Moshe Glikson, "Al haperek" [On the agenda], *Ha'aretz* 28.3.1929. See also: editorial letter, *Ha'aretz* 8.3.1927.
[60] Abrahams 1982; Helman 2006: 388–89.
[61] Sassatelli 2007: 1–6.

Chapter 2. "Travelling to Esther": A Civil-Religious and Pilgrimage Event

> The location—a community center in a distant Samarian village. The main protagonist, she who charms and attracts the whole *Yishuv* from Metula to Ruhama, Tel Aviv, does not appear on stage. She shows her charm and enchantment over there, on the Mediterranean coast. Here in the village, they desire and yearn for this beauty queen, think of her, hallucinate and dream about her.[62]

While noting the obvious promoting tone, we can discern here the usual mythical discourse about Tel Aviv. In this instance, the viewpoint is from the periphery, revealing the provincial desire for city life with its imagined congestion, hedonism, and freedom. Since these qualities were attached to the specific *locus*, this annual ritual of traveling to Tel Aviv provided the opportunity to experience mythic urban Jewish life, which, during the rest of the year, was mere hearsay.

When provincials arrive at the great city they had heard so much about, they experience both desire and repulsion, and do their best to assimilate into the urban environment. However, since in this case the pilgrimage center was not a specific shrine but the entire urban space, the pilgrims' attention was not directed towards a specific location but diverted by a sequence of distractions.[63] A sharp-eyed metropolitan observer, the young poet Nathan Alterman (1910–1970), wrote such an imagined provincial-in-the-big-city carnival account, in the well-known song "The Couple on the Roof" (written for his satirical review for the theater), which gently mocks this imagined provincial behavior. His protagonists, a man and a woman, have come from distant Afula in the Jezreel valley, both wearing their fanciest clothes. Watching the procession from the roof, they experience the crowding, the pickpockets, the jostling by other spectators, and the temptation to look at (but not touch!) other potential objects of desire. When the man displays excitement at the performance, the woman silences him: "Don't be such a provincial! Haven't you ever seen a carnival?" Soon after, she loudly expresses her own admiration. When she catches sight of Baruch Agadati, filming the carnival, she thinks that they are now being filmed, and orders her companion: "Let's not

---

[62] Shlomo Hillels, "Le-Tel-Aviv (bedihah le-Purim)" [To Tel Aviv (A comic tale for Purim)], CZA KKL5/49171/1.

[63] Simmel 1997.

sit here like dummies! Use your miming skills and kiss me! All Afula will be amazed!"[64]

In the frequent periodical discourse, Afula was usually mentioned as a place in which nothing happens.[65] Indeed, the song was written from the imaginary provincial's point of view, with their typical nervous sensitivities when participating in such a massive event. The city is a dangerous place, due to its urban crowdedness, but the greatest danger, beyond congestion and pickpockets, was that of the gaze. The man in the song has to promise that he "will keep with faith/ like before the wedding," since the city, as is well-known, is characterized not only by pretty and tempting women but also by an atmosphere of sexual recklessness.[66] However, the real problem of people from the provinces is that they tend to suspect that everyone is watching and judging them. This exaggerated self-consciousness makes the woman think that the cinematographer's lens is directed at her.[67] Her fantasy of being seen as an authentic metropolitan woman includes a passionate kiss with her "dummy" mate, to make her local provincial friends green with envy. This potential nationwide visibility does not make her worry about social sanctions at home, since everyone will concede that whatever she did took place at the licentious Purim carnival in Tel Aviv. This was a realization of one of the carnival slogans, according to which "from Dan to Beer-Sheba/ from Metula to Nahalal/ [people] will come to Tel Aviv/ to see and be seen in the carnival."[68]

We can assume that the urban experience of the masses who came to Tel Aviv from all over Palestine was not as extreme as the scene depicted by Alterman. Obviously, Hebrew urban life appeared much more glamorous on Purim than on any other day. The mass pil-

---

[64] Nathan Alterman, "Pizmonot le-Purim tartzag" [Songs for Purim 1933], *Turim* 29–30 (28.2.1933); reprinted in Alterman 1979: 213–215.

[65] Troen 2003: 136.

[66] The danger of using the hands for different purposes—theft or "sexual harassment"—stood at the core of a parody written by poet Avraham Shlonsky on this song (see: Halperin 1997: 266).

[67] The shots filmed by Agadati at the carnival were indeed edited for a five-minute episode in the film *Zot hi ha'aretz* [This is the Land, 1934], Spielberg Jewish Film Archive, Hebrew University, Jerusalem, VT DA330. See: Shoham 2011b.

[68] Announcement of carnival committee, *Ha'aretz* 11.2.1931.

grimage to Tel Aviv for the Purim carnival enhanced the mythical discourse of the young and "miraculous" city, helping to bolster it as the "core area" of the Jewish sector in Palestine on a symbolic level. The imaginary provincial experience described by Alterman had an obvious ideological goal: to create and empower the urban myth of Tel Aviv, and to position the city at the "center" of the *Yishuv*.[69] In the context of the three elements described here—culture (solemn ideology), economy (commerce), and entertainment—the self-image of a new Jewish capital city seemed hard to refute.

But how exactly was this imagined urbanity connected to the Jewish nationalist project? To understand more specifically the content of the myths and ideology of Urban Zionism, let us now turn to the meaning of the pilgrimage.

Urban Zionist Ideology

The meaning of every pilgrimage can be analyzed on two levels: the cultural, including the specific myths, symbols, and ritual practices; and the social, including the social relationships that are reconfigured through the act of pilgrimage.[70] On the cultural level, I will focus on two eminent biblical symbols: Queen Esther and the Persian capital, Shushan.

For some people, traveling to Tel Aviv on Purim became the classic religious pilgrimage. I mentioned above the large Bukharan family who told Karniel, "we are traveling to Esther." Karniel himself associated this reply with the traditional ceremony of chanting the Book of Esther at the tombs of Mordechai and Esther in Akhmadan, Persia, which popular opinion identified with biblical Shushan and which attracted many pilgrims every Purim.[71] The Akhmadan site preoccupied Purim celebrators in Palestine as well, and remained the focus of several articles and polemics in professional and popular

---

[69] See Azaryahu 2007b: 171–77. On Alterman's mythical urban project, see Eidar 2003.

[70] Morinis 1992: 22–24.

[71] "Amar Azmavet," *Doar-Hayom*, 25.3.1932.

publications.[72] To the extent that Tel Aviv was indeed a substitute for Akhmadan, Esther became a popular saint. As the patron of the celebrations, she "owned" them, bestowing her name upon them.

This interpretation was further circulated by the decision of the organizing committee to build the street theater "Esther's Palace" in 1932. Unlike the two male statues of King Ahasuerus and Mordechai, the Queen Esther stood upright, 30 meters high, watching over her celebrations.[73] This giant figure can be seen as a substitute for the flesh-and-blood Queen Esther, after the cancellation of the Hebrew Queen Esther beauty contests in 1930. Whether represented by a human body or a giant mannequin figure, Esther was symbolically given sovereignty over Tel Aviv during festival time. Like other local festivals in the world, the Tel Aviv celebrations had a patron-saint.

While Esther represented current Jewish sovereignty over urban space, similarities were also drawn between Tel Aviv and biblical Shushan. The slogan "The city of Tel Aviv rejoiced and was glad," which echoed the biblical verse about Shushan [Esther 8:15], appeared everywhere. Mayor Dizengoff even chose this phrase to conclude his annual speech at the opening ceremony.[74] This was quite unusual in terms of Zionist ideology. Indeed, journalists such as Uri Keisari questioned the cultural benefit of these comparisons, and wondered why "the first Hebrew city" should exalt a beautiful mistress who saved her people by manipulating the carnal lust of a corrupt king. Moreover, why should the Hebrew city compare itself to a decadent cosmopolitan city best known for its multilingual atmosphere, not to mention its multitude of feasts and banquets?[75]

---

[72] See N. Abrahamov, "Purim be-eretz Haman" [Purim in Haman's land], *Krovetz le-Purim* (1935): 11; Ze'ev Vilna'i, "Kivrah shel ha-malkah" [The Queen's gravesite], in Lewinsky 1955: 15.

[73] For additional photos of Esther's Palace, see Fisher 1984: 96; fragments 71–76 from Axelrod cinema news broadcast, Spielberg Jewish Film Archive, Hebrew University, Jerusalem, VT ax10; unidentified British film, Spielberg Jewish Film Archive, Hebrew University, Jerusalem, VT 00034; and a contract for the construction of this project, 25.2.1932, TAMA 04–3219c.

[74] "Lamrot ha-matar: Purim mutzlakh be-Tel-Aviv" [Despite the downpour: A successful Purim in Tel Aviv], *Doar-Hayom* 5.3.1931; Meir Dizengoff, "Birkat he-hag" [The festival's greeting], *Ha'aretz* 18.3.1935.

[75] Uri Keisari, "Ester, Akhashverosh, Haman, Mordekhai et Kompani…" [Esther, Ahasuerus, Haman, Mordekhai, and co.], *Doar-Hayom* 22.3.1932;

This artistic-ideological choice can be understood only by analyzing it within its own ideological framework—that of Urban Zionism—rather than judging it in terms of competing Zionist doctrines. The carnival celebrated the building of a "thoroughly Hebrew city," an exclusively Jewish public sphere, and a stratified and diversified Jewish society, which could not be populated only by farmers and warriors. Unlike other civic-religion events in the Yishuv, which emphasized the return to the soil, heroism, or nationalist sacrifice, the Purim carnival emphasized the flourishing of commerce, the sovereignty over urban space, and the personal freedom of every individual Jew—somewhat anti-macho (Esther) and cosmopolitan (Shushan), but still nationalist ideology. I will elaborate on this in the concluding chapter.

Communitas *and the* Zionist Masses

The cultural aspect cannot fully explain the powerful gravitational force of the carnival, given its relative lack of artistic value or any other aesthetic virtue, which was remarked upon by many visitors and even by some of the carnival's enthusiasts and spokespersons. Alterman, for example, wrote about a street light in the form of a carousel: "the astonishing lack of taste of this anonymous creation irritated none of the open-eyed wanderers who crowded around the crib of the newborn carnival. For me, this was the first clue that Tel Aviv is inspired with a mood of forgiving festivity."[76] Alterman implied that the carnival's power was not to be found in its artistic and aesthetic achievements, but elsewhere. So what was it that attracted all these people to the carnival?

This question may be answered by turning our attention to the social aspect of the carnival. Many modern sites and events attract tourists by claiming to display the society that lives at the site or is reflected in it.[77] In our case, this claim was explicit: even the carnival's

---

idem, "Ester, Ester, mizgi lanu yayin" [Esther, Esther, pour us some wine], *Doar-Hayom* 24.3.1935. See Halperin 2011.

[76] Aluf nun [Natan Alterman], "Adloyada be-Tel-Aviv" [Carnival in Tel Aviv], the Israeli center for documenting stage arts, file 62.3.7.

[77] MacCallenn 1975: 48.

harshest critics, who mercilessly condemned it as poor, banal, unoriginal, and overly commercial, admitted to feeling some satisfaction in the huge national gathering of so many Jews in Tel Aviv.[78] In other words, the main pull of the carnival did not lie in any artistic sophistication, the procession, or the attendant activities, but in the mass gathering itself, that is, the audience. According to a foreign account of the Purim procession by a British tourist, "[The procession] was neither grand nor distinguished, but the passion which had made it still held Tel Aviv in its grip. The air was alive. The faces of the people glowed with conquest. They had built the only Jewish city in the world."[79] In other words, the powerful tourist attraction was the new, exclusively Jewish urban public sphere. It was this that stirred everyone, and it was this that generated the tangible excitement in the air. More than anything else, the Tel Aviv Purim carnival was an *ideological attraction*.

Moreover, the concentration of such a massive number of Jews in a large capitalist city provided a real urban experience of congestion and alienation within a mass of people, so familiar from the literature of Western urbanism and hence desired by cosmopolitan Zionists.[80] There was a significant gap between the actual everyday experience of living in or visiting the city, which, after all, was not such an alienated place (at least until the mid-1930s), and the mythical discourse linked to it, which emphasized its metropolitan character as a key component of its Western "normalized" self-image.[81] Nevertheless, the Purim carnival provided an annual opportunity to experience this discourse, for the local population and pilgrims alike. In other words, it was a ritualistic experience, alien to the participants' ordinary life. The annual ritualistic obfuscation of individual faces in favor of the urban mass

---

[78] For example: R., "He'arot u-reshimot: Purim be-Tel-Aviv" [Notes and impressions: Purim in Tel Aviv], *Hapo'el Hatza'ir* 5.4.1929, 15–16; G. Hanoch, "Sidrei-hayim (Reshimot be-ikvot ha-Purim)" [Ways of life (Notes on Purim)], *Hapo'el Hatza'ir* 5.3.1926, 14–15.

[79] Bolitho 1933: 107.

[80] This genre is well illustrated by works of many authors, from Friedrich Engels, Charles Dickens and Charles Baudelaire to Ferdinand Toennies, Georges Simmel and Walter Benjamin. See, for example: Simmel 1997.

[81] Eidar 2003: 197–231; Tammy Razi, "Tel Aviv as Dystopia" (work in progress).

created a sort of *Communitas* in Turner's sense: the Purim urban mass was created by a temporary suspension of every previous life-context—age, peer group, gender, ethnicity (to some extent, even Arabic), profession, political affiliation, residence—except for Jewishness. As in western urban literature, the carnival physically presented the masses as an independent social entity. But unlike that literature, this was a positive presentation, displaying the emerging Jewish masses in Palestine as a true historical force, rather than a merely discursive construction.

This civil religion and its ideology were thus prescriptive rather than descriptive. The regular moral imperative of the tourist: "You ought to be there, experience and see this," became a concrete ideological imperative: "You *ought* to be there, to experience the happiness in our new homeland."[82]

Conclusion: A Local-National Tradition

Every site of pilgrimage has its own "catchment area."[83] As we saw, the Tel Aviv carnival was particularly powerful in the sphere of domestic tourism, so its catchment area was the whole *Yishuv*. The evolution of the local invented tradition of Tel Aviv into a nationwide event demonstrated the growth of Tel Aviv not only as a regional commercial and cultural capital, but also as the symbolic center of the new Jewish Palestine, and as a central social site of Zionist identity construction. The annual mass gathering of such a large proportion of the Jewish population highlighted the symbolic importance of Tel Aviv, far beyond its geographical boundaries. The comparison with biblical Jerusalem, noted above, was not out of place: Tel Aviv turned into the non-official capital of the *Yishuv*—that is, of the national Jewish society.

The Purim carnival in Tel Aviv created the new Jewish public sphere in a circular manner: it celebrated its own existence and simultaneously represented and re-created it, thus realizing Durkheim's conception of a modern "secular" religion, in which a society

---

[82] MacCallenn 1975: 9–10.
[83] Turner 1974: 178–79.

worships itself without any supernatural mediation.[84] Nevertheless, unlike ordinary forms of civil religion, in which the concept of society is an abstraction, these Purim celebrations *physically* and *visibly* presented the Jewish masses, which were *revealed* as the Nation. In a typical Durkheimian circular manner, this nation was both the subject and the object of civil religion, both the exalting and the exalted. It turns out that the only ideological element that could attract such a mass of Jews to one place and constitute a Jewish public sphere was precisely Urban Zionism.

In other words, when analyzed as a mass movement rather than a monastic one, Zionism appears to be much more pro-urban than the frequency of anti-urban rhetoric suggested. The following chapters will discuss the particular outlooks of Urban Zionist ideology regarding the relationship between tradition and modernity (chapter three), the new Jewish body (four), the Zionist attitude toward non-Jews (five) and gender roles (six). Urban Zionist opinions in these issues will be examined through their appearance in the carnival's performances, and in the interpretational discourse about them, with special attention paid to the use of traditional themes in the modern urban context. I shall begin with an examination of the uses of the concept of tradition in the Tel Aviv Purim carnival.

---

[84] Moore and Myerhoff 1977; Durkheim 1915: 214.

CHAPTER 3

"A Little Bit of Tradition"

The Concept of Tradition

This tension between continuity and rupture is characteristic of all modern nationalist movements. In general, it may be said that for several decades, scholars of modern nationalism have been divided into two camps. "Modernists" (such as Gellner) viewed nationalism as embedded (as an outcome or a cause) in the collapse of pre-modern "traditional society" and thus emphasized the modern rupture. Those of the second camp are "perennialists" who emphasize modern nationalism's continuation of pre-modern identities. This dichotomy is actually based on a classical dichotomy in social science between "tradition" and "modernity" as two opposed ideal-types. Many scholars who followed this typology noticed the actual mixture of the two ideal-types in modern nationalism, but chose to underscore one of the two as the determinant.[1]

The same division may be found among scholars of Zionism, who frequently considered the tension between continuity and rupture "the bedrock of Zionist discourse."[2] The actual mixture of tradition and modernity in Zionist thought and praxis was viewed as an ongoing modernization process, while scholars seemed to disagree only about its success. However, both sides—whether they speak about successful or failed modernization—agree that the continuous presence of tradition should be attributed to the "irrationalism" of nationalism, and that tradition is an anti-modern or non-modern phenomenon, a residue from pre-modern life. Among other factors, this narrow point of view resulted from the traditional historiographic

---

[1] For example: Brubaker 1996: 13–22; Smith 2000: 27–51; Gorski 2000; Pecora 2001: 25–29.

[2] Penslar 2007: 3. See also: Roshwald 2004; Saposnik 2008: 9–16.

focus on Zionist pioneers, who incessantly talked about their "rebellion" against Jewish tradition.[3] As we shall see here, in Urban Zionism "tradition" and "modernity" did not clash and were even associated with each other to create new cultural formations. The classical dichotomy of modernity and tradition, even if generally rejected and roundly criticized as too rude, firm, abstract, and Eurocentric, has not been replaced by a methodological substitute and still permeates the study of modern nationalism.[4] To avoid the use of this overstated meta-theory, I shall suggest a new working definition for the concept, followed by a close examination of its uses in the modern urban context.

Elsewhere, I defined "tradition" as "a socio-cultural practice that assigns temporal meaning."[5] In other words, rather than an ontological entity, tradition is a symbolic activity that attributes traditional qualities to certain sectors of life that are understood as binding together different times to create a continuous identity. This paradigm allows tradition to include various modes of temporality—long-range and short-range, past-oriented and future-oriented, cyclical and linear, fragmented and continuous—in all their possible permutations and combinations, along with modes of different social units. Importantly, this sense of temporality does not necessarily imply total continuity, but can also function as a conceptual frame for grasping changes and discontinuities.

Such temporal meanings were assigned both to Purim celebrations since 1920 and to the entire Jewish pre-modern tradition. As we shall see, the relationships between the two were conceptualized through the term "tradition," which was taken to assign different temporal modes to the practice of Purim.

Hence, this chapter will focus on the accurate functions of the concept of tradition as a socio-cultural mechanism, that is, the explicit discourse on tradition and its role in Zionist identity construction, as exemplified in the Tel Aviv Purim carnival. The discourse on tradition was much wider than that on traditionalism, that is, the narrow debate

---

[3] The literature is voluminous. See, in a nutshell: Katz 1979: 6, 85–108; Shapira 1988: 72; Berkowitz 1993: 5–7; Raz-Karkotzkin 1993; Shapira 1997a; Eisenstadt 1998; Bartal 2002.

[4] See critiques of the classical dichotomy: Shils 1981: 7–10; Eisenstadt 1983: 98–114; Heelas 1996: 7–11; Taylor 1999.

[5] Shoham 2011a: 315.

regarding affirming or negating tradition. This discourse included the four aspects discerned by Thompson: the hermeneutical aspect, the normative aspect, the legitimization of authority, and the construction of identity.[6] A study of the discourse on tradition reveals the centrality of the concept of tradition as an identity-constructor, alongside additional "modern" connotations that were added to the concept in the industrial era.

As a conceptual framework for understanding the relationship between the invented tradition of Purim in Tel Aviv and the pre-Zionist tradition, we may use, and somewhat alter, a classical distinction between "great" and "little" traditions made by the anthropologist Robert Redfield several decades ago. For Redfield it was a *spatial* distinction between traditions of great civilizations that are "consciously cultivated and handed down" and local or folk traditions that are "for the most part taken for granted and not submitted to much scrutiny or considered refinement and improvement."[7] Displacing these conceptualizations to the discursive realm, I suggest that there are great and little traditions *in time*: great old traditions that are perceived as given, as having a long history, and hence as beyond current human intervention, such as "the Jewish tradition" as opposed to young little traditions that are perceived as novel and thus (unlike in Redfield's opinion) more easily submitted to scrutiny and improvement. In the industrial era, these were what the historian Erik Hobsbawm designated "invented traditions"—cultural practices consciously invented as human artifices, though they conducted complicated dialogue with great traditions—such as Purim celebrations in Tel Aviv.

I will begin by tracing concrete uses of the word "tradition" to describe the celebrations, including the carnival procession and the dance balls, as indicating a conscious reflection on these practices as new traditions. Then I will map the semantic field of the concept, which was broadened to include "modern" connotations such as "progress" and "expertise," alongside pre-modern meanings, and demonstrate its actual effect on the institutionalization of the celebrations. The chapter will end with discerning two discourses regarding the relationship between past and present, which will be designated "folklorist" and

---

[6] Thompson 1996: 91–93; Sagi 2008: 6. On differences between tradition and traditionalism see: Boyer 1987; Gadamer 2002: 280–281; Sagi 2008: 8–10.

[7] Redfield 1960: 42.

"modernist." Interestingly, despite the differences between the two, there was similarity regarding their use of the concept of tradition.

Purim Celebrations as an Independent Tradition

Although Zionist Purim celebrations began in the late Ottoman era, the concept of them as tradition appears in sources only after World War I. The balls that had been organized since 1908, and the street processions that began in 1913 or 1914, were not defined as traditions. In the British Mandate period, however, both the balls and the street carnival were talked about as small traditions. The year 1920 was retroactively determined as the point of their genesis, while the existence of any Purim celebrations in the *Yishuv* before World War I was forgotten.

A notable example of this discourse on tradition can be found in descriptions the balls of Agadati. The first was organized in 1921, and as early as 1922 the ball was advertised as "the traditional Purim ball," with no additional explanation.[8] In 1925, Agadati's ball was defined in a report as "the traditional"—without even the noun "ball."[9] From that year and onward, the announcements of Agadati's balls numbered the years of the ball's existence, with 1920 as "year zero." "The ball's first decade"—1930—was markedly celebrated.

Agadati was not the only entrepreneur to title his balls "traditional." In 1923, a Purim ball in "Eden" theatre was also reported as "a matter of tradition, for already quite a few years."[10] Actually, it had existed for four years, at most.[11] Other organizers, such as the *"Hamaccabi"* club in Haifa, or the *"Hakumkum"* theatre, defined their balls as "traditional," although not all of them announced the number of years they had existed.[12] "Tradition" could thus refer to a very short time span. For example, although the first Hebrew Queen Esther

---

[8] Announcement of "Sha'ar Tzion" library, *Doar-Hayom* 14.3.1922.

[9] *Doar-Hayom* 12.3.1925.

[10] "Purim be-Tel-Aviv" [Purim in Tel Aviv], *Doar-Hayom* 7.3.1923.

[11] See announcement about "Eden" ball, dated to 1919, in: Ze'evi 1988: 481.

[12] Ad of *"Hakumkum"* [pot] ball, *Doar-Hayom* 21.2.1928; Ad for "Hamacabi" ball in Haifa, Purim 1929, and an ad for a ball in "Eden" Haifa, in the posters collection, national library, file V1969/3; announcement 1 and 2 on Agadati's ball, Purim 1930, and announcement of the ball of "Macabi avsh-

election gala was organized in 1926, it was already defined as a "tradition" in 1928.[13]

In common discourse, the "traditional" Purim balls indicated the involvement of a non-profit organization with cultural, educational, or political orientation—as opposed to "private" balls that were organized in cafés, restaurants, and hotels. For example, it was reported in newspapers that the traditional ball of the "Ohel" theatre would take place in the "Mugrabi" theater, whereas, by contrast, a private ball would take place in the "Ophir" theater.[14] This distinction was important for the Zionist media, particularly because the two types of balls were not necessarily different in practice or in financial motivations on the part of the organizers; both types of balls sought to earn money from their events while deducting allocations to the JNF. Needless to say, the Zionist media was interested in the traditional balls, considered them central cultural loci, and reported many minor details: the atmosphere, who wore what, cultural and commercial innovations, and of course who was elected "Queen Esther" of the ball. The "private" balls were generally neglected.

Indeed, as we have seen in chapter one, during the 1930s there was a gradual diminution in the balls' status as a site of identity construction. Increasingly, media and municipal documents spoke of "dance balls" instead of "costume balls," with an increasing number of private balls at the expense of traditional ones.[15] In 1935, there were already several dozen private balls before Purim.[16] Apparently, some of these balls were not commercial, but private parties that were habitual gatherings of friends, which included women's talk about "clothing, cosmetics and recipes" alongside men's talk about "commerce while listening to the notices of London's stock market in the radio-gramophone. Then, at twelve o'clock exactly everyone stood up, expressed

---

alom" Petah-Tiqwa, in the posters collection, national library, file V1969/4. See also: Ze'evi 1988: 485, 487.

[13] "Tel-Aviv," *Ha'aretz* 7.2.1928. See also the announcement of Agadati's election ball in Purim 1929, in the posters collection, national library, file V1969/4.

[14] "Bulmus ha-Purim be-Tel-Aviv" [Purim craziness in Tel Aviv], *Doar-Hayom* 13.3.1930.

[15] Internal memo of the Tel Aviv municipality, 3.4.1929, TAMA 04–3218a.

[16] *Ha'aretz* 17.3.1935.

good wishes and affirmed that 'they were never so delighted as they were this evening,' and with the blessing 'see you next Purim' they went back home to their boring everyday lives."[17] These parties may have differed from other parties only by virtue of the Purim costumes. Mostly, these were dance parties which resembled the usual parties held in Tel Aviv.

After 1936 and the decline of the carnival, there were still many Purim parties held throughout the *Yishuv*, with costumes, dancing, and all the related activities. However, in 1938, a newspaper sadly announced that "only the *Hamatat'e* theatre is organizing a traditional costume ball this year, in the *Mugrabi* Theater."[18] All the other balls were private and hence had no public meaning for the Zionist media, which no longer reported on Purim balls in the late 1930s. *Hamatat'e* was the only institution that tried to organize traditional Purim balls after 1936, but these were quite unsuccessful and were probably discontinued after 1938.

A similar process may be detected in the street carnival. If we ignore for the moment the last-minute cancellation of the 1920 carnival and the forgotten 1914 procession, the first costume processions were organized by *Kapai* (the Palestine worker's fund) between 1921 and 1923. In 1924, after a public debate regarding the right to organize the carnival as a fundraiser, it was announced that "this year *Kapai* will organize the traditional procession."[19] In order to fundraise, *Kapai* urged the public to purchase its ribbons and revenue stamps: "By purchasing the ribbons, the public will show appreciation for the effort of the *Kapai* organization over several years to create a popular and pleasant festival with added educational value."[20] The educational value of the "popular and pleasant festival" was indicated by the fact that they organized the festival "for several years" and had created temporal continuity.

The definition of the carnival as a "tradition" was a crucial argument in favor of its institutionalization, for example in the context of

---

[17] *Iton Meyuhad* 27.3.1938.

[18] *Ha'aretz* 13.3.1938.

[19] "Tahalukha shel masekhot be-Purim" [A costume procession in Purim], *Ha'aretz* 21.2.1924.

[20] An announcement on "masks and costumes festival" by *Kapai*, in the posters collection, national library, file V1969/4 (reprinted in: Carmiel 1999: 230).

the 1928 debate between the JNF and the municipality described in chapter one above. The main reason given in favor of the carnival was that it had already been in the process of becoming a local tradition.[21] In due course, the carnival's financial instability caused annual rumors about its possible cessation, which generated loud protest. Bialik, for example, emphasized that "the cancellation of Purim celebrations, which have already became a tradition and might become a true folk festival, for the benefit and fun of the masses—is inconceivable."[22] The concept of tradition, alongside the public's enjoyment, was thus imperative in justifying the demand to maintain the celebrations.

After Bialik's death in 1934, some suggested cancelling the 1935 carnival to publicly mourn his passing. However, this suggestion was rejected by the committee, which argued that

> With his healthy folkish sense, Bialik always objected to cancelling folk tradition, since, *when isn't there some mourning for Israel?* [Commemorating him in the celebrations] will be more reverent to Bialik, may he rest in peace, than turning a traditional-popular festival into a day of boredom and idleness.[23]

Under the auspices of the municipality's organizing committee, the carnival indeed received greater public recognition as a stable and constant tradition and an important site of national identity construction, along with becoming the largest invented tradition in the *Yishuv*. Everyone was proud of the capacity of the young city to develop a steady and significant tradition.

---

[21] An editorial letter by Y. Ben-Ya'akov and A. Kamini (members of JNF national committee), *Ha'aretz* 14.2.1928; "Tel-Aviv ve-yafo" [Tel Aviv and Jaffa], *Ha'aretz* 17.2.1928; "Yafo ve-Tel-Aviv" [Jaffa and Tel Aviv], *Doar-Hayom* 20.2.1928; "Tel-Aviv ve-yafo: Hakarnival yesudar" [Tel Aviv and Jaffa: The carnival will be organized], *Ha'aretz* 22.2.1928; "Moda'a ravreva" [Great announcement], *Doar-Hayom* 26.2.1928. See some protocols of city council meetings: Helman 2006a: note 25.

[22] *Yediot Iriyat Tel-Aviv* 4, 1933, 116.

[23] From the association of writers and artists to municipality, 23.12.1934, TAMA 04–3220c; from the association of painters and sculptors, 15.1.1935; a formal press release from the municipality, undated, TAMA 04–3222. Emphasis original.

This was precisely why the cancellation of the carnival in 1936 created a public scandal.[24] The carnival had been cancelled once before, in 1930, but the reason then was security concerns in the wake of the riots of summer 1929. In 1936, the sole and obvious reason was clearly the municipality's organizational incapacity, described above.[25] The cessation of the tradition was perceived as more than just an organizational failure. It was viewed as a real cultural menace, due to the failure of cultural entrepreneurs to create an authentic culture.

In order to understand why it was so important to maintain tradition, we should analyze the connotations of the concept's semantic field in contemporaneous discourse: expertise, linear progress, authenticity, spontaneity, and stability.

Discourse on Tradition

In his studies about traditions in urban contexts, Redfield understood the concept of tradition as linked to large civilizations with developed urban centers, in which the tradition is handed down by the particular caste of intellectuals, who received the knowledge of previous generations and further refurbished it. Redfield and Singer made an analogy between the development of tradition and urbanization, both seen as a process of progress.[26] This time-perception was generally accepted as the temporal framework for the balls, and even more so for the street carnival. There was constant talk about the carnival's advancement, improvement, and progress, as a major temporal framework.

In many documents, it was repeatedly and clearly stated that beyond its economic benefits, the main motivation for organizing the carnival was either (1) that it had already become a tradition and could not be discontinued; or (2) that with the right institutional investment in money, manpower, and thought, it had the potential to become a stable tradition. Both arguments were habitually integrated so as to complement each other. Tradition was thus understood as a temporal praxis, stretched between the adjacent past and the distant future as

---

[24] Announcement of the carnival committee, 29.1.1936, TAMA, file 04–3222.
[25] "Tel-Aviv," *Doar-Hayom* 8.3.1936.
[26] Redfield & Singer 1969: 225–227; Singer 1972: 42–43.

a progressive process of linear advancement. Whether one looks back and observes its progress until the present, or looks forward in order to gain an overview of its future progress,—the present should fulfill its task and link the past with the future. In practical and normative terms: tradition must be continued.

It should be noted that at first, when Agadati advertised "his" balls and announced the number of years they had been held, the reason was clearly commercial. He used his reputation to guarantee the expertise of the organizers who conducted the most spoken-about ball since the earliest days of Tel Aviv's Purim celebrations in 1920, and he also sought to sell tickets: "This year, as every year, B. Agadati is organizing his traditional masquerade balls."[27] It was agreed that "Agadati's traditional balls are becoming more sophisticated every year and are attracting a large crowd," or, in other words, that his expertise had gained ground over the years.[28] Agadati was described and branded as "the authorized expert for Purim affairs" along with his "ministry."[29] Similarly, the "*Hamataté*" theatre claimed that "its members are authorized as having established inventions in amusements."[30] In these contexts, the "tradition" referred to the experience accumulated throughout several years of managing the business. The experts mentioned here were performative experts, such as painters, actors, directors, clowns, and others, as well as administrative and financial experts and scholars. The concept of tradition indicated the improvement of the events through temporal continuity.

Another connotation of tradition was the repetitiveness of an event that was organized once a year on a Jewish festival. When Agadati was asked by a reporter about his return from abroad, he responded: "The month of Adar [the Hebrew month of Purim] is approaching. You know, we can't forget the tradition."[31] The annual

---

[27] "Nishfey hamasekhot hamasortiyim shel B. Agadati" [Agadati's traditional masquerade balls], *Doar-Hayom* 6.3.1927.

[28] "Yerushalayim yom yom: Neshef Agadati"[Everyday Jerusalem: Agadati's ball], *Doar-Hayom* 13.3.1927.

[29] "Erev Purim be-Tel-Aviv" [Purim evening in Tel Aviv], *Doar-Hayom* 24.2.1929.

[30] Ad of "Hamatat'e" [groom], *Doar-Hayom* 18.3.1932.

[31] Uri Keisari, "Im hazerem …: Im Agadati, al kos teh" [Along the stream …: A cup of tea with Agadati], *Doar-Hayom* 13.2.1928.

recurrence of the day directs the attention not so much to the "great tradition" or the Hebrew calendar, but to the previous or next year, that is, the small invented tradition, which compelled Agadati to return from abroad. Unlike Redfield and Singer's model, the "progress" was not made over the course of generations but over a much shorter time span—several years. The element of repetitiveness was connected to the element of progress in the range of possibilities for mass entertainment in Tel Aviv.

The discourse on small tradition was highly reflective. It relentlessly described and analyzed its own development from its outset. In many cases, the decorations at the balls were paintings or photos of Purim celebrations from previous years, including one ethnographic exhibit about the topic that was organized for a Purim ball in 1935 (Agadati tried to organize such an exhibit as early as 1925).[32]

Some of the retrospectives went as far as the "pre-history" of the balls. The writer Bracha Chavas (1900–1968), for example, remembered in 1929 the intimacy of the *Akhuzat-Bayit* balls of her youth before World War I. They were still organized in private spaces but emphasized costumes and artistic floats instead of the Purim meal, *Shalach-Monos*, and other traditional practices. From her perspective, the story of Purim balls was the story of the "outing" of Jewish joy from indoors to outdoors. Needless to say, by no means was Chavas the only one to be nostalgic about pre-urban Tel Aviv Purim celebrations, as opposed to the present urban and alienated celebrations.[33] However, the balls of *Hapo'el Hatza'ir* before World War I were generally forgotten, and 1920 was retrospectively determined as the genesis point of the tradition in its current form.[34]

---

[32] "Tel-Aviv ve-yafo" [Tel Aviv and Jaffa], *Ha'aretz* 24.2.1928; ad of Agadati ball, *Doar-Hayom* 13.3.1930; "Tokhnit hagigot ohel Purim be-ulamey hata'arukha" [Program of Ohel Purim celebrations in the exhibit halls], *Doar-Hayom* 6.3.1935; "Likrat nishfey Purim be-Tel-Aviv" [Toward Purim balls in Tel Aviv], *Doar-Hayom* 17.3.1935; "Mikhtav galuy shel B. Agadati" [An open letter of B. Agadati], *Ha'aretz* 10.3.1925.

[33] Bracha Chavas in: Lewinsky 1955: 279–280; "Mah she-ani ro'eh ve-shome'a be-Tel-Aviv" [What I see and hear in Tel Aviv], *Do'ar ha-yom*, 25.2.1934

[34] For example: Simcha Asaf, "Purim bitefutzut yisrael" [Purim in Israel Diasporas], central Zionist archive KKL5/4917/2 (unpublished, but disseminated through JNF propaganda materials); Uri Keisari, "Keitzad hayim

When it came to the street-carnival, it was generally agreed that "today we don't find the depleted form that we previously had. Today we have a big carnival, multi-branched, multi-sights, and powerfully expressive."[35] The progressive discourse was dominant and prevented sentimental yearning for the early years. Nostalgia became dominant only after the cancellation of the carnival in 1936.[36]

In many cases, this reflection on the development of the small tradition was identified with the progress of the city itself. In the mid-thirties, when the carnival was strongly institutionalized, it was frequently thought that "it is our past heritage to celebrate Purim in Tel Aviv with splendor—a simultaneously secular and Jewish-traditional splendor."[37] Again, the "past" referred to here is no longer ago than 14 years. To take another example: toward Purim of 1934, it was written that "the program continues the city's customs that have accumulated over 14 years, while adding some more parts and customs."[38] "The customs of the city" were understood here as an accumulated knowledge that represented the progress of the city itself. In that year, the city celebrated its twenty-fifth anniversary, and another writer attributed a commemorative quality to Purim:

> Despite the hatred and the obstacles and the decrees, we can discern significant progress during the twelve months that passed from Purim to Purim. The *Yishuv* will gather to celebrate the Hebrew city, a "city and a mother" in the *Yishuv*, which gained so much strength during twenty-five Purim days.[39]

The identification of the city with the festival was projected to an imagined retrospective, according to which the city was established on Purim. Actually, as I have shown elsewhere, the retroactive

---

etzlenu: Divrey tuga misaviv leyod dalet be'adar" [How do we live: Sad things around the 14th of *Adar*], *Doar-Hayom* 19.2.1935.

[35] "Lamrot ha-matar: Purim mutzlakh be-Tel-Aviv" [Despite the downpour: A successful Purim in Tel Aviv], *Doar-Hayom* 5.3.1931.

[36] Tidhar 1959: 3579; Perski 1944: 147–150. See also: Arieh-Sapir 1997.

[37] *Ha'aretz* 1.3.1934.

[38] *Davar* 1.3.1934.

[39] B.D. "Me-inyaney hayom" [Daily affairs], *Doar-Hayom* 28.2.1934.

determination of spring 1909 as the founding date of the city had a lot to do with Purim and the tourist season of "spring events" in Tel Aviv.[40] In this text, Purim functioned as an annual day of self-reflection for the city.

The progressive time-perception of the tradition's development was not merely descriptive, but also normative. It ceaselessly demanded that tradition be "improved," that faults be repaired, that aesthetic breaches be sealed.[41] Thus, for example, when distributing the prizes for the best performances in the procession, the judges explained their decisions by dividing the performances into two parts: those whose "progress is noticeable" and who won prizes, and those who "still need to further progress."[42] The underlying assumption that the celebrations must progress implied that new practices must be introduced every year. Simultaneously, the organizing committee itself made great efforts to keep improving the festival from year to year.

This normative-progressive discourse concealed an apprehensive discourse regarding the insecurity of tradition, as is indicated in the above-mentioned public petition, written by Bialik and signed by many intellectuals, artists, and writers:

> Cancellation of Purim celebrations, which have already become a tradition and might become a true folk festival, for the benefit and fun of the masses—is inconceivable. Nevertheless, the festival organizers are obliged to add more artistic content and value; to improve and enhance both its external form and the musical and literary material.[43]

The text raised the problem of human agency within tradition, embodied in the tension between normative and descriptive progress: on one hand, the tradition was going to, or should have, or had already, become a "true folk festival," that is, an authentic expression of folk spirit. On the other hand, it would not happen without a proper

---

[40] See: Shoham 2012. See also: Fireberg 2003a; Azaryahu 2009.
[41] Compare Hobsbawm and Ranger 1983: 6.
[42] Protocol of *Adloyada* judges committee, *Doar-Hayom* 6.3.1934.
[43] Supra note 22.

investment of thought, money, and manpower. The new tradition was thus both artificial and authentic.

The petition assumed that the celebrations were already established as a tradition, but at the same time assumed that they would be transformed into a "true folk festival" only with appropriate public investment, together with the imposition of meticulous cultural standards. In other words, in order to exist, the tradition should be constantly improved. Actually, the recurrent calls for "improvement" reflected a somewhat nervous and insecure discourse. This discourse demanded relentless progress and growth, otherwise the tradition would meet with extinction. Moreover, the "inconceivable"—cancellation of the festival and the disruption of the continuity of tradition—may pose a real threat to the authenticity of the New Hebrew culture. As we shall see below, this prophecy fulfilled itself and eventually caused the discontinuation of tradition.

Needless to say, the "inconceivable" for the celebrations' fans was, in fact, quite conceivable. In contrast, one opponent of the Purim carnival wrote that

> The content of this festivity was poor this year just as it was in the previous one. To the extent that this Purim festivity becomes a "tradition," its flaws and emptiness become more and more apparent.[44]

In a minority opinion, this writer assumed that the transformation of a cultural practice into a tradition does not necessitate a positive attitude toward the culture under discussion, which would be measured not only in terms of authenticity and popularity, but also in terms of content. Unlike for Bialik in the public petition, for this writer (who wrote as early as 1929) the tradition seemed rooted enough, and its cancellation was indeed—and perhaps unfortunately—inconceivable. In any case, both sides admitted the dependence of tradition on human acts, decisions, resources, and ability to administer the public sphere. Both understood tradition as a significant cultural practice with an "authentic" continuous grip on social life.

---

[44] "He-arot u-reshimot: gimmel. Purim be-Tel-Aviv" [Comments and notes: c. Purim in Tel Aviv], *Hapo'el Hatza'ir* 24, 5.4.1929, 15–16.

Another connotation of the tradition was thus determinacy. The writer quoted above feared that if the carnival would indeed become a "tradition," its emptiness would be fixed in the *Yishuv*'s public life. For Bialik as well, the cultural level of the festival should have been raised precisely because it was in the process of becoming a tradition. One of the Hebrew Queen Esther critics made this point very clear:

> Just a few comments. The thing itself is not to be criticized. Such a gathering of Jews in Tel Aviv is not dismissible. This is one of the agreeable nationalist demonstrations, which happens as by itself, unintended, and Tel Aviv is the happy city to be given that reward due to the national effort of building the only Hebrew city in the world. Well, precisely because of its importance, it is my duty not to conceal the fundamental flaws of this festivity, so that they will not be added to the tradition and determined as permanent customs.[45]

The main motivation for this writer to express his protest directly was the understanding that new customs become tradition in its formative stage. He was afraid that if a corrupt custom (applauding the parading Queen) would be integrated into tradition, it would become indisposable. Similarly, the organizers of the "Ohel" ball in 1935 declared their struggle against "the acceptable frame of routine dance balls, which became a substandard tradition in Tel Aviv."[46] Once a cultural practice is made into a tradition, it becomes determinate and continuous and would be hardly opposed throughout following generations.

The progressive discourse entailed an understanding of tradition as a linear practice in a process of becoming, stretched between the adjacent past and the far future. Although the carnival was understood as a small tradition, open to human intervention, it was assumed that at some point it would become a "real" tradition that would be protected from such intervention.

---

[45] Y. Avizohar, "Yemey Purim be-Tel-Aviv (mikhtav lama'arekhet)" [Purim days in Tel Aviv (a letter to the editors)], *Ha'aretz* 1.4.1929.

[46] "Tel-Aviv: Ohel Purim bata'arukha" [Tel Aviv: Ohel-Purim ball in the exhibition (halls)], *Doar-Hayom* 28.2.1935.

The discourse regarding tradition thus included "modern" connotations such as expertise and linear progress, but also connotations that were not necessarily modern, such as repetitiveness. At the same time, it had contrasting connotations, such as authenticity and determinacy, which implies the exact opposite: that tradition is a stagnant cultural practice, perhaps retained over the course of generations, rather than a developing and dynamic one—whether descriptively or normatively. Tradition was discussed as a spontaneous practice protected from human intervention, yet, at the same time, bitter cultural wars took place over the right way to construct tradition before it would become totally fixed. Before we explain how these connotations came into play simultaneously, let us demonstrate the power of the progressive discourse in quite a prosaic matter: the cancellation of the carnival in 1936.

"A Bit of Tradition": A Discourse on Progress and the Cancellation of the Carnival

Interestingly, this discourse on progress proved crucial in the cancellation of the carnival in 1936 due to a lack of funding. As we have seen earlier (chapter one), the real problem was the constant increase in the carnival expenditures, which was not the result of an increase in the number of visitors to the carnival, since that would have only increased its tax income. It was due to the unrelenting and uncompromising demands to keep improving the carnival's "artistic level." This demand had viable implications—greater employment of professional artists, stage-hands, administrators, and others—which entailed greater expenditures. In 1929, for example, the budget was 390 Palestine pounds—much more than the JNF's carnival through 1928. It was covered by several income sources, and only 50 pounds came out of the city's budget. In 1935, the expense was somewhere between 2,600 and 3,000 pounds, while the income was only 31 pounds! The municipal council was forced to allot 1,000 pounds to cover the deficit, and many months later, debts were still claimed by creditors and suppliers.[47]

---

[47] Unpublished municipal resolution, 28.1.1935; carnival expenses during 1935, with no exact date—both in TAMA, file 04–3221a; Purim carnival

One direct consequence of the sharp increase in public expenditure was a sharp decrease in the public's participation in the events, in terms of both monetary contributions and performances. This was unlike the 1920s, when amateur performers were at the forefront of the festivities, and the public order was maintained somewhat more loosely as a consequence. As the experts pushed toward a "higher artistic level" and better organization, the public was pushed from active participation into passivity.

From this perspective, the main cause of the carnival's failure was "over-professionalism," which was simply not in keeping with the modest material resources of the *Yishuv* institutions. The linear discourse of progress that had augmented the invented tradition in the first place now demanded that it be constantly and incessantly improved, and that new innovations be introduced each year. It may be said that the demand was to relentlessly re-invent the tradition each year. Hence, toward the mid-1930s, the tradition acquired greater importance in the public consciousness, and was perceived as permanent and steady. This brought many people—artists, municipal officials, administrators, merchants, and others—to assume that their baby was large, mature, and strong enough to walk by herself (Hebrew nouns are gendered, and "tradition" has a feminine form). They thought that this tradition could grow spontaneously, without the "artificial" effort of seeking financial resources, inventing a program, and organizing a complex mass event. As these institutional efforts grew, the public awareness of their existence dwindled. Thus, the public did not respond to the municipality's desperate calls for financial assistance during the winter of 1936. Even city's the merchants, who profited considerably from the carnival and were the first to protest its cancellation, did not volunteer to help.[48] It turned out that the carnival's symbolic power was not matched to Tel Aviv's bureaucratic reality. But it also appeared that a tradition cannot move forward without the intervention of human agents.

---

[48] committee protocol, 10.2.1935, TAMA, file 04–3221c; protocol of 167th meeting of the municipal management, 28.1.1935, TAMA, file 04–3222.

From Tel Aviv and Jaffa merchants' association to municipality, 20.2.1936; from Palestine industrialists' association to municipality, 2.3.1936; from Mayor Dizengoff to Palestine industrialists' association, 3.3.1936: all in TAMA, file 04–3222.

This tension between authenticity and artificiality in the discourse about the "progress" of culture was ironically exemplified by one sharp-eyed newcomer, the young poet Nathan Alterman. After the cancellation, he published in the daily newspaper *Ha'aretz* his "Lullaby for *Adloyada*":

> Adloyada, quiet! Don't cry loudly.
> My heart is stressed of mercy on you
> Nap in protocols
> Don't dare show yourself outdoors
> People said: let's create a new way of life
> Let's have you as our established tradition
> Well... there you see, we made a little bit of tradition
> And it's finally over. Enough for now![49]

The song opens with parodying a tragic biblical lamentation [imitating Psalms 83:2], but its language is gradually transformed into prosaic speech, from the "stressed heart," through the napping in the protocols, and slipping into the ending ironic chatter—"well," "enough." The tension between the prosaic and the sublime is built into the concept of tradition itself, not as inherent contrast but as one-way movement, in which the sublime collapses into the prosaic. The flowery talk about tradition as an authentic "new way of life" collapsed with everyday problems such as financing and protocol books, just as the biblical language collapses into the prosaic one.

The direct targets of Alterman's criticism were, of course, the Zionist cultural entrepreneurs, who failed to sustain a durable tradition. However, the prosaic tone of the song's language challenged critics as well. Unlike the stern and clear voice of "people" who demand "an established tradition" in third person, the extent of the sarcasm in the first person plural voice in the final verse is not clear, when "enough!" is said to tradition. The author did not make a clear distinction between "established tradition" and "a little bit of tradition." Ironically, it seems that at least part of the cultural power of tradition is derived from the intentional and planned, though contingent and prosaic, manner in which it begins and may also end. In a sense, the

---

[49] Nathan Alterman, "Shir Eres La-Adloyada" [Lullaby for the carnival], *Ha'aretz* 6.3.1936, 8. Reprinted in: Alterman 1976: 232. All punctuation marks are in original; only the first two stanzas were quoted here.

prosaic aspect of tradition that eventually led to its cessation indicated a real connection between the tradition and historical human lives. In our case, the authenticity of the invented tradition was derived from its connection not to traditions from time immemorial, but precisely to the "artificial" efforts of the people to maintain it through its institutions.

"A Second Tradition (!), a Modern One"

So far we have seen how the concept of tradition referred first and foremost to the small tradition that was consciously invented in Tel Aviv. However, the great Jewish tradition was also there, at least as an interlocutor with which to develop the small tradition. Still, the conceptual differences between the allegedly stagnant, authoritative, and spontaneous great tradition, and the new small, dynamic, prosaic, reflective, and conscious one, were too striking to go unnoticed. In public discourse, there was a clear understanding of the differences between the two traditions, along with a questioning of the logic of designating both phenomena with the same word, "tradition," as Uri Keisari noted:

> As in every year, and in this year as well, we take on the brims of the Book of Esther and continue a generations—long tradition in making noise, eating *Hamantaschen*, and loudly singing outdoors and indoors.
>
> To this tradition, which was established from time immemorial for thousands of years, a second tradition (!), a modern one, was added, the tradition of balls, of masquerades and the tango and Charleston with the varieties, and our gals with their very short dresses, all these products of our twentieth century, the century of good happy days, the century of the emptiness and the excessiveness and the jazz and the radio....[50]

The difference between the two traditions was intensively sharpened in Keisari's text. Whereas the great tradition is a-histori-

---

[50] Uri Keisari, "Im hazerem: Beshuley megilat ester" [Along the stream: In the brims of the Book of Esther], *Doar-Hayom* 8.3.1928. Ellipsis, parentheses, and reading marks are all in origin.

cally attributed to a time-span of thousands of years, the small one is ironically located in the twentieth century and its sources are clearly located in capitalist mass entertainment. The designation of the new festive forms as "tradition (!)" is made problematic by the added exclamation mark between parentheses. Nevertheless, the two do not seem to differ in their values, as both convey notions of popular joy, albeit in somewhat different cultural means. Keisari himself noticed this elsewhere, and complained about the relatively minor use Tel Aviv Purim celebrations made of the traditional customs such as *Shalach-Monos* and eating *Hamantaschen*.[51] Moreover, he ridiculed the ignorance of the youth regarding the great Jewish tradition. Still, he observed, "the opponents, who are not always wrong, claim that this entire business of Purim celebrations is nothing but chasing amusements," not unlike other amusements. Nevertheless, to justify the escapism,

> One must rely on something. Hence this something is placed nearby; namely, a tale about a blond girl who slept in the king's court to relieve his loneliness — this entire crowd relies on Esther and cries:
> — Long live tradition![52]

At this point the writer described an imagined conversation with a Tel Aviv girl who "looked like a Hollywood dancer." He interrogated her regarding the connection between contemporary festival customs and the traditional Purim customs or the Book of Esther. The girl evaded his attack and responded with one of her own: "Must one be happy for a reason? What does it have to do with it? Who cares about some event that happened some thousands of years ago?" The connection between the great tradition and the invented one was described in his texts as loosened, but eventually, the writer arrived at the conclusion that "if Purim had not existed, we should have invented it." In other words, the inventiveness of the new tradition and its reliance on the great tradition reveal an inventive dimension in the great tradition as well.

---

[51] U.K. [Uri Keisari], "Hamutar lanu lomar? Masoret Purim holekhet ve-ovedet!" [Can we say so? Purim tradition is getting lost!], *Doar-Hayom* 24.3.1935.

[52] Uri Keisari, "Keitzad anu tolim …: Ester, ester, mizgi li yayin!" [How we hang …: Esther, Esther, pour me wine], *Doar-Hayom* 24.3.1935.

These texts introduce the problem well, but do not clarify the historical and interpretive relationships between Tel Aviv's Purim celebrations and previous festive forms. This problem has been discussed at great length in contemporaneous public culture via two different discourses, which I will designate as *folkloristic* and *modernist*.

The *folkloristic* discourse attempted to establish the continuity of the invented tradition with the past tradition and considered Tel Aviv's celebrations as "folk culture" continuous with previous folk cultures. For this discourse, both past and present cultures share common authenticity with a true "folk spirit." The *modernist* discourse attempted to establish a rupture with the past, while focusing on the internal continuum within the new tradition toward the future, and marked a clear border between the new culture and what preceded it, which was degraded as "uncivilized" or "primitive" ("exilic" in Zionist terms), and hence irrelevant as a cultural source for modern tradition. As we shall see, both discourses merged together through the concept of tradition, which was used by both as a core component of identity.

Within the folkloric discourse, the invented tradition was described as a natural extension of the previous great folk tradition. Folklorists who dedicated articles, anthologies, or monographs to Purim customs through the ages used markedly folklorist methodology and language to position Tel Aviv's carnival on that traditional continuum. No rupture between tradition and modernity was noticed, since the Tel Aviv carnival was never attributed essentially different modern characteristics. Relying on contemporaneous images of Purim merriments as superficially carnivalesque and hence particularly folksy, the folklorists situated the Tel Aviv carnival within the continuum of Jewish folk culture through the ages.[53] In this manner, the carnival presumed to convey the mythical connotation of folkism and its identification with authenticity.[54]

The folklorist discourse was apparent, for example, in the following public speech by Bialik, who, toward Purim, emphasized that

> The supplement to our traditional festivals is not aimed at changing acceptable norms, but at filling in the frame. The nice

---

[53] See: Doniach 1933: 3, 126,154; Goodman 1949: 329; Lewinsky 1955: 277–296; and: Simcha Asaf, supra note 34.

[54] Burke 1987: 3–22; Bendix 1997.

custom of the first fruit is organized on the day after Pentecost.[55] Also, the folk festival, Tel Aviv's Purim carnival, takes place after the day of Purim, after the familial domestic festival, in a meal with friends and "sons like olive saplings" [PSA 128:3] around the table. The home is the origins of the joy for the Jew. "You shall rejoice in your festival with your household" [see Deuteronomy 16:14]. And from there—[the joy spreads] everywhere. And when the joy is over the edge, it breaches out—to the streets, slight intoxication—until one doesn't differentiate between cursing Haman and blessing Mordecai [BT Megillah 7:2], but without alcoholic drunkenness, which was always alien to the spirit of Israel through history, before and after Purim.[56]

By no means was this speech a reliable source regarding the relationship between the public and the private in Zionist Purim celebrations, which generally neglected the private sphere.[57] As a prominent activist for Tel Aviv's Purim carnival, Bialik portrayed a spatial virtual fantasy that in the first conceptual phase differentiated the domestic sphere that he identified with the old tradition from the public sphere he identified with the new one. In the second phase, however, both spheres were organized hierarchically, and the organized joy of the public sphere was depicted as a direct outcome of the spontaneous joy of the domestic sphere—that is, of the original tradition. The extension of domestic norms into the public sphere explained the civilized character of the festival, allegedly consistent with the traditional Jewish home, while ignoring the wild character of historical exilic Purim celebrations. In any case, the legitimization of the public-modern sphere was based on its portrayal as a mere extension of the domestic-traditional.[58]

---

[55] And not on the holiday itself in order not to violate orthodox laws concerning the observance of the festivals—implying Bialik's compromising position in this religious-secular dispute (Helman 2006a).

[56] "Hagigot Purim be-Tel-Aviv" [Purim celebrations in Tel Aviv], Ha'aretz 13.3.1933, 1.

[57] Arieh-Sapir 1997: 238.

[58] On incidental correlations of myths of traditional Jewish family with bourgeois ethos, see: Kaplan 1991; Hyman 1995. On the centrality of familial ethos in the constitution of Zionist public sphere, see Razi 2010.

Let us now turn to the modernist discourse, which attempted to establish an unbridgeable rupture between the new traditions that were considered a mere human production, and the pre-modern tradition that was a-priori given. This discourse was loudly sounded, first of all, in the Jewish Orthodox opposition to invented traditions. A. Z. Rabinowitch, who was a main opponent of Purim celebrations, attacked the very notion of an invented tradition: "A traditional ball—woe is such a tradition." Instead, he claimed, the people "turned aside from the real path of tradition, the path of morality and modesty," referring to the immodesty of Hebrew Queen Esther pageants.[59] For Orthodoxy, there was an unbridgeable gap between invented tradition and the great tradition it perceived as meta-historical and protected against human intervention.

Not a few non-Orthodox opponents of the carnival also emphasized the unbridgeable gap between the two traditions. An opponent wrote, "We used to have nice and useful tradition-foundations for our nation. In our times they were dismissed, and their place was taken by new ones, unforeseen by our ancestors, such as the tradition of the balls."[60] In a column critical of Purim balls in *Hapo'el Hatza'ir*, it was written that "the traditional masquerade balls are not traditional and add nothing [to our culture]."[61] The impossibility of any connection between the two traditions was assumed to attack the new invention as not only corrupted in itself but also artificial, that is, not a real tradition.

In a somewhat more complicated manner, the modernist discourse employed a rhetoric of alienation and detachment in the creation of the new culture that was particularly common among the pioneers and members of Labor Movement circles:[62]

> From year to year Purim is going and being more and more consecrated as a folk value. Tradition—is still absent. This word means: an account of many years, perhaps generations.

---

[59] Azar [A. Z. Rabinowitch], "Hirhurim" [Reflections], *Davar* 5.3.1929.

[60] Abraham Shvadron, "Ke-ein krovetz la-carnival" [Alleged ode to the carnival], *Ha'aretz* 11.3.1931.

[61] N., "He'arot ureshimot: aleph. Purim be-Tel-Aviv" [Notes and columns: a. Purim in Tel Aviv], *Hapo'el Hatza'ir* 21, 16.3.1928, 13.

[62] Shapira 1997a; Ze'ira 2002; Sagi 2007.

After surveying the carnival's merits and shortcomings, the writer added:

> Along the years, the contents and form will probably be improved. Some original lines may be added. Such things are done almost spontaneously, with no artificial wisecracks. The result of such wisecracks to invent "original" contents for this folk festival is evident in the barbaric suggestion, published in [the journal] *Ketuvim*, to create a mannequin figure of Haman and arrange a mass *auto-da-fé* for it.[63]

This anonymous text criticized the suggestion, made by poet Avraham Shlonsky, to revive rituals of symbolic violence, to be discussed in chapter five. Shlonsky's folklorist attempt to conduct a dialogue with Jewish great tradition was condemned, not only because of its "barbarian" character, but also for being a "wisecrack," that is, for negating the linear, uncontrollable, and gradual way in which traditions should develop over the years, or over generations. This attempt was so smart-alecky because of Shlonsky's denial of the gap slashed between the new reflective culture and the old barbarian tradition, as well as his attempt to bridge this gap in a desperate search for authenticity.

A more comprehensive systematization of the modernist discourse was offered by Labor Movement educator and writer Gershon Hanoch, who in a programmatic article agreed that the concentration of so many Jews in Tel Aviv was a positive phenomenon in and of itself,

> But I believe that those who looked at the "masquerade procession," that is, its pseudo-contents, and its artistic forms; the tasteless and disorganized stream of the masses; the wisecracking inventions of the carnival's costumes and their aesthetic taste; and those who generally look at our "Hora" [the folkish Hebrew dance] dances in the streets, our "recreation" in the festivals, and our "orders" of mass celebrations, can see the revelation of the curse of unrootedness and some sudden cutting of folk-tradition without corrective innovation. Although we are not yet used to discussing these issues, I think that this problem of the absence of traditional ways in our renewing life, the

---

[63] Supra note 61.

absence of any platform and frame for public-popular rules and "customs," particularly in the life of our rapidly developing city [...], is one of our toughest and [most] painful problems.[64]

As we have seen, Hanoch was not the only critic who viewed the carnival as too hedonist, commercial, unoriginal, and full of kitsch. However, instead of making a personal or group attack on the festival organizers, or a call to immediately cancel it, Hanoch recognized alienation from Jewish tradition as the main problem—particularly in the rapidly changing and impatient city that prevented cultural trends from turning into stable traditions. This constant discontinuity deprived the new culture of any authenticity, so that every cultural practice, song, or dance generated "some sense of imitation—either to our past or to others' present [...] without self soul." Eventually, he summarized, the new culture lacks "a frame of cultural tradition."

Like others who dealt with cultural entrepreneurship, Hanoch thought that unlike buildings, settlements, and factories, "tradition is not created by hands, and ways of life for a land and a society are not made on one day." Nonetheless, he called which was in "creation of the elementary platform to develop the new tradition, at least in the realm of mass public." The municipal and cultural institutions, as well as artists and intellectuals themselves, should have been engaged in that project.

Hanoch brought the logic of modernist discourse, which emphasized the discontinuity with tradition, to an extreme edge, claiming that this disengagement resulted in alienation and detachment as essential characteristics of the New Hebrew culture, especially in the urban context. The lack of authenticity was evident not only in the conscious imitation of "others' present"—that is, the Christian-Mediterranean carnivals—but also of "our past"—which was no longer usable as a cultural source.

In other words, Hanoch did not think that a new culture could be created without the concept of tradition, and his conclusion was just the opposite: the public culture should be more punctiliously inspected, so as to gradually create "traditional ways in our renewing

---

[64] G. Hanoch, "Sidrei-hayim (reshimot be-ikvot ha-Purim)" (Ways of life [Notes after Purim]), *Hapo'el Hatza'ir* 5.4.1929, 15–16. Quotation marks are original.

life" according to appropriate aesthetic and moral standards. Only in such a reflective and highly organized manner would the new culture eventually be authentic—that is, it would be weaved into the natural fabric of society, and become a new tradition, a real one. The cultural engineering was supposed to function as no more than temporary scaffolding that would one day be removed when the new building would be populated, and it would feel as though it was always there. In the modernist discourse, then, the concept of tradition had a key role of legitimizing, not as the historical basis for the present, but as a normative concept of the desired goal.

The spokespersons who addressed the *Yishuv*'s invented traditions did not cease talking about the need to create a national culture for many generations, and develop a traditional orientation. The *Yishuv* was indeed understood by "modernists" as a new creation, unlike all that preceded it. Still, the rupture could occurr only once, since it should create a new era, which, it was hoped, would last for a long time and create a new, stable identity. Besides the alleged break with all traditions, it should creat new traditions which would last throughout generations. Some of the disputes described and analyzed below seem nowadays to slightly over-estimate the importance of the field of cultural entrepreneurship for the new Jewish identity. It was the understanding of the present as a formative period in the creation of a new tradition that may last for future generations that strengthened the emotional tone of these "*kulturkampfs.*"

Despite the obvious differences between the folklorist discourse and the modernist one, the two had much in common. Both agreed with the need for institutional organization in the cultural public sphere. The "authentic" and "spontaneous" traditional culture that develops by itself, without reflective and intended efforts, was perceived as belonging to a time other than the present, whether as the past origins of the invented tradition or as its future goal. Both discourses shared a common understanding of the present tradition as reflectively and "artificially" created by humans, but in a certain time dimension—in the past (for folklorists) or future (for modernists)—some life segments might somehow lack reflexivity and hence were or would be totally authentic.

In other words, the relationship between the folklorist and the modernist approaches was far from identical with the dichotomous relationship between tradition and modernity. Rather, these were two different ways to talk about tradition as assigned temporal meaning and a desired authenticity. For both discourses, the great Jewish tradition of Purim was perceived as given and unchangeable, while the little tradition of Tel Aviv's carnival was perceived as invented, shaped by human agency. The folklorist discourse attempted to establish the continuity of the great tradition with the little invented one, so as to make the latter more authentic. The modernist discourse neglected the great tradition as a cultural source, and instead focused on transforming the invented tradition into a novel great tradition that would eventually be rid of the consciousness of inventiveness in favor of spontaneity and naturalness.

However, the simultaneous use of the concept of tradition for both great and little traditions connected them to each other in the hermeneutical aspect, enabling mutual borrowing of cultural practices. Both discourses were actually active in the cultural entrepreneurship, assuming that tradition is *de facto* experienced as a human product in the present, while desiring to weave the invented tradition into the life fabric so as to become spontaneous. In fact, consciousnesses of both rupture and the development of were necessary to constitute Purim celebrations in Tel Aviv as a "tradition" that would be both artificial and spontaneous, both folksy and institutional.

Assigned Temporal Meaning

As we have seen here, the concept of tradition was in use to assign temporal meaning to the celebrations. However, it was flexible enough to include various, often irreconcilable, time-perceptions: long-range and short-range, past-oriented and future-oriented. The tension between continuity and rupture was thus not a tension between "tradition" and "modernity," but was embodied in the concept of tradition itself as a tension between the great tradition and the invented one. Titling the new cultural practice "tradition" granted it an aura of authenticity, which enabled it to become an arena for bitter cultural disputes.

Anthropologists usually assume that ambivalent cultural sites are overloaded with meanings and have a significant role in identity construction.[65] The tempo-social concept of tradition embodied the tension between rupture and continuity. This tension exists in every

---

[65] For example: Douglas 1975: 47–59.

identity construction, but was discursively overemphasized in modern Jewish nationalism.

The study of the discourse about tradition in a particular invented tradition reveals various temporal perceptions and a rather complicated ideology regarding the relationship between past and present, continuity and rupture. The cultural significance of the concept of tradition stood in direct contrast to the anti-traditionalist image of Zionism that has been overstated in literature, as discussed in chapter seven below.

The discourse about tradition described and analyzed here is arguably characteristic of various nationalist movements and numerous additional cultural phenomena of the industrial age, which witnessed not only the invention of new traditions but also the elevation of new temporalities.[66] The following three chapters will be dedicated to the integration of particular performative and discursive motifs from traditional Purim into the Tel Aviv celebrations. Precisely because of the commercialized and global character of the carnival, these elements were what granted it its unique local aura. Moreover, from the scholarly perspective, the appearance of these past motifs broadens the interpretational framework to reveal hidden elements of Urban Zionist ideology and the transformations in Jewish lifeit entailed.

---

[66] Koselleck 2002: 168.

Chapter 4

The Civilized-Carnivalesque Body

The Carnivalesque and the Bourgeois

This chapter (and the two to follow) will analyze the appearance of implicit elements which were not always reflected upon. Such motifs appeared in what theoretician Julia Kristeva calls the "inter-textual space." As a scholarly paradigm, inter-textuality does not look for conscious influence between cultural formations, but rather examines the textual space in which the specific motif appears.[1] This chapter will discuss Zionist transformations in body perception as performed in the Tel Aviv Purim carnival.

The body has recently become a major object for study in Judaic studies, in what some scholars designate "the corporeal turn."[2] A variety of scholarly works deal with the Jewish body as a noticeable focal point of social, cultural, and political tensions, and with discourse about the body in wider contexts.

Within this corporeal turn, Zionist bodies are mostly studied as revolutionary, assuming that the pioneers' discourse, which demanded refinement of the exilic docile body perception, indeed dominated the new Hebrew culture.[3] Among other factors, these studies assumed that Zionist discourse rid itself of "exilic" folk culture.[4] The following chapter strives to demonstrate that this was just one part of the story. Rather than the pioneer ethos, we will focus here on two other ideologies which framed the Zionist body perception: folklorism and bourgeois respectability or civility.

---

[1] Kristeva 1980: 49–51, 65–66; Kristeva 1986: 36–40.
[2] Eilberg-Schwartz 1992; Kirshenblatt-Gimblett 2005.
[3] Biale 1997; Neumann 2009.
[4] Boyarin 1994.

Like most nineteenth-century European nationalist movements, Jewish nationalism did embrace the romantic ethos of folk culture (despite the hostility of some Zionist intellectuals toward Jewish folklore, discussed above). The new Hebrew culture was considered an extension of the "true folk spirit," which throughout the ages was mainly evident in folk culture.[5] However, as revealed by Mosse and a number of his disciples, the bourgeois ethos of "respectability" also proved vital for European nationalism in the industrial age. Although it was understated in historical literature, bourgeois ethos was omnipresent in various fields in the Yishuv.[6] When it came to the body, these two discourses were not conceptually consistent, since folklorist body perception was considered unrespectable and uncivilized.

Indeed, the body traditionally performed in pre-Zionist Purim was a *carnivalesque* body. Following the influential definitions of Bakhtin, the classical carnival is considered a subversive site, in which the body's lower stratum is emphasized and themes of fertility and growth are expressed through obsessive talk about food and sex. Bakhtin, along with many other scholars, saw in late medieval and Renaissance carnivals a unique social site in which oppressed groups had opportunities to experience some form of egalitarian utopia and a disdain for social hierarchies and strict church ideology.[7] Despite the shred of romanticism in these definitions—which overlooked the possibility of violent occurrences due to the temporary suspension of social hierarchies—these definitions became commonplace and acquired dominance in the voluminous historical, philosophical, and anthropological literature on carnivals, divided around the question of whether the symbolic inversion embodied a real threat to the hierarchies or a conservation of the social order.[8]

Pre-modern Purim celebrations, dating from the late Middle Ages (and even earlier) were indeed seen by many modern scholars, Jews and

---

[5] On the Zionist-folkloristic body see: Roginsky 2007.

[6] Helman 1999; Helman 2010; Hirsch 2008.

[7] Bakhtin 1968: 10, 81; Bakhtin 1981: 146–224; Bakhtin 1984: 156–160. Also: Kristeva 1980: 78–80.

[8] See: Le-Roy Ladurie 1979: 305–324; Davis 1978: 163–171; DaMatta 1984; Burke 1987: 182–204; Davis 1987: 119–123; Chartier 1988: 115; Muir 1997: 91–92. for criticism see: Hayman 1983; Stallybrass & White 1986: 6–26.

non-Jews alike, as "the Jewish carnival."[9] On one level, there was some direct mutual borrowing of specific cultural practices, such as costumes, parodies, public drunkenness, and gluttony. Also, there were typically carnivalesque themes, such as the war of the sexes and vulgar language, which were specifically characteristic of early modern *Purimspiels* (special Purim plays by Yeshiva students). Moreover, the two phenomena were also considered similar with regard to their capacity to threaten public order and destabilize social hierarchies. The debate regarding the line between symbolic and real subversion in Christian carnivals was echoed regarding Jewish Purim: historian Elliot Horowitz mentions many cases in which its wild practices undermined the social order, while literary scholar Harold Fisch emphasizes the semiotic-ritualistic character of this subversiveness and its imagined nature.[10]

Like Christian carnivals, Purim was "civilized" and "pacified" during the modern period, as Jewish leaders and rabbis (of all religious affiliations) sought to create a greater distance between the sacred and the profane by attempting to banish "barbarian" habits. Parallel to the "civilizing process" of the Christian carnival, wild and anarchic Purim customs were also diminished. Purim practices that were cast out included cross-dressing, public drunkenness and gluttony, and publicly offending community leaders and rabbis. "Reformers" devoted particular attention to rituals of symbolic violence, to be discussed in depth in the next chapter.[11]

In due course, modern Jewish folklorists romanticized these Purim practices—much as the practices of Christian carnivals were romanticized—and lamented their diminution. In line with the other folklorism movements of the industrial-age, they assumed, justifiably or not, that folk cultures disappeared or were "contaminated" with the advance of modernity.[12] In 1912, the historian Israel Abrahams lamented that "criticism [...] hasw killed the Purim joy."[13]

---

[9] Frazer 1994: 646. See: Horowitz 1994; Belkin 2002: 56–65. Le-Roy Ladurie even thinks that there is possible influence of Jewish Purim on Christian carnivals (Bar-Navi 1986: 64).

[10] See: supra note 8; and: Gaster 1953: 221–232; Haris 1977; Mantgen 1994; Fisch 1994; Hanegbi 1998; Horowitz 2006.

[11] Belkin 2002; Har'el 2004;

[12] See, for example: Burke 1987: 15–16.

[13] Abrahams 1912: 272.

Chapter 4. The Civilized-Carnivalesque Body

On its folkloristic aspect, the Tel Aviv Purim carnival made extensive use of subversive carnivalesque discourse about the body, in which the individual body was diffused in the collective one. This seemed to contradict the bourgeois discourse about the body, which mainly focused on preserving the individual body. The tension between folklore and modernism as the building-blocks of the new culture was thus understood not only temporally, as discussed in the previous chapter, but also corporeally. The case of the Tel Aviv Purim carnival enables us to discuss the transformation of the Jewish subversive folk tradition of Purim into a bourgeois festival and the Judaization of bourgeois values of respectability and civility. Nevertheless, the conceptual contradiction between folklorism and the bourgeois value-system regarding the body was reconciled in the ideology of Urban Zionism, as we shall see hereafter.

Indeed, the cultural practices of Tel Aviv's carnival did not, by any means, reflect the carnivalesque spirit. As is convincingly shown by Helman, the Tel Aviv carnival was a bourgeois tourist event, which actually conveyed "serious elitist ideals and rituals"; maintained existing "social and political hierarchies" within *Yishuv* society; clearly "distinguished between actors and spectators"; and enforced exceptionally strict order.[14] Traditional corporeal carnivalesque Purim practices, such as public drunkenness, public gluttony, rude language, or rude sexuality, were strictly rejected. Only rites of symbolic violence were at some point accepted, and this will be discussed in detail in the next chapter.

It might surprise contemporary Israelis that in general, the Tel Aviv Purim carnival was highly civilized, and that order was perfectly kept, at least before 1934–1935, when there were problems of overcrowdedness and some fights. City officials, not to mention British rulers, were extremely intolerant of social disorder. The concept of "order" was considered a key factor not only for the economic success of the carnival but also to prove that the Jews were a civilized nation, worthy of political self-assertion. The municipality repeatedly warned the public to maintain public order: not to walk on the saplings, to obey the marshals, not to overcrowd balconies and roofs, and to follow many other such directives.[15]

---

[14] Helman 2006a: 386.

[15] See: Ze'evi 1988: 503–507. Exemplar of "Mor'e-derekh la-hagigot velakarnaval be-Purim tartza" [A guide for carnival and celebrations in Purim 1931],

Order was maintained not only in terms of law, but also in terms of morals, employing the bourgeois term of *civility*. The carnival floats and performances were very sensitive about not offending anyone, including rivals of Zionism.[16] Internal political disputes were ideally concealed. Vulgar language was unheard. Indeed, according to one sharp-eyed observer, the crowd's laughter at the parade was at most "chuckles," rather than "uproarious."[17] Performances of role reversals of men and women were also not to be found, and potential hostility between the sexes, let alone rude sexuality, was concealed, as we shall see in chapter six below. Public drunkenness and grotesque eating were also absent, although a float presented by the wine factory *Carmel Mizrahi* "urges the people 'drink, friends, be drunk, friends,' but in vain: no drunken people are seen."[18] Other traditional anarchic customs such as beating each other and grabbing items from each other joyfully, or publicly insulting community leaders (this last done by a "Purim Rabbi"), were also unheard of. Not only was the latter practice eliminated, but one float that criticized Mayor Dizengoff regarding a political controversy was taken out of the procession, "due to the impolite behavior towards the city's elected official."[19]

The carnival was thus anything but subversive.

Despite this bourgeois character, and alongside it, there was ceaseless talk about the carnivalesque spirit as representing the true folk spirit in the Bakhtinian manner. To bridge the gap between talk about the carnivalesque body and the actual bourgeois body perception that was the only one to be legitimized by the celebrators, contemporaries employed the cultural mechanism of *romanticizing*. However,

---

TAMA 04–3218b; from Dizengoff to carnival committee, 25.2.1931; from Y. Gefen and A. Aldema to police inspector; and from Jewish agency management to Tel Aviv's mayor, 30.12.1930: all in TAMA 04–3218a.

[16] Undated municipal announcement (from 1937), TAMA 04–3222; "Yom Ha'Adloyada be-Tel-Aviv" [Carnival day in Tel Aviv], *Doar-Hayom* 14.3.1933; *Ha'aretz* 2.3.1934; see Carmiel 1999: 49.

[17] *Palestine Post*, 2.3.1934.

[18] "Ha'hagigot be-Tel-Aviv: Hemshekh" [The celebrations in Tel Aviv: Continuation], *Doar-Hayom* 6.3.1931. See also, regarding drink and food: Carmiel 1997: 97; Ze'evi 1988: 492; Harari 1947: 96; S. Samet, "Eikh paramti et haneshef harishon" [How I "Purimized" my first ball], *Ha'aretz* 13.3.1933.

[19] "Reshimat Ha'hovevim" [List of amateurs], TAMA 04–3221b.

these were not only past Purim celebrations that were romanticized, but also contemporaneous Tel Aviv celebrations. Let us now turn to examine in detail the folkloric discourse about Purim in general and about the Tel Aviv Purim celebration in particular.

"Secular and Democratic": Folkloric Carnivalesque Discourse

In 1921, Eliezer Ben-Yehuda published a newspaper article in which he glorified the folk spirit of Purim. Responding to the claim made by biblical scholars who viewed the events described in the Book of Esther as fictional, Ben-Yehuda explained that unlike other festivals, which commemorated historical events, Purim was created by the folk's "free will." The people celebrated Purim not "with reverence like the other festivals" but rather with "drunkenness and joy and much jocularity." The power of Purim is thus its anti-institutional, even anti-ideological, character, expressed by its lack of seriousness. Ben-Yehuda's conclusion was far from anti-nationalist, though: he suggested an innovation in which the custom of *Shalach-Monos* would be conducted as organized assistance to new Jewish immigrants, not only for humanitarian reasons but also so that "the rumors about them will awake in the hearts of their brethren in their Diasporas the desire to walk in their path" and immigrate to Palestine.[20] The folklorist discourse was thus recruited to support nationalist goals.

How and why was the seemingly folklorist anti-ideological Purim linked to Zionist ideology? Yitzhak Lufban (1888–1948), a major Labor Movement journalist, gave a hint:

> Purim is the stepson of our people's festivals [… and] many rabbis and community leaders objected to it throughout all generations, since the ancients. Notwithstanding, "ordinary people" [*amkha*] observed it with devotion. Indeed, this secular and democratic festival should to be demeaned by snobs. Purim […] is constantly renovated in the spirits of periods and eras. Purim is

---

[20] E. Ben-Yehuda, "Purim shel aliya" [Purim of immigration], *Doar-Hayom* 25.3.1921.

the festival of the joke and the prank, of the mask, the costume, and multiple forms of the search after the form.[21]

For Lufban, this folkloric spirit was the ideological background of the search for the "right formula" for Purim celebrations. The text emphasized the connection between the "folkish" character of the festival and its dynamism. The festival survived, despite multiple enemies—rabbis, sacred texts, and ideologies—which sought to annihilate it, by virtue of its capability to transform itself during its journey across different times, places, and varied cultural needs. This miraculous capability bears witness to the festival's special bond with the true spirit of the Jewish folk. To keep up with this historical continuum, Purim celebrations in Tel Aviv do not have to be similar to Purim celebrations in Kasrilevke, Tzan'a, or Shushan: they have to suit themselves to the cultural needs of the folk, just as they did in Kasrilevke, Tzan'a, or Shushan. Now Zionist ideology was that need, and, hence, it was identified with the folk.

In other words, not only were past Purim practices romanticized, but so were the present Purim celebrations in Tel Aviv, which were often described as carnivalesque and subversive, contrary to the actual bourgeois practices employed in it.

Some observers portrayed the Tel Aviv carnival as bearing a symbolic reversal, which allowed for a temporary suspension of social hierarchies, as in the following description of the carnival preparations: "Even the maids prepare themselves to the carnival, that is, that one can't tell who the lady is and who the maid is. And you move aside and dare to ask nothing from them, lest they get angry at you. And the children—they totally rebel against their parents and teachers."[22]

Although this was far from a true description of the carnival's atmosphere, it was the common discourse. Within this discourse, many interpreted the Yemenite participants gaining first place, and particularly the ascension of Yemenite milk-distributer Tzipora Tzabari as the victor in the 1928 Hebrew Queen Esther pageant, as an expression of

---

[21] A. Borer [Yitzhak Lufban], "Purim taratz" [Purim 1930], *Ketuvim* 20–21, 14.3.1930.

[22] Hegay ben Hegay, "Erev Adloyada be-Tel-Aviv" [Carnival evening in Tel Aviv], *Ha'aretz* 21.3.1932.

the "redemption" of the Yemenite Jews from their inferior socio-economic condition.[23]

In addition, some residents wrote to the organizing committee and suggested ways to enhance the carnivalesque spirit in the carnival. One suggestion was to place sales counters for glasses of wine throughout the city, "in order to increase wine popularity and elevate the mood." Another suggestion, following the decision to make "*Adloyada*" the Hebrew word for carnival, was to have an authentic Purim meal as part of the procession, on a large truck bed with real people drinking real wine, who would really become drunk. This was intended to enable the audience to experience the original anarchic meaning of the Talmudic phrase that was the source for the term *Adloyada*, as we shall see below. These suggestions were rejected.[24]

Another expression of carnivalesque discourse may be found in a song chosen by the organizing committee, along with a few dozen other songs, to be printed and distributed to the masses during the festivities. The song "Purim 1932," written by Avigdor Heme'iri, is better known as "Give a Shoulder" [*"Ten Katef"*]. The song is mainly about overcoming personal troubles through song and dance:

> Let us go wild/ with no thought and brain/ don't look at your worries!/ damn!/ Until you've no longer strength/ abandon your heart, lung, liver.
> [Refrain:] Give a shoulder/ let's hug together/ Peretz, Uri, Pnina, and Ruth!/ heart to heart/ up to fever!/ We have Purim/ we will never die![25]

The carnivalesque spirit is expressed here not only in the disregarding of everyday worries, but in the neglect of appropriate body

---

[23] Azov [A.Z. Ben-Yishai], "Regaim: Halom hamalkhut" [Moments: Royal dream], *Ha'aretz* 9.2.1928. This description with almost identical wording can be found in JNF's propaganda: "Purim be-eretz Yisrael (mitokh hachronica shel hayey hayomyom)" [Purim in Palestine (everyday chronics)], CZA, KKL5\4917\1; Doniach 1933: 156–158. See also: Spiegel 2001; Stern 2006; and below, chapter six.

[24] David Zvi Zak, accepted in municipality on 31.12.1933, TAMA 04–3221b; Reuven Nodorolsky, undated, TAMA 04–3219a.

[25] Avigdor Hame'iri, "Purita tartzab," TAMA 04–3219c; printed in Lewinsky 1955: 277.

maintenance, assuming that when hugging together, "we will never die."[26] The body is deconstructed in the song, which focuses on the internal organs, "with no brain," while the abandonment of the liver also hints at the consumption of alcohol. With this mistreatment, the individual body can survive only by being absorbed into the collective body, which celebrates its victory over death through Purim.

Another telling example of the carnivalesque discourse romanticizing the Tel Aviv Purim carnival was a comic silent film, entitled *"Vayehi Bimey"* [In the Days of Yore; Tel Aviv, 1932]. This was the first fiction film ever produced in Palestine, but it was fictitious in more than one sense.[27]

The film is a short (18-minute) comedy of errors, which tells the story of mix-ups among three couples at the carnival. The three couples—ultra-Orthodox, American-bourgeois, and pioneers—are involved in a series of mis-identifications in which they are masked and mistaken for one another. The main plotline is focused on the ultra-Orthodox couple, and the struggle of Mendel the tailor for liberation from his overbearing and domineering wife. As part of this struggle, he runs away from home, dresses himself as a pioneer, gets drunk, sings, and dances, while she looks for him all over the city.[28]

Between the staged scenes of the movie's plot, the producers added documentary footage of the Tel Aviv Purim carnival (18% of the entire film). Nevertheless, this carnival was described in the film in a manner unfamiliar in any historical source: as a real carnivalesque carnival. Extensive use was made of carnivalesque objects such as costumes, face-masks, and alcohol; carnivalesque themes such as the war of the sexes (with misogynic tendencies); and drunkenness that distorts the perception of physical space (presented, for example, through 360-degree upside-down camera movement, which represents Purim as a topsy-turvy day) and consequently seems to subvert bourgeois family values. The carnivalesque space distorts the clear judgment of

---

[26] See: Bakhtin 1968, in particular chapters 5–6.

[27] "Vayehi Bimey," Studio film Palestine Production Company, screenwriting and shooting: Natan Axelrod, directed by Hayim Halachmi. Spielberg Archive, VT DA016. I would like to thank Mr. Yossi Halachmi for allowing me to possess a copy of the film.

[28] On the film see: Bursztyn 1990: 40–44; Tryster 1995: 155–160; Halachmi 1995: 114; Shoham 2011b.

Chapter 4. The Civilized-Carnivalesque Body

all the participants, who fall victim to material lusts, disguises, and identification fiascos.

In other words, the people who created or watched the film thought that this film, with its farces and disguises, indeed represented the Tel Aviv Purim carnival, and that the depiction of the Tel Aviv carnival as a truly subversive carnival, like those of contemporary Latin America, made sense.[29] It is worth mentioning that the film was generally well-accepted by the *Yishuv*'s audience, which had firsthand knowledge of the real Purim carnival, and knew, for example, that no one there wore face masks. Moreover, contemporaneous commentators in the media, who were very sensitive to unrealistic cinematic representations, did not make any comment on this misrepresentation of the carnival.[30]

The film was not "realistic" in any strict sense, but it was part of the carnivalesque discourse. It relied on the rich literary and theatrical tradition of Yiddish satires and farces, which also had some cinematic continuity, for example in the Soviet-Yiddish film *Jewish Luck* (1925).[31] This Yiddish carnivalesque tradition found its successor in the carnivalesque discourse on the Purim carnival in Tel Aviv. Only within this discourse is it possible to understand how a film like *In the Days of Yore* could presume to describe the Purim carnival.

The carnivalesque discourse was most obviously articulated in 1932, when the organizing committee declared a contest for a Hebrew word for "carnival." A special committee of literati received from the public no less than 253 letters, including some from abroad, which included 209 suggestions. The name determined by committee members, "*Adloyada*," was not among these suggestions, but was suggested by a committee member, the writer Y.D. Berkowitch (1885–1967).[32]

The linguist and writer Dan Almagor thinks that "Berkowitch's suggestion is one of the most brilliant and successful Hebrew neologisms." The idea was to play with the Russian echo of a grandiose event, such as "*Olympiada*" [Russian form for "Olympic games"

---

[29] See, for example: DaMatta 1984.

[30] Zimmerman 2001b: 90–94; Feldstein 2009: 72–77.

[31] On the film see: Hoberman 1991: 92–96. Thanks to Olga Gershenson.

[32] From Dizengoff to newspapers *Davar*, *Ha'aretz*, and *Doar-Hayom*, 24.12.1931, TAMA 04–3218b; letters of suggestions, and the decision in favor of "*Adloyada*," committee protocol, 27.1.1932, TAMA 04–3218c.

which was adopted in Modern Hebrew], while gendering the word as feminine in contrast to the "Gentile" carnival, which was heard in Hebrew as masculine.[33]

Above all, however, it echoed the carnivalesque Talmudic saying that "a man must be drunk on Purim to the extent that he will be unable to differentiate between cursing Haman and blessing Mordechai" (BT Megillah 7:2). The Hebrew/Aramaic words "*Ad-Delo-Yada*" can be read as "beyond cognition" or "beyond knowledge" of good and bad.

The original Talmudic context of this saying is an extremely strange anecdote, even in terms of rabbinic literature. This saying is first brought in the Talmud in the name of the sage Rava, and immediately afterward, the Talmud relates a story about the Purim meal of that same Rava with his friend, Rav Zeira. They ate and drank, and at some point, Rava was so drunk that he slaughtered his friend. The next day, Rava realized what he has done, prayed for his friend, and brought him back to life. The next year, Rava again invited his friend to drink with him at the Purim meal, as though nothing had happened. Rav Zeira refused to come, replying, quite understandably, that "miracles do not happen every day."[34]

A detailed analysis of this Talmudic story is beyond the scope of this study, but its eminently carnivalesque features cannot be overlooked, particularly the central theme of dying and returning to life on one day.[35] Yet the revived Rav Zeira was terrified enough by this experience to refuse to participate in another Purim meal with Rava. In other words, the story introduces both the vital power of the carnivalesque experience and its perils. This tension is apparent in the Halakhic debate which arose from this Purim tale, regarding the question of drunkenness on Purim—is it a requirement, a permitted act, or a prohibition?[36]

This carnivalesque spirit, with its vitality and perils, was deeply imprinted in the consciousness of Purim celebrators in Tel Aviv by

---

[33] See: Almagor 1993: quote from p. 54; Lewinsky 1955: 291–292.

[34] BT Megillah 7:2. In the printed Talmud the story is about Raba. On the different versions see: Spiegel 2004.

[35] See: Gaster 1969: 831–834; Polish 1999, and also: Frazer 1994: 646, 664–665, 675. The latter goes as far as to claim that Jesus' crucifixion was actually part of Purim ritual of symbolic violence (ibid., 667–673).

[36] See: Tavori 1990: 19–20; Rafeld 1998; Arand 1999; Spiegel 2004.

the Hebraicized term of *Adloyada* for carnival. Interestingly, the choice of the word provoked a surprisingly agitated debate, and many protests were received in the municipality. Indeed, some of the opponents of the word claimed it implied that "only drunk people participate in the procession, while we actually know that only sober people do so."[37] Although this description was entirely correct, this was the precise idea behind the new word: to locate the Tel Aviv carnival on the historical continuum of subversive Purim celebrations throughout the generations. The *Adloyada* positioned the vitality and violence of pre-Zionist Purim as the pretext and genre of the current celebrations.

The term was roundly criticized for several other reasons, including "the rules of Hebrew pronunciation disable any option to accept it; this is a kind of unparalleled linguistic barbarism!"[38] Quite naturally, many criticized the biased selection procedure, in which the suggestion of a committee member was preferred. Indeed, since the competition offered a monetary prize, the municipality probably did not complain about this decision, which saved money. So many letters were received by the newspaper *Doar-Hayom* that after several of them were published, the editors noted: "With these two letters we hereby finish the polemic regarding '*Adloyada*' and apologize to all the letter-writers, amounting to legions, thank God, which were not printed here due to lack of space. We hope that this name will be off the agenda and will be remembered only in humoristic Purim newspapers."[39] But it was not off the agenda: on the next day the term appeared in a commercial ad offering "Purim amusements and *Adloyada* needs" for sale.[40] Quite promptly, songs were written which glorified the *Adloyada* as a young woman, looking for a groom.[41] Despite the criticism of the new term,

---

[37] Avshalom Ofri to carnival committee, 7.2.1932, TAMA 04–3218c.

[38] Meir, "He-arot" [Comments], *Ha'aretz* 29.2.1932.

[39] *Doar-Hayom* 25.2.1932. See more protests: Avshalom Ofri, supra note 37; an open letter of Avraham Tenenbaum to carnival committee, *Doar-Hayom* 21.2.1932; open letters of lawyer Avraham Shaul Lubarsky and S. Lavonsky, *Doar-Hayom* 25.2.1932.

[40] Announcement of "Globus," *Doar-Hayom* 26.2.1932.

[41] "Hamotar metuyar (mitokh tokhnit matate Purim)" [Leftover is superfluous (from the program of Purim balls of the mataté theatre], *Ha'aretz* 18.3.1935. This song was written by Avraham Shlonsky (see: Halperin 1997: 276–277).

which many saw as archaic, alien, and awkward, it was immediately integrated into everyday language.

This prosaic matter generated a surprising burst of excitement. The writer Daniel Perski exaggeratedly described this mini-storm: "Everyone ... in the streets, cafés, theatre, cinema, and synagogue—in every place and time, what are Jews talking about? Of course, about Hebraizing carnival." He thought that this excitement was derived from the fact that "this was the only attempt in Jewish history in which the question of a necessary Hebrew word was not decided by a single writer or scholar, but was handed over to the people itself."[42]

The huge flood of letters regarding the "*Adloyada*" sent by lawyers, bookkeepers, farm-hands, and workers to the daily newspapers and the municipality, indeed revealed a deeper cultural tension regarding Zionist "folk culture." This may be attributed not just to the rare opportunity for the public to be involved in Hebraizing a word, but to this specific word—carnival—which denoted the folk culture, the authentic expression of the people's life. In semiotic terms, it might be said that the sign was supposed to be chosen by the signified itself—the people. It was allegedly a "folkish" choice, and this unique unification of signified and signifier drew many people to participate in the process. Eventually, the apparent not-folkish way in which the decision was made revealed the paradox of "formal folk culture," that is, the crucial role of individual culture agents, and the non-spontaneous and well-managed dimensions of this "folk culture."[43]

The carnival was talked about as if it were a carnivalesque event, in the Bakhtinian sense, despite the evident lack of carnivalesque cultural practices. However, there was one exceptionally carnivalesque practice which supported the carnivalesque discourse: the widespread popular use of play caps and guns. These were a part of the celebrations as long as they were held (and are used in contemporary Israel). The loud booms were heard throughout the city several days, or even weeks, before the festival, and were thus reported as a harbinger of Purim.[44] The poet Nathan Alterman described the preparations for the festival: "With a thunder of bombs/ with the voice of destruction/ the

---

[42] Perski 1944: 152–158.

[43] See introduction, supra note 53.

[44] "Beyafo uve-Tel-Aviv" [In Jaffa and Tel Aviv], *Ha'aretz* 4.3.1923; "Hag Ha-Purim beyafo" [Purim in Jaffa], *Ha'aretz* 28.3.1921.

young devils (*Takhshitim*) of Tel Aviv applaud: forcefully strike down/ even a newborn, a baby in a crib/ fires a gun in front of his wet nurse!"[45]

The municipality repeatedly, though ineffectively, warned the public to avoid these dangerous toys. In 1935, the organizing committee notified the police and the public of its decision to officially prohibit them. A few days after this notification, a man named Yesha'ayahu Operman complaint: "My apartment's windows were shot by toy guns and as a result of the explosives the duvets in the bedroom and the clothes in the cupboard were burned and we were left with no duvets and clothes." The damage was estimated to be more than 150 Palestine pounds, which he demanded from the city as compensation. Not surprisingly, the municipality refused, but agreed to recompense him with 10 Palestine pounds, going "beyond the letter of the law."[46] Only after the outbreak of "the Arab revolt" in April 1936 was this prohibition efficiently enforced. The citizens were repeatedly warned that they were committing a criminal act, but it seems that only a real security threat made an impact.[47]

The explosives were a carnivalesque element not only because they were used despite their prohibition, and because of their disruption of civil order, but also because of the aggressive nature of the game itself. Although some blamed the Arabs for this bad habit, explosives were actually part of the traditional noisemaking upon the mention of Haman's name during the reciting of the Scroll of Esther, within and outside synagogues, since as early as the sixteenth century, when gunpowder arrived in the Middle East and Europe. This noisemaking became a main target of criticism by the above-mentioned "reformers."[48] The popularity of this extremely dangerous play in Tel Aviv (and elsewhere) stood in direct contrast to the "pacification" of Purim. In addition to the burnt linens in the Operman apartment,

---

[45] Agav [Nathan Alterman], "Regaim: Al saf Ha'Purim" [Moments: On the threshold of Purim], *Ha'aretz* 15.3.1935; reprinted in: Alterman 1976: 112–113.

[46] Letters from Zalman Churgal to Rokach and to the police, 27.2.1935; from Yesha'ayahu Operman to the municipality, 19.3.1935, TAMA 04–3222; *Ha'aretz* 19.3.1935.

[47] Undated municipal announcement (1937); from Neve-Shalom neighborhood committee to Dov Hoz, 18.2.1937, TAMA 04–3222.

[48] See Ratzhabi 1988: 223; and particularly Har'el 2004.

several children were reported to suffer severe eye injuries.[49] Beyond the physical danger, the idea of the game is to create war-like noise, using materials similar to those used in real modern weapons, waging a game-like war in the spirit of the carnivalesque tradition.

Harmonized and Carnivalesque

In principal, the alleged carnivalesque character of the Tel Aviv Purim carnival was not considered as negating its bourgeois character. Carnivalesque discourse was romanticized and understood as harmonious, as evident in the film *In the Days of Yore*. The film portrayed an imagined national space in which everyone is Jewish, and every Jew is eventually happy. At first, the confusions and misidentifications create a distorted space of imagined wild freedom. Eventually, after all the comedy's errors are resolved, no one is hurt, the human bodies remain hale and hearty, no irreversible sexual conduct takes place, and the three cinematic couples live happily ever after. The imagined loosening of the moral rein during the carnival led to enhanced harmony on the collective level and thus, at the end, to the reinforcement of the social order. The carnivalesque space represented a harmony among the different parts of Jewish society: the religiously Orthodox, the pioneers, and the bourgeois. This fictional depiction of Tel Aviv both reflected and created its most notable myth, as "the first Hebrew city," describing the collective Jewish body as proliferating in the urban space.

The carnivalesque discourse was an interpretational frame through which the bourgeois carnival was understood. Except for the gunpowder, which was by no means encouraged, it had no practical anarchic implications. The carnivalesque genre was not intended to be replicated in the present, but rather to be interpreted through the riddle of the civilizing process. Only traditional expressions suited to the ethos of bourgeois respectability were considered culturally use-

---

[49] Dr. A.D. Friedman, "Pur Ha'einaim be-Purim (Lishlom hatzibur veha-yahid)" [Lottery of the eyes in Purim (Public and individual safety)], *Ha'aretz* 12.3.1933; "Venishmartem le-einekhem" [And thou shall care about your eyes], *Ha'aretz* 28.2.1934

able. Public order was important for the Jewish image of the civilization process, as described in the following summary of the carnival:

> [There was] no tasteless debauchery. Everything was in measure and tempo, the joy was somewhat restrained, as if it was played by musical notations, with no grating dissonances. The order was also kept this time. The crowd didn't enter prohibited places, and listened to the marshals.[50]

Tel Aviv spokespeople praised their carnival for its order, and talked about it as evidence of the success of the Jews' civilizing process and "the high cultural level of our public, capable of organizing celebrations and assemblies [...] with no accident, no crime, no drunken people drifting through the streets, no thefts and brawls and so on"—as opposed to notable carnivals in the Christian world.[51]

The politico-cultural significance of this order-maintaining can best be explicated through a comparison with the equivalent Jerusalem carnival in the 1920s. During that decade, there were unofficial festivities on Jaffa Street in Jerusalem on Purim. A large crowd gathered on the streets, dancing, singing, and watching many people in masquerade who wandered about. Some presented street performances, walking or driving back and forth. Most asked for, and received, pocket change from the passers-by, whether the request was made on behalf of charitable institutions or for personal need.[52] Generally, the event posed an annual threat to public order, and a burden for the police force.[53] One year, when Purim fell on a Saturday, it was reported that people in masquerade took to the street for three days—from Friday to

---

[50] "Hakarnaval Ha'Purimi be-Tel-Aviv" [Purim carnival in Tel Aviv], *Ha'aretz* 24.3.1932.

[51] "Aharei hahagigot" [After the celebrations], *Yediot Iriyat Tel-Aviv* 5 (1935), 132. See also: G. H. H., "Le-ahar hagigot Ha'Purim" [After Purim celebrations], *Ha'aretz* 6.3.1931; M. G. [Moshe Glikson], "Al haperek" [On the agenda], *Ha'aretz* 28.3.1928.

[52] "Yerushalayim" [Jerusalem], *Ha'aretz* 7.3.1928.

[53] "Birushalayim" [In Jerusalem], *Doar-Hayom* 2.3.1926; "Mifga'ei hanehagim hamishtovevim" [Hazards of irresponsible drivers], *Doar-Hayom* 22.3.1927.

Sunday.[54] The carnival thus did not have clear boundaries in time and space, or between performers and audience.

Some of these performances were classically Zionist, such as a performance by the Jewish train workers, who paraded back and forth through the streets in a paper train engine with a Zionist flag and lit candles.[55] According to the Jerusalem newspaper *Doar-Hayom*, most years the majority of the people who participated in the masquerade on Jaffa Street were identified ethnically as Persian and Urphali (from Urfa, in southeast Turkey of today) Jews. One float of Persians represented the entire gallery of the figures of the Book of Esther: Mordechai, riding on horseback, Queen Esther, Haman, and Ahasuerus, as well as secondary figures such as Harvona, Bigtan, and Teresh. All "passed through Jaffa street back and forth, by horses, carriages, and foot, and sang Hebrew songs in Arabic form: one loudly chants and everyone repeats. One of them did magic tricks by raising knives beyond his head."[56]

These sights recurred every Purim in Jerusalem and provoked criticism, or more accurately disgust, in the Jewish press. The newspaper *Ha'aretz*, for example, reported that in Jerusalem, "the streets were filled with sooty people, wearing sort of rags for so-called costumes, dancing and singing to the sound of flute and drum and so forth."[57] These criticisms were repeated each year, and at some point the newspaper reported, somewhat desperately: "And their "praise" should be said to their faces: there is no taste in their costumes, and there is no taste and beauty in their alleged acting as well, and in their singing and music, but the crowd is not quite punctilious, and hundreds of people are attracted to these groups."[58] In 1927 there was an attempt to organize a carnival in Jerusalem in the well-structured style of the Tel Aviv carnival, and it was defined as "the first carnival in Jerusalem." The Jewish press clearly did not view the Jaffa Street carnival as the

---

[54] "Purim birushalayim" [Purim in Jerusalem], *Ha'aretz* 7.3.1923.

[55] "Yerushalayim" [Jerusalem], *Ha'aretz* 28.2.1921.

[56] "Hag ha-Purim birushalayim" [Purim festival in Jerusalem], *Doar-Hayom* 12.3.1925.

[57] "Yerushalayim" [Jerusalem], *Ha'aretz* 7.3.1928; see also: "Yerushalayim" [Jerusalem], *Ha'aretz* 12.3.1925; "Ata klila" [Some lightness], *Doar-Hayom* 23.3.1927.

[58] "Yerushalayim" [Jerusalem], *Ha'aretz* 21.3.1927.

predecessor of the organized carnival (though ultimately the latter carnival failed).[59] Here there was no fascination with the charm of spontaneous folk culture, but only self-distinction from its "uncivilized" and "unaesthetic" character.

The discrepancy between these reports and the enthused reports about the "folkist" nature of the Tel Aviv carnival is illuminating. In the 1920s, when the organization in Tel Aviv was not yet very meticulous, a similar carnivalesque atmosphere was reported in Tel Aviv: "The familial joy began. Every home turned into a tiny carnival. And then began the primitive concerts on cans and basins and benches. Wine came in—song and dance came out."[60] The positive connotation of the word "primitive" is striking here, particularly when compared with the disgust expressed with regard to the carnival of the Persians and the Urphalis in Jerusalem. It could possibly be explained as ethnic prejudice or cultural patronage, but it seems it was more than that: rather, the disorganized Jerusalem carnival was perceived as a real threat to the Zionist civilizing process.

In other words, the "true folk spirit" itself bridged the gap between Tel Aviv's respectable and orderly tourist event, and the praised subversion and wildness of the pre-modern Purim practices. In Tel Aviv, it was allegedly the new folk itself that desired perfect order. The folkloric discourse was actually integrated into bourgeois ideals regarding the proper maintenance of the body, and the two were thought to harmoniously complement each other.

In a summary report of the 1927 carnival, which took place during an economic downturn, it was emphasized that "the joyful mood was not artificial but natural, as if everyone was determined to halt the bad spirit."[61] The discrepancy in describing the lack of "artificiality" of the good mood is quite apparent: if the good mood is a result of conscious determination, isn't it artificial? The conscious institutional attempt to direct and manage emotions in the public sphere was talked about as if it was spontaneous and natural. The same contradiction came to the surface in the report quoted above:

---

[59] "Yerushalayim yom yom" [Everyday Jerusalem], *Doar-Hayom* 13.3.1927. See supra, chapter two, note 14.

[60] "Purim be-Tel-Aviv" [Purim in Tel Aviv], *Ha'aretz* 11.3.1925.

[61] "Hakarnaval be-Tel-Aviv" [Tel Aviv carnival], *Ha'aretz* 21.3.1927. See also: Goldberg 2005: 98–100.

Everything was in measure and tempo, the joy was somewhat restrained, as if it was played by musical notations, with no grating dissonances.[62]

The image of the musical harmony matched the pastoral image of folk culture, which if given the freedom to develop without inhibition would be miraculously harmonious. This enforcement of social order by the ethos of civility proved no less efficient than a state law enforcement, which Zionists could not execute.

A most telling example of the romanticizing of the contemporaneous Tel Aviv carnival in light of the "civilized folklore" discourse was a suggestion made by Baruch Agadati in 1928 in the context of the agitated public debate regarding the future of the carnival. Agadati suggested that the carnival be delimited within a fenced space, and that visitors be required to wear a paper hat to be sold for ten mils (a mil was a thousandth of one Palestine pound) at the entrance points.[63] This was meant to resolve the funding issue, but was also intended to achieve cultural goals, as explained in another editorial letter. Agadati thought that the crowd should not be static and passively wait for the parade procession. Instead, he suggested that "multiple processions will simultaneously depart from different places in the city, led by bands, passing through the city, and before evening will consolidate to one big conglomerate." The itineraries of the many processions should not be predetermined, and instead, the order would be maintained by using the everyday rule: "walk on your right." In other words, there would be no need for marshals, or physical barriers between audience and performers such as ropes, but rather, "the order will be maintained by the crowd itself." Everyone would decorate their houses and cars, and the guiding principle would be "not standing and curiosity, but movement, activity, proverbs and stories which provoke laughter and make worries and troubles be forgotten, surprising inventions, funny games, and so on."[64]

Agadati actually suggested designing the carnivalesque space in a fashion similar to that of his balls, which were designed to conceal

---

[62] Supra note 50.

[63] "Lesidur hakarnival bu-Purim (mikhtav lama'arekhet)" [About organizing Purim carnival (editorial letter)], *Ha'aretz* 17.2.1928.

[64] B. Agadati, "Lesidrey hakarnaval be-Tel-Aviv" [Organizing Tel Aviv carnival], *Ha'aretz* 4.3.1928.

any spatial distinction between performers and audience: "Our balls are not supposed to be a show, but merriment! Not a spectacle, but life! Not a place in which one merely gazes, but a place to fulfill one's potential!"[65] In the same manner, the wanderer (or *flâneur*) in the urban street-carnival should have been endlessly surprised by encounters with unexpected performances, instead of passively waiting in the audience to watch them.

Agadati suggested the production take place in a utopian space in which the entire "people" is wandering through the streets in a spontaneous and disorganized manner, thus creating a miraculous order and harmony. Agadati saw in folk culture more than a source for legitimacy and interpretation: he viewed it as a desired socio-political structure similar to what Simmel had designated "festive sociability."[66] Of course, this should have been enabled only by the physical enclosure of the carnival in a concrete space to which one must purchase an entrance ticket. In the suggested cultural performance, each person becomes a float and a viewer at once, the social hierarchies are temporarily suspended, the senses are overstimulated, and the people's spontaneous joy is harmoniously expressed. In order to maintain the public order when many processions are moving along random routes, all that was needed was to adhere to the civil rule, "walk on the right." That is, public order should have been maintained not by hierarchies or political power, but by an ethos of civility and manners.

We can assume that this suggestion was not seriously discussed because it seemed impractical to fence in an urban space for one day. It is also possible that the organizing bodies were afraid of losing control—which is precisely what Agadati desired. Agadati's gradual disengagement from the organizing committee of the carnival, after many years of activity, probably was linked to the rejection of his suggestion. In fact, following 1928, the carnival followed the opposite path—more institutional involvement, less amateur participation.[67]

---

[65] A guide to Adagati's traditional costumes balls, p. 2, archive of Israeli center for stage arts, file 62.3.7.

[66] See supra, introduction, note 38.

[67] See a letter from the committee to Agadati: "We wonder why you do not visit our office, and request you to come over and take a more active part in our work" (29.2.1932, TAMA 04–3219b).

Nevertheless, this suggestion reflects a common understanding of the problem of social order within carnivalesque discourse. The carnival was indeed perceived as a spontaneous expression of folk culture. The extraordinary public order that was kept during the carnival was presumed to be the authentic expression of a civilized people, rather than an outcome of institutional enforcement by higher authorities. The folklorist discourse was linked not only to the past, but to the present as well, since the urban space of Tel Aviv was perceived as a place that belonged to all of the Jewish people, beyond the rule of any authority.

Discourse of Civilized Folklore

As implied before, Western academic and literary writing about the carnivalesque somewhat romanticized it. The romanticizing of the carnival is thus embedded in carnivalesque discourse itself. According to common Zionist discourse, these wild past practices were developed in exile, when the symbolic subversion was necessary to preserve the mental survival of the persecuted Jewish people. Nowadays, or so the explanation went, there we are no authorities to whom the Jews ought to protest and no social order to subvert, since "the first Hebrew city" belonged to the entire Jewish people. Zionism understood itself as institutionally legitimizing the real Jewish folk culture, for the first time in history. Hence, the Purim carnival was no longer wild because the authorities the original Purim was meant to subvert no longer existed as such—be they the rabbinic establishment or the Gentile authorities (the latter was challenged in 1933, as we shall see in the next chapter). The city of Tel Aviv appeared as a place in which the collective body could prosper, regardless of any authority, as in Bakhtin's classical definition of the carnivalesque. The Jewish joy, which was suppressed for ages in private and semi-public spheres, was now freely present in the public space. Within folkloric logic, the bourgeois order was understood as the result of the harmony of "true" folk spirit, which is now given true freedom. This "civilized folklore" discourse settled the obsession regarding order-maintaining with the alleged suspension of hierarchies during the carnival, using the metaphor of musical harmony. In Tel Aviv, or so the explanation went, there was no need of wildness to express folk spirit because it was already free from hierarchies anyway.

The frequent talk about Tel Aviv's free atmosphere was supported by Tel Aviv's hedonist and permissive everyday public culture, as described by Helman, who concludes that "Tel Aviv's overwhelmingly secular and notoriously free society was in no dire need of a specific yearly safety valve." Contemporaneous observers agreed.[68]

In a recent book, the historian Boaz Neumann analyzed what he describes as the Zionist body perception. Discussing a small group of pioneers who indeed produced voluminous mythical writings about their erotic relationship with the soil, Neumann demonstrated how pioneers immersed their bodies in the soil via body-liquids such as sweat, and body wholes.[69] Conversely, the Urban Zionist perception of the body was mainly of bourgeois character, emphasizing the preservation of the body. The folkloric discourse, on the other hand, immersed the individual body not so much in the land but rather in the collective body. Rather than educating people to sacrifice their bodies to the land or nation, this "civilized folklore" discourse attempted to harmonize the individual body with the collective one.

The next two chapters shall demonstrate the tension between bourgeois and carnivalesque traditions with regard to two significant carnivalesque elements: rites of symbolic violence and sexuality. These two notions were dealt with via cultural performances of two key scenes from the Book of Esther, which functioned as the interpretational frame for these historical transformations: the scene in which Mordechai rides a horse, which replaced the scene of the hanging of Haman as the key political scene in the book; and the scene in which King Ahasuerus chooses his queen, which was the key sexo-political scene. The two following chapters will be dedicated to analyzing the performance of these two scenes in the Tel Aviv Purim carnival. Let us begin by discussing rites of symbolic violence and their modern transformations.

---

[68] Helman 2006a: 388. See also: Yosef Shaked, "Likrat hasimkha heyehudit hahadasha" [Towards a new Jewish merriment], *Ha'aretz* 8.3.1933.

[69] Neumann 2009.

Chapter 5

"Mordechai is Riding a Horse":
Political Performances

Political-Cultural Performance

These next two chapters will analyze the cultural performances of biblical figures in the carnival. The term "cultural performance" refers to non-verbal expressions, via the body, objects, and sounds, which include rites, rituals, songs, dances, theatre, and other expressions in one analytical category. For the anthropologist Milton Singer, who coined the term, the analysis of processes of cultural transformation through cultural performance seemed somewhat corrective of interpretive manipulations by cultural agents. In this sense they are unlike mere "high" ideological texts, and hence more observable.[1] Victor Turner further developed the term as a general approach to the study of culture, but unlike Singer, Turner emphasized the liminality of cultural performance, in which common social rules are suspended in favor of an enhanced reflectivity, which enables (though does not necessitate) for the social system a degree of self-criticism.[2] Thus, the analysis of cultural performance and its transformations over time can reveal, or extract, implicit ideological motifs.

In this chapter, I will explore symbolic and mythical dimensions of Zionist power, which proved crucial in the creation of the Zionist sphere of civil society and identity construction. In accordance with Alexander, "power" is understood here as "also a medium of communication, not simply a goal of interested action or a means of coercion. It has a symbolic code, not only a material base."[3] The very symbolic

---
[1] See: Singer 1972: 64–65, 71.
[2] See: Turner 1987: 21–32. According to Kertzer (1988: 9), this reflexivity is the core definition of the ritual.
[3] Alexander 2006: 48.

dimensions of Zionist power are revealed and analyzed here through their cultural performances in the Purim carnival.

Hereafter I will discuss the performance of the biblical scene in which Mordechai is Riding a Horse. The performative centrality of the scene provides a thick clue regarding the dynamics in Zionist conceptualizations of its significant Others and understandings of political power. The unique variation of Urban Zionist perception of power is hinted at in the shift from symbolic violence in pre-Zionist performances into rites of rationality; but as we shall see, unlike other "uncivilized" rites, the rejection of symbolic violence was far from conclusive.

Mordechai and the Horse

A debasement and mockery of a fictitious "king" are general carnivalesque themes, and Bakhtin thought, for example, that the numerous scenes of grotesque coronation in *Gargantua and Pantagruel* are intended to mock Jesus' passion.[4] Historically, popular Purim performances in most Jewish Diasporas through the ages focused on symbolic violence toward evil Haman, situating this biblical scoundrel as the main performative antagonist-protagonist. The general structure of the performance was relatively homogeneous, consisting of performing acts of symbolic violence on mimetic figures of Haman in different variations. Some created mannequins of Haman in varied sizes, which were then set aflame, hanged, stabbed, or even shot by gunfire after a staged procession. Sometimes a real actor was hired to play Haman, and his role was to be led in a street procession, spat upon and humiliated by the crowd, and finally disposed of in a simulated execution in the street. The biblical scene of the hanging of Haman (Esther 8:10) was a significant performative basis for European Jewish popular theatre. Many Jewish communities observed this performative ritual despite the fact that it could be seen as taunting Christian religious sensitivities. Many European Christians (not without reason) perceived this custom as an overly fervent or ludicrous imitation of Jesus' passion, and in a few historical incidents, Jews paid a heavy price for the performance. This performance was accompanied by other customs, such

---

[4] Bakhtin 1968: 198.

as making noise when Haman's name was intoned (or blotting out his name through other means) during the liturgical chanting of the Book of Esther in synagogues.[5]

Beginning in the eighteenth century, and during the nineteenth, as part of the "pacification" noted above, there was a visible diminution in Haman's theatrical role. Rabbis, intellectuals, and community leaders declared a moralistic war against traditional revenge customs. In many places where this "reformation" took place (within all Jewish religious streams, to the same extent), the beating of Haman found no adequate performative substitute, and gradually, popular-traditional Purim performances faded away.

The Tel Aviv carnival was the first significant Purim celebration in the Jewish world to suggest a "pacified" performative substitute, which pushed Haman to a secondary role. Instead of the hanging, the scene of Mordechai riding horseback, led by Haman on foot (Esther 6:11), became the most common and popular visual motif that accompanied Purim celebrations in Tel Aviv. Throughout the years when the carnival was held, there was not one procession in which this motif was not included. This scene was usually at the center of the performance of the "oriental youth" (*Tze'irey Hamizrakh*) club, and won several prizes.[6] This motif was not only performed in the main procession, but it also appeared in many posters, caricatures, and decorative items published by various organizations as an informal symbol for the carnival. Consider this caption from a JNF poster entitled "Purim's masks":

---

[5] This performative structure recurred, with some variations, at least since the fifth century CE (see Linder 1983: 171–172; Thornton 1987), throughout the Middle Ages and the Renaissance (Roth 1933; Roth 1959: 244; Belkin 1997) and the early-modern era (Goodman 1949: chap. XV; Gaster 1953: 221–232; Lewinsky 1955: 107–120; Kapakh 1961: 40; Ratzhabi 1988: 222 and note 31; Sperber 2002: 5–10; and more). For a general overview see Lewinsky 1947; Horowitz 2006; Hanegbi 1998; Har'el 2004. Mantgen (1994: 346) cites offended Christian interpretations, and following Roth (1933), he also suggests that the parody of the hanging of Haman/Jesus contributed to the development of blood libels.

[6] See, for example: "Purim be-Tel-Aviv" [Purim in Tel Aviv], *Ha'aretz* 1.3.1926; "Purim be-Tel-Aviv" [Purim in Tel Aviv], *Ha'aretz* 20.3.1927; "Hakarnaval be-Tel-Aviv" [The carnival in Tel Aviv], *Davar* 28.3.1929; "Lamrot ha-matar: Purim mutzlakh be-Tel-Aviv" [Despite the downpour: A successful Purim in Tel Aviv], *Doar-Hayom* 5.3.1931; from Dizengoff to "the group of Yemenite youth," 15.3.1933, TAMA, file 04–3220a.

Chapter 5. "Mordechai is Riding a Horse": Political Performance

A joyful sailor, working people/ a hasty clown, JNF box/ Mordechai rides a nice horse/ let us sing "the people of Israel live!"[7]

The transformation in the performative-interpretive emphasis of the biblical text may be exemplified in an interesting notebook in which Yemima Aberman, a preschool teacher-in-training, documented the activities of a preschool day that happened to take place before Purim. The notebook includes an abbreviated version of the Book of Esther as told to the children. In Aberman's story, the hanging of Haman is completely omitted along with any hint of a brutal vengeance by the Jews, probably to spare the children the bloody scenes (Jewish children were not spared these scenes in previous generations, of course).[8] Instead, Haman's leading Mordechai on horseback is relocated to the end of the story and told in detail, after the exposure of Esther's Jewish identity—unlike in the biblical narrative, in which the parade precedes Esther's exposure. In other words, according to Aberman's version of the story as told to the preschool children, Haman's only punishment, and the fullest manifestation of the Jews' redemption, is conveyed in the procession of Mordechai, the royal horse, and Haman through the streets of the city.[9]

From the perspective of contemporaries, the immediate interpretation of the motif was, first and foremost, political: to allude to Jewish self-sovereignty. Consider this song, titled "The singing of the Jewish masses [during the bringing of Mordechai on horseback]":

— What happened?
— Who came?
Who leads, who is led, and who gave the order?
And who will have the victory—the descendants of Haman or Judea?

---

[7] CZA, file KRA 196. See also KRA 439; KRA 1766. See also: "Kishutei rehov be-Purim" [Purim street decorations], Sha'ar Zion, Beit Ariela library, photos collection, festivals file, Purim 1960; TAMA, file 01–06, pictures p-1431, p-1432. A caricature, "Kakha Ye-ase la-ish" [Thus it shall be done to the man; Esther 6:11], *Ha'aretz* 18.3.1935.

[8] On transformations in children's stories see: Shavit 1986.

[9] Purim Notebook by Yemima Aberman, CZA, file J17/7225.

> Who's happy? Who moans? Who was defeated?
> Who's riding on the king's horse? Who has the merriment?
> — We are with the victory, and Haman with the defeat.
> Mordechai, a Jewish man, see—has honor and greatness.
> He's riding the king's horse, wearing azure-purple.
> The crown on his head—and the horse is led by Haman.[10]

The actualization of the scene was even more explicit in the following description of the opening ceremony of the 1931 carnival in "Esther's palace":

> "Queen Esther" is revealed. The Jews of Shushan with their white garments are revealed, and then Mordechai, riding his horse, led by Haman, and Zeresh [his wife] with their entire household are walking after them, whining.—Thus shall it be done to the man whom the King desires to honor! [Esther 6:11]— Horrible Haman is walking and declaring in his awful, hoarse voice. And Mordechai is rejoicing on his horse with his song: "our God's deeds"... "turning over all his curses into blessings, turning over all his evils for good"... (While the heart of the mass crowd is happily dubbing: turning over all his black books to white).[11]

The surprise element of Mordechai's royal horseback procession in a seemingly hopeless situation was appropriated by the writer to express the hope of reversing the plot in the Zionist story as well, after the 1929 "White Paper," which imposed limitations on Jewish immigration and land purchase in Palestine.

It should be noted that the question of the scene's narrative function within the biblical story was the source of broad-scale discussion among ancient and modern commentators. A detailed literary discussion is beyond our scope here, but from the Zionist point of view, it is safe to say that this scene is about national honor: it is the

---

[10] "Pizmonot betekes haptikha shel hakhag" [Songs for the opening ceremony], *Krovetz for Purim 1935*, VII.

[11] "Lamrot hamatar: Purim mutzlach be-Tel-Aviv" [Despite the downpour: A successful Purim in Tel Aviv], *Doar-Hayom* 5.3.1931. Ellipses are in original.

first event in the plot in which Mordechai gains honor by his own virtue and not through his family connection to Esther. According to this approach, a major consequence of Mordechai's royal parade was the awe and respect he later received from all high officials of the Persian Empire (Esther 9:3–4). Zionist-oriented commentators of the Book of Esther define national honor as both an independent political goal and a political means that may be converted to enhanced power. In that sense, the scene redeems Mordechai from his despised dependency on a woman and women's dishonorable business, and its performative centrality in Tel Aviv redeemed the entire festival from the feminine means of rescue and made the shift toward respectable masculine heroism.[12]

Zionists interpreted the scene as symbolizing the way in which the Jews (men) take their destiny into their own hands, out of God's hands and Gentile rule, and national honor was now made tangible by the man riding his horse in Tel Aviv's streets, as in the following statement:

> Every Israelite person is being transformed nowadays, not only in terms of masks, but in reality. The depression and sadness are gradually disappearing, going away, and new Jews, happy and joyful, with their elderly, children, and grandchildren, are walking in the streets with lightened faces.
> Blessed are we: Haman—is cursed. Mordechai—is blessed, and he is the one to ride the horse.[13]

The writer alluded to the carnivalesque Talmudic saying that encouraged drunkenness and loss of consciousness (*Ad-Delo-Yada*) to the extent of impairing one's ability to make the distinction between cursing Haman and blessing Mordechai. This carnivalesque reversal

---

[12] See: Segal 1999 (with some more explanations for the scene's function in the story); Hazony 1995. The frequent criticism on the use of "feminine tricks" in the book of Esther was integrated with a criticism on the "exilic" nature of Purim. See, for example: Dr. A. Teneboym, "Hirhurim le-Purim" [Reflections for Purim], *Doar-Hayom* 8.3.1936; Uri Keisari, "Hamutar lanu lomar? Masoret Purim holekhet ve-ovedet" [Are we allowed to say? Purim tradition is getting lost], *Doar-Hayom* 24.3.1935.

[13] Supra note 11. See BT Megillah 7:2.

was now re-inverted to deepen the distinction between good and evil. The imagined political power explicit in riding the horse was what set the cursed apart from the blessed.

It is not surprising that performative riding on horseback was not limited to Mordechai. Sometimes Mordechai was accompanied by an entire royal entourage of horsemen. Occasionally, "Queen Esther" also rode in a carriage, led by horses. The procession of 1928 was led by a horseman trumpeter, followed by a horsemen's guard, holding national flags. In due course, groups of horsemen from the surrounding Jewish villages, wearing colorful costumes, were added to the parade.[14] The horse motif was further elaborated on 1932, when Mayor Dizengoff began to lead the entire procession, accompanied by Avraham Shapira, a legendary guard from Petah-Tikva, the first colony—both rode their horses. The Mayor riding his horse immediately became one of the most familiar and common symbols of the carnival. A publicity pamphlet about Tel Aviv published in several languages included the statement, somewhat exaggerated, that "the carnival's peak is the procession, led by the mayor, riding his horse." In a flattering song to Dizengoff, written by Kadish Y. Silman, there is a refrain: "like Mordechai—Dizengoff rides his horse."[15] This symbol penetrated the collective memory. In 1998, the Tel Aviv municipality organized an *Adloyada*, and Mayor Roni Milo headed the procession on a horse, in homage to the remembered processions.[16]

The signifier of power was thus the horse, rather than Mordechai. Its politico-cultural functions should therefore be analyzed separately, not as a mere image but as a physical presence of power.

The Horse

Animals were always a grey zone in the human imagination. Animals were used in art, religion, literature, and performance to explore human limits. Toward the modern era, animalistic metaphorization

---

[14] All sources in supra note 5.
[15] Ben-Yishai 1936: 8; "Me-inyanei deyoma" [On current affairs], *Ha'aretz* 13.3.1933; "Hakarnaval Ha-Purimi be-Tel-Aviv" [Purim carnival in Tel Aviv], *Ha'aretz* 24.3.1932, 1. See also: Lewinsky 1955: 277; Carmiel 1999: 246.
[16] Carmiel 1999: 251.

was utilized to maintain the borders between humans and animals, or between nature and culture. However, perhaps more than in art and literature, the animal's physical presence in performance has a presence beyond its mere symbolic function. The performative signification of the alleged border between nature and culture in the body of a real animal calls attention to the fragility of the borders between the animal and the human.[17] In our case, the performative use of animals reveals the attempt to signify a border between nature and culture as a crucial component of Zionist identity construction, particularly in the urban context.

From its very beginnings, the civilizing discourse of Tel Aviv combined the ecological with the political. The act of delineating the neighborhood on the empty sands was the core of the powerful foundation myth of Tel Aviv.[18] It was understood as imitating the Genesis story — a recurrent structure in stories on the foundation of cities, narrated as the emergence of Cosmos from Chaos, of culture from nature.[19] The clean, organized, and controlled city functioned as a clear antithesis to the wild and primitive desert. However, a border was not drawn between humans and all other life forms. Humans ought to rule not only over nature itself, but also over other humans who enable themselves to be ruled by nature, that is, those who live in poverty, disarray, and filth, and thus enable "nature" — diseases, ghouls, robbers, and others — to control their lives. For theories of social contract, beginning with Hobbes, such uncivilized elements represent the wild "state of nature" from which humans should be redeemed by taming the "animalistic" human tendencies through the political sphere. The assumption that the new Zionist man should rule his destiny was linked to his rule over nature and its related human populations — the Arabs and, to an extent, Arabic Jews (or "Mizrahim"). The new Jewish man was thus not only the new Jew but a new human (as opposed to an animal). The

---

[17] Berger 1980: 5; Derrida 2002; Wahrman 2004, 127–153. On animalistic performances see: Read 2000; Chaudhuri 2007; 2009. My deep thanks are given to Noam Gal for passionately introducing me into the challenging world of "animality studies."

[18] Arikha 1969: 5. See: Fireberg 2003a; Eidar 2003: 197–231; LeVine 2005: 126–132; Mann 2006: 75–76; Azaryahu 2007a: 54–60; Shoham 2012.

[19] See: Eliade 1954: 12–21; Tuan 1978. The closest inspiration for Tel Aviv in that matter was Odessa (Zipperstein 1985: 1–3, 25, 33–40; Mann 2006: 12).

wilderness was a significant Other of Zionism, while technocracy was worshiped, not only as a means, but as a cultural goal in itself.[20] Tel Aviv, "the first Hebrew city," was mythologized as a place in which the Jews took their destiny into their hands and ruled over nature, other nations, and their own pre-civilized "exilic" features—with all these feats taking place simultaneously. This discourse influenced, for example, the choice of the distant location of *Akhuzat-Bayit* as the first neighborhood. In order to create their oasis, the planned suburb with street lighting, running water, and sidewalks, they wanted to distance themselves from both Jaffa's "diseases" and its "Arabness," wrapping nationalism with technological modernization, targeting wilderness as the main enemy.[21]

This ecological context of Zionist perceptions of power can explain why, beside the horses, only domesticated animals were displayed in the carnival processions: sheep, cattle, chickens, donkeys, and camels. Regarding at least some of these animals—in particular camels and sheep—there was also an Orientalist analogy between these alleged docile and patient animals and the Arabs, who should have patiently lingered to enjoy the Zionist technology and the progress it brought to the East.[22]

The domesticity of the horse was more complicated, due to its two opposing cultural aspects: on one hand, its wild species symbolizes free nature, or anarchy. More specifically, it symbolizes the barbarians who threatened the ancient Roman world and the Christian medieval world, or, more recently, pirates, cowboys, and American "Indians," who captured the imagination of twentieth-century masses. On the other hand, a tamed horse, quietly walking, and a man— knight, soldier, or king (in some cases, princesses or ladies as well) — seated on its back symbolizes power in its splendor.[23] European aristocratic sport (hunts, races and related activities) is but one notable cultural performance that uses horses to embody the rule of "civiliza-

---

[20] Penslar 1991.

[21] Katz 1986: 409.

[22] Cohen 2003.

[23] This perception echoes in Greek myths of contours (Clutton-Brock 1992: 53), as well as the biblical association of Egyptian empire with "the horse and its rider" (Exodus 15: 1). This perception was absorbed by every culture in which horses were domesticated (ibid., 178–181).

tion" over nature. The ethos of sportsmanship expresses control not only over extra-human nature, but also over inner-human "animalistic" aggressive impulses.[24]

As is convincingly demonstrated by Bartal, these two contradictory aspects of the horse were introduced into Zionist mythology from Eastern Europe through the image of the Cossack, who was transformed into a Bedouin Zionist Orientalist mythology. In Russian political myths and culture, the Cossack was known as the frontier horseman who allegedly threatened to release the subordinated peasants. The Cossack's ability to rule over the wild horse represented the Janus-faced imagined frontier experience: freedom from imperial government, alongside control over nature. The Cossack could tame nature, and, at the same time, be an integral aspect of nature. The horse simultaneously represented organized political power, alongside the anarchic wildlife and the "the state of nature."[25] Horse races organized for Tel Aviv's carnival emphasized the sportsmanship ethos. With the occasional participation of Bedouin men from the southern desert, this ethos was utilized as a possible platform for fraternity among nations.[26]

The horse that walked patiently in the city's streets beneath the rear end of the new Jewish man embodied controlled nature. The ability of the rider to control and maneuver the tall animal exemplified the new Jewish man's distinction from nature, and his ability to control and suppress the non-civilized elements, be they the desert, inner aggressive impulses, or human groups which resemble nature.

In Tel Aviv, horses not only symbolized Jewish sovereign power, that is, the Jews' ability to control nature via culture, order, and restraint, but also corporeally embodied and exhibited this power. First, there were the horses of the municipal police force, which supervised the public order, and occasionally headed the procession to clear the anticipated route of crowds. Nevertheless, the horses of the British police were also present, as a reminder that the actual political power was, in fact, not in Zionist hands. In other words, it was an allegedly non-violent perception of power.

---

[24] Elias and Dunning 1986.

[25] Bartal 1998.

[26] "Hakarnaval Ha-Purimi be-Tel-Aviv" [Purim carnival in Tel Aviv], *Doar-Hayom* 24.3.1932.

Since the horse was such a crucial emblem for Jewish rule over well-designed urban space, it was important, from the Zionist point of view, to make sure that the right protagonist rides the horse. Let us now turn to our abandoned antagonist-protagonist, Haman, in order to understand what happened to the rituals of symbolic violence.

Haman, Evil, Nationalism

The old performative emphasis on symbolic violence towards Haman mythologized a meta-historical evil, which was traditionally embodied in the concept of *Amalek*. This word referred originally to a vagabond tribe that taunted Israel in the Sinai desert after its escape from Egypt. *Amalek* was defined as Israel and God's nemesis, and hence God commanded its elimination from history (Exodus 17: 8–16). However, throughout the centuries, the concept's meaning was expanded to include varieties of world evil. According to the typology suggested by Paul Ricoeur for myths of evil, this is an eschatological myth, within which evil was created by an ancestor during history and would be destroyed within history as well. Accordingly, *Amalek* and *Israel* were considered counter-protagonists, representing meta-historical evil and good.[27]

The customary Purim performances relied on the genealogical hint given in the Book of Esther that Haman's actual origins were with *Amalek*.[28] These performances dealt with the existence of evil in the world by understanding the Jewish people as chosen and hence persecuted. The grotesque display of a total battle against evil constituted the ontological and historical presence of evil in the "Other" as a mirror-image of the good in the Self. To confront its perpetual political inferiority, the chosen-persecuted group created a performance of inversion in which evil was personified, mimetically persecuted, and destroyed. After this catharsis, order was regained when the "good" people return to their political inferiority, which embodied theological superiority. The performance had an apparent cohesive function for

---

[27] Ricoeur 1967: 171–174, 235–243.

[28] In the Book of Esther, Haman is referred to as "the Agagite" (e. g. Esther 3:1), which is understood in rabbinic literature as indicating his ethnic origins from Agag, the king of *Amalek* in the days of Samuel (Samuel I, 15: 2–33).

Jewish communities, and the imitation of the "Other" via the wild carnivalesque behavior, particularly drunkenness, practiced putting oneself in the Other's shoes, in order to re-signify the psychological barrier between the groups.

In a sharp contrast, in Tel Aviv's Purim celebrations, the behavioral characteristics of a persecuted-chosen group were eliminated, whereas the performative presence of evil was altered and had a different social function. The scene of Mordechai riding a horse was not a reversal of social order, nor was it carnivalesque. Unlike the Italian comedies, for example, here the servant—Haman—never dared to trick his master. The performance was perfectly static, with no drama and no comedy, in keeping with static power relations. The implicit assumption was that evil should not be fought to be destroyed, but like the horse should be tamed to respectfully serve the good (who was still, of course, the Jew). The performative language had changed from ethnocentric grotesque into a "realist" representation of ideal power relations. This performance neutralized evil from its meta-historical charge and attempted to control it by creating a stable hierarchical public sphere. Instead of imagining a cruel and brutal revenge of their oppressors, the Jews now imagined a rational management of the public sphere that concealed any resistance. This performance both symbolized and created the new public sphere. The fight against evil thus moved from the meta-historical realm to the civil-political one. It was a psychological transformation from political inferiority to sovereignty, which included a transformation in political rituals as the meta-historical myth was replaced by a political one. However, the new perception was no less mythical than the former, as we shall see.

The dramatic focus of the parade changed accordingly: so far, Haman was the antagonist-protagonist, playing the role of absolute evil and meta-historical Other. Now, the protagonist was Mordechai, the "I," the sovereign, whereas Haman was his obedient (and unimportant) servant. The uncompromised war, to the last day, was transformed into a possibility of peaceful co-existence, as long as there was clarity regarding who rides the horse and who leads it by walking, who is the master and who is the servant.

With regard to representations of biblical figures, evil was indeed miniaturized in Tel Aviv's carnival. One hermeneutic technique was the replacement of Haman by his sons and, in particular, the youngest one, Uaiezatha. Alterman wrote that "Haman was hanged on a tall gallows [tree]/ and Uaiezatha on a planter."[29] The character of Uaiezatha, who was never a folkloric figure before the Zionist era, gained surprising popularity in songs and media. The above-quoted song by Yehuda Karni, which described Mordechai riding his horse, concluded with the following words: "Zeresh is mourning/ her heart is blowing/ Haman is ready for the rope/ but in town there is no tree/ and his ten sons/ are pale like lime/ and every donkey and mule/ will tell their deeds."[30] The characters who used to be the nation's worst enemies in previous Jewish cultures were now transformed into a group of small, frightened children who could easily have had the hell punched out of them, so to speak. The inability to hang Haman (satirizing the lack of greenery in Tel Aviv) did not matter, since the Jews were now visibly in power and revenge was no longer necessary.

Another hint of the miniaturization of Haman is to be found in the re-naming of a central city square during the festival. The square was called the "and Haman restrained himself" (Esther 5:10) square, alluding to the public restrooms in that square.[31] Here evil was associated with the one who walks through the city streets but needs the bathroom. In the Zionist sovereign consciousness, as expressed in the carnival, Arab resistance to Zionism was essentially no different than the lack of greenery or public restrooms in Tel Aviv. All these phenomena could be addressed by technological progress, proper management, thoughtful planning, and consideration for economic welfare. Evil was interpreted not as an ontological-meta-historical force, but as a socio-historical phenomenon, perceived as the result of a lack of education and civilization. All one needs to do to struggle against this evil is to ride the horse.

Anthony Smith, the scholar of comparative nationalism, suggested a distinction between two sorts of nationalist movements, which he named *ethnocentric* and *polycentric*. Ethnocentric nationalist movements demand national rights for themselves, contending, justifiably or not, that they are persecuted more than others. Polycentric

---

[29] Natan Alterman, "Pizmonot le-Purim tartzag" [Songs for Purim 1933], *Turim*, no. 29–30 (28 February 1933); reprinted in Alterman 1979: 213–215. See above, chapter two, note 64.

[30] Supra note 10.

[31] See above, chapter one, p. 27.

nationalist movements demand a right which they consider universal.[32] In Zionism, the eminent spokesman for polycentric nationalism was Theodore Herzl (1860–1904), the founder of the World Zionist Organization. He perceived the roots of hatred between Jews and Christians as the outgrowth of their symbiotic social relationship throughout generations. Hence, he thought that an exclusively Jewish public sphere would release both sides from the hatred by liberating Judaism from its ethnocentric chosen-persecuted image. Such a fully-controlled public sphere should educate the Jewish people to an enlightened *Bildung,* in order to deal with the world's evils via proper social, economic, and cultural planning. Thus, the success of Herzl's project would depend, among other parameters, on the stabilizing of social hierarchies and power relations in the public sphere.[33]

In 1920s Tel Aviv, the replacement of the hanging of Haman by Mordechai riding a horse was indeed emblematic. An ethnocentric attempt at a signification of tough borders between "I" and "Other" was replaced by polycentric nationalism, capable of containing Others within the public sphere, on the condition that the hierarchy between Jews and Gentiles be stabilized.

An interesting example of polycentric nationalism can be found in a description of the children's carnival procession by A. Z. Ben-Yishai (1902–1977), later the editor of the municipal bulletin, who commented on the absence of Haman, as everyone wore only costumes of Mordechai, Esther, and Ahasuerus. He thought that nowadays Haman evokes not anger, but only jocularity: "[Haman] is like the pre-revolution Russian cops. In the case of a man who was mercilessly hanged every year, and then in his death was still stunned by noisemakers — his sins were in the meantime exonerated."[34] After so many years of uncompromising hatred, Haman can be forgiven, due to the diminished importance of his role as the scoundrel in the drama of Jewish history.

This sharp transition in Zionist culture away from previous Jewish cultures did not pass unnoticed, but modernists and folklorists

---

[32] Smith 1971: 170–171.

[33] See, for example: Herzl 1998: 96; Vital 1984: 256–266; Shavit & Sitton 2004: 21–24; Shoham 2008.

[34] A. Z. Ben-Yishai, "Rega'im: Purim shel tinokot" [Moments: A children's Purim], *Ha'aretz* 6.3.1928; CZA, file KKL5/4917/1.

judged it differently. The poet Avraham Shlonsky (1900–1973) wrote a long folkloristic article in which he surveyed the wild history of Purim, from Talmudic sources to the *Purimspiel*, and wondered:

> Isn't there here a seed for a new tradition? Consider Purim festival—the most folkish and bright among the festivals [...] But what form and style are these of our annual carnivals? [...] We found neither form nor frame. It is necessary to make this custom of burning Haman into the procession's pivotal point. This is the peak and the final point. The effigy of Haman the Agagite is being led, heading the procession; the entire people is flowing to the large square—in which the burning ceremony will take place; and then the burning, and that's it! The freedom of expression—to the people!"[35]

Shlonsky's suggestion lacked a measure of political correctness, and indeed provoked an agitated debate that even slipped into the daily press. Many attacked "the barbarian suggestion to create an effigy of Haman and make a mass *auto-da-fe*."[36] Shlonsky, from his folklorist point of view, considered these past practices evidence of the miraculous ability of Jews to be happy even in the darkness of exile, and ignored the ethnocentric image of these practices. His "modernist" critics, however, did see the connection, and called for the ethnocentric practices to be abandoned in the new Hebrew culture, with its attempt to designate Jewish identity in sovereign and polycentric terms. A mimetic execution for symbolic evil was inappropriate not only as an irrational "voodoo" act, but mainly because it was unnecessary in a world in which the evil wa perceived as controllable and manageable.

The dominance of polycentric nationalism in the 1920s was well-expressed by the considerable Arab presence in the carnival. Tens of thousands of Arab visitors came not only from nearby Jaffa, but also

---

[35] Eshel [=Abraham Shlonsky], "Purim (Al-pi mekorot yeshanim ve-khadashim)" [Purim (According to ancient and new sources)], *Ketuvim* 5.3.1928, 1–2.

[36] "He'arot ureshimot: Purim be-Tel-Aviv" [Comments and notes: Purim in Tel Aviv], *Hapo'el Hatza'ir* 21, 16.3.1928, 13.

from Samaria, the southern desert, and Jerusalem.[37] Arab peddlers, usually unlicensed, wandered around the city, selling food, beverage, "traditional" costumes, and other merchandise. Some Jews expressed ethnocentric concern, not only for the livelihood the carnival provided for the Arabs, but also due to apprehension about the very social and spatial mixture of Arabs and Jews in the "Jewish" city. After the cancellation of the carnival in 1936, one man thanked the municipality and wrote, "Last year in Tel Aviv carnival I was terrified. I saw in the streets more Gentiles than Jews." For such Jewish purists, the danger was not only a matter of security, but also a matter of civility, since the Arab peddlers worked "unlicensed (and with no sanitary inspection) and violate the sanctity and beauty of the city."[38]

Nonetheless, for many Zionist contemporaries, the steady visits of Arabs to Purim carnivals proved the capability of polycentric Zionism. The influential editor of *Ha'aretz* newspaper, Moshe Glikson (1878–1939), wrote that

> Purim joy in Tel Aviv revealed the lies of [Palestinian] nationalist inciting, and witnessed how baseless the loud propaganda is, by proclaiming emotions of hatred and revenge, where they are actually absent, and attempting to build a wall between neighbors who live together safely. Purim joy in the streets and neighborhoods of Tel Aviv is turning into a popular-civil carnival, with no distinctions of religion and nationhood. Thousands of Arabs were among the celebrators.[39]

Reacting to a violent incident between Jewish and Arab youngsters on Purim eve in 1924, Glikson implied that the civil ethos of the carnival threatened the "corrupted" Arab leadership. Another

---

[37] See, for example: "Ha-karnaval ha-purimi be-Tel-Aviv" [The Purim carnival in Tel Aviv], *Doar-Hayom*, 24.3.1932; "Yom etmol be-Tel-Aviv ha-hogeget" (Yesterday in celebrating Tel Aviv), *Davar*, 27.3.1929; "Falastin modi'a" [The newspaper *Falastin* announces], *Ha'aretz*, 21.3.1935. Reports on the participation of Arabs in the carnival recurred every year, in the Arab press as well. See the photo in Carmiel 1999: 49.

[38] From H.S. Yemini to Tel Aviv municipality, accepted 9.3.1936, TAMA, file 04–3222.

[39] M.G. [Moshe Glikson], "Al Ha-perek" [On the Agenda], *Ha'aretz* 22.3.1924.

commentator wrote a decade later that "the Arabs also took their share in the joy: they came in masses to participate in the fun, and in their childish oriental imagination, our Purim was probably influential for coming closer, more than any "round table" conferences and common interests."[40] Just like Herzl's *Altneuland*, this Orientalist-utopian approach suggested not wasting time on political negotiations with Arab leaders, and instead gaining the population's support through economic development, which would eventually provide them with personal happiness in the face of Arab nationalism. The Arab participation in the carnival's "celebration of the economy" seemed, in the eyes of many Zionists, to be the realization of this utopian vision.

The following text was titled "The day of friendship between Arabia and Israel:"

> *Id al Maskhara*[41] attracted tens of thousands of Arabs to Tel Aviv's streets. In these happy hours, no one thought about the Mandate, the White Book, Arlozorov, and Jamal Al-Huseini.
> "Nothing is like the *Yahud*," said a *fallakh* to his friend. "Such a festival can take place only once a year."[42]

This miraculous fraternity can exist only assuming that "Nothing is like the *Yahud* [the Jews]," that is, when Jews prevail in the public sphere. Indeed, in light of the 1936 cancellation of the carnival, and the increasing violence with "the Arab revolt," many developed nostalgic views of the idyllic fraternity of Arabs and Jews in the carnival, before Arab leadership "sparked the clash."[43]

Palestinian-Arab nationalist media had repeatedly underscored the massive Arab attendance at the carnival. However, from its perspective, this attendance was attacked as in congruent with their

---

[40] A.S. Yuris, "Purim shehushbat" [An interrupted Purim], *Hapo'el Hatza'ir*, 22, 9.3.1934, 12–13.

[41] A Hebrew-Arabic language game, referring to Purim as both "festival of masquerades" and "festival of commerce."

[42] "Sodot Min haheder (shemuot porhot be'olamenu uva'olam hagadol)" [Secrets from the room (rumors in our world and the bigger world)], *Doar-Hayom* 25.3.1932.

[43] "Inyanim: Idiliya min hayamim harishonim" [Affairs: An idyll from the first days], *Ha'aretz* 28.2.1937.

nationalist resistance to Zionism, as even "a purchase of a soda in the street from people who refuse to employ Arab workers" was perceived as a pro-Zionist act.[44] From the perspective of the Palestinian media, the power of polycentric nationalism was clearly understood. They viewed this participation as an exemplar of Palestinian national humiliation, a submission to the capitalist and licentious cultural agenda of Urban Zionism.

The Arab presence was prominent not only among the carnival's audience but on the stage as well. The representation of Arabs in Purim street theatre was quite different than in contemporaneous Hebrew theatre, where Arabs were represented only in negative terms, as corrupt and backward.[45] In the carnival, conversely, they were represented (not too often, though) as potential members of the new society. For example, a performance on the biblical Levites displayed the sacrificed cattle, led by their Arab shepherds, who were probably their true owners.[46] Another float, created by the JNF and called "The Progress of the Nation," included a moving truck which displayed a variety of Zionist characters: pioneers, bourgeois—and an unmistakable Arab man with his recognizable apparel—*Galabiya* and *Abaya*.[47] For the Arabs, this representation established a significant role in the new society, and valued their contribution to "the progress of the nation." This utopian exposition is strikingly similar to the exposition of the figures of Herzl's utopian novel *Altneuland*.[48]

This representation of the Arabs corresponds with the argument made by some scholars that Zionism had no significant Other against which its identity was constructed—not the British, nor even the Arabs. What historian Anita Shapira calls "the defensive ethos"

---

[44] See, for example: "Ba-itonut Ha'arvit" [In the Arab press], *Doar-Hayom* 12.3.1933; "Me-ha-itonut Ha'arvit" [From the Arab press], *Ha'aretz* 15.3.1933; "Iton hamufti al Purim be-Tel-Aviv" [The *Mufti*'s newspaper about Purim in Tel Aviv], *Ha'aretz* 5.3.1934; "Purim celebrations in Arab newspapers," *Ha'aretz* 22.3.1935; *Yediot Iriyat Tel-Aviv* [Tel Aviv municipal bulletin] 5, 1935, 138; and more of the same every year.

[45] Urian 1996: 19–32.

[46] *Ha'aretz* 2.3.1934.

[47] The picture is found in: Carmiel 2004: 198–199.

[48] Herzl 1987.

was part of a wider symbolic system of polycentric nationalism.[49] However, despite the dominance of the defensive ethos in the pre-1936 *Yishuv*, the power component of polycentric Zionism was clearly seen by the Palestinian media. Urban Zionism, in its Herzlian-polycentric variation, could, of course, include Arab men and women with their traditional costumes—but not their nationalism. Some Jewish writers did not fail to notice the power component of polycentric Zionism. Avigdor Hame'iri (1890–1970), for example, wondered about Haman leading Mordechai on horseback: what would the Jewish reaction be if any other nation would have depicted the Jews as their obedient servants?[50] Polycentric nationalism was not abstraction of power, but yet another perception of power, more civil-political and economic than military. The riding of Mordechai on the horseback symbolically emphasized the bureaucratization and rational management of the public sphere as a means of political control. Thus, the defensive ethos was far from pacifist.[51]

As noted above, polycentric nationalism had its own symbols, myths of evil, and public rituals according to which the Other is not really evil, but just requires guidance in the proper direction to achieve clarification of political hierarchies. Polycentric nationalism thus seemed capable of mobilizing non-Jews to support the Zionist project by abandoning ethnic nationalism and overcoming the ethnic limitations of Jewish identity. The new identity should, or perhaps really could, have been based on social planning, economic partnership, and civil solidarity. Tel Aviv's public events, the Purim carnival among them, were probably the only cultural site in which there was indeed such a symbolical-economic partnership between Arabs and Jews. Notwithstanding, even this Zionist illusion was shattered after 1936, when the carnival (along with the Levant Fair) ceased to exist and the ethnic dimensions of the conflict became more apparent. But the dominance of polycentric nationalism as a paradigm for the construction of Urban Zionist identity was already confronted with a serious challenge a few years before those events.

---

[49] Shapira 1992: 83–126; Shapira 1995; Eisenstadt 1998.

[50] Avigdor Hame'iri, "Al mot la-karnaval" [A lament on the carnival], *Ha'aretz* 8.3.1936.

[51] Cohen 2003.

1933: And Haman is Back

On the seventh of Adar (March 5), 1933, the notorious elections in Germany resulted in the rise to power of a man who was seen until then as a political caricature—Adolf Hitler. The shock caused by this political turning point resulted in an immediate transformation in the Zionist understanding of the relationship between evil and the Jews. Once again, the Jews were understood to be eternal victims of meta-historical evil powers. In the carnival of 1933, only a week after the German elections, there was already a thematic change, which was further enhanced in consecutive years and continued throughout the 1930s and the Second World War.[52] Uaiezatha did not disappear, but his father came back to the central stage, along with Shlonsky's rejected suggestion.

One float in the 1933 procession displayed Hitler, riding his horse along with his *Sturmabteilung* (SA), tyrannizing two beaten and injured Jewish men. The caption read "Hitler is persecuting and Palestine is closed" [that is, for immigration], and the tableaux was performed by the Petah Tikva association of Caucasian Jews. Although the direct target for the political protest was British immigration policy, it infuriated the German consulate in Jerusalem, which immediately sent a harsh protest letter to Mayor Dizengoff, demanding an apology. Dizengoff refused, claiming that the float was private—although he forgot to mention that the municipal committee assisted this float with two Palestine pounds, and then granted it a prize of two more pounds. More profoundly, however, Dizengoff added that "obviously, this representation is but a spontaneous reaction, reflecting a public opinion which will not accept the fate of the Jews in Germany. Actually, it is quite amazing that the protest was not stronger."[53]

---

[52] About the immediate association of Haman with Hitler and *Amalek* with Nazi Germany, in different circles, see, for example: Perski 1944: 159–161; Goodman 1949: 243; Lewinsky 1955: 309, 320; Piekarz 1990: 276–278; Horowitz 1994: 11–12; Horowitz 2006: 85–86, 90–93.

[53] "Yom Ha'Adloyada be-Tel-Aviv" [The Day of the *Adloyada* in Tel Aviv], *Doar-Hayom* 14.3.1933; "Masa Ha'Adloyada" [The *Adloyada* procession]," *Ha'aretz* 14.3.1933; from the German consul to Dizengoff, 22.3.1932; from Dizengoff to the German consul, 29.3.1933, TAMA, file 04–3220a; expense report for Purim 1933 (mentioning giving a prize to this performance), TAMA 04–3220b; judgment committee report, *Doar-Hayom* 16.3.1933; "Likrat Purim" [Towards Purim], *Doar-Hayom* 21.2.1933.

The float, with its caption "Death to all Jews," as well as Dizengoff's proud response and his refusal to apologize for demeaning the new German leadership, and most importantly the performative act of putting Hitler on horseback instead of Mordechai, all expressed a new direction regarding the presence of evil in the street performance. This old-new evil belonged to another category, against which the usual measures of rational management would not suffice. It was now necessary to use expedience and language of a different sort.

This tendency was augmented in the following year, when a bigger number of floats dealt with the Nazi regime. The topic of the main float, sponsored by the organizing committee, was "Israel's tribes." The Jews of Germany were represented as tyrannized by Hitler, who rode a dragon with three monster heads, beating and injuring Jews. Obviously, the horse of the previous year now seemed a bit too earthly. However, this year, the drama it did not stop there. In the closing ceremony of the festival, that evening, a staged "trial of the books and their burners" took place in the city square. This street-play on "The trial of antisemitism," as it was referred to by reporters, was written by Bialik and Shlonsky, directed by Moshe Halevi, and erformed by real actors (not all of them professional, though), instead of mere extras as in previous performances. The characters were Jewish writers whose books were publicly burned in Nazi Germany, such as Karl Marx, Henry Wassermann and others. When Wassermann, said, "I loved the spirit of Germany," for example, the audience responded with booing; but when Marx said that there are no nations but only oppressors and oppressed, the audience applauded (at least according to the Labor Movement newspaper *Davar*). The accused was that very dragon on which Hitler had ridden earlier that day. After a legal discussion it was found guilty, and after a torch dance and another torch procession, it was burned in Dizengoff square, and the crowd "was swept into the dancing circle around the bonfire." The *Palestine Post* summed up the day in one sentence: "it was a bad day for Hitler."[54]

---

[54] *Davar* 2.3.1934; "Masa Ha'Adloyada in Tel-Aviv" [The Adloyada procession in Tel Aviv], *Doar-Hayom* 2.3.1934; Yuris, supra note 40; "Carnival depicts Jews' past and present," *Palestine Post* 2.3.1934, 1; Ze'evi 1988: 507; *Krovetz for Purim 1935*, 8; "Ha'Adloyada" [The Adloyada], *D'var Ha'shavu'a*, 2.3.1950. On the performance see: Carmiel 1999: 248.

The reactions to this staged trial were much milder than one would have expected before 1933. Obviously, there were those who were astonished by the sudden appearance of "such a barbarian method for the struggle of an enlightened nation, particularly in the first Hebrew city." Those protesters thought that this was a non-Jewish approach, and warned that the use of such murky practices lowered the Jews to the moral level of their barbarian enemies.[55] Nonetheless, the very cultural entrepreneurs and critics who disdained Shlonsky's suggestion in 1928 arrived at the same conclusion six years later: evil must be put on trial, sentenced, and executed in the city square.

In the 1935 procession, Haman had already fully acquired back his traditional role. In one float, Haman paraded with his ten sons, all hanged on the gallows as in the biblical story, and for the first time Haman was publicly hanged in Tel Aviv's streets, in the best of ethnocentric tradition (and again, this float attracted harsh criticism for its "ugliness"). Hitler, his modern descendant, received his due as well, of course, and was again represented as threatening a Jew with a gun and a knife. The crowd responded to this float by intensifying the firing of their toy guns. The "committee for the boycott of German products" contributed its own float to the procession, in which the swastika was displayed wrapped by a snake.[56] The new atmosphere of uncompromising symbolic war against evil penetrated other cultural loci as well. During the liturgical reciting of the Book of Esther in Tel Aviv Central Synagogue, transmitted by loudspeaker to Allenby Street, the name of Haman was greeted with extreme noise in keeping with the traditional custom, using toy-guns and caps, with the crowd loudly shouting "Boo Haman! Boo Hitler!"[57]

Besides performative rituals, the association of Haman with Hitler was also conveyed in rhetoric. Newspapers published songs

---

[55] From Gershon Peshkov, Netanya, to Mayor Dizengoff, 27.2.1934, TAMA, file 04–3220b.

[56] "Simkhat Purim be-Tel-Aviv" [Purim joy in Tel Aviv], *Doar-Hayom* 19.3.1935; MT, "Inyanim: Ketzat sikumim le-Purim tartzah" [Affairs: Some summaries for Purim 1935], *Ha'aretz* 22.3.1935, 4; "Yom Ha'Adloyada be-Tel-Aviv" [The Adloyada day in Tel Aviv], *Ha'aretz* 21.3.1935; "Masa Ha'Adloyada be-Tel-Aviv" [The Adloyada procession in Tel Aviv], *Doar-Hayom* 21.3.1935.

[57] "Petikhat Hakhag" [The festival's opening], *Ha'aretz* 1.3.1934; "Purim tartzad be-Tel-Aviv" [Purim 1934 in Tel Aviv], *Doar-Hayom, Ha'aretz,* 1.3.1934.

with calls for revenge on Haman and his modern descendants.[58] In the opening speech of the celebrations, Dizengoff declared, in the English version of the speech: "We will celebrate our victory upon Haman's heirs through the ages."[59] The special municipal carnival bulletin, *Krovetz*, published a photo of an antisemitic float from the carnival of Köln, Germany, with the caption: "'Purim, of the heirs of Haman in Germany." This oppositional association between the two carnivals further sharpened the new symbolic interpretation of the symbiotic relationship between the two nations.

This association of evil with Haman was elaborated to more general contexts than the specific struggle against Nazism. A column that attacked the routine inflation of pricing during Purim concluded with the words: "Do we really want to place a sword in the hands of Agagite Haman?"[60] In other words, Haman was ubiquitously used as a specific reference to Hitler and Nazism, and a general reference to the Jews' enemies.

After 1933, it would never have occurred to anyone that "we are doing a significant injustice to Haman," as Ben-Yishai wrote in 1928.[61] No humbling or demeaning attitude would be considered unfair to such a wicked evil. Hitler's rise to power, alongside the raw violence toward Jews in Germany, put the talk about sovereignty in Tel Aviv in proportion. Beyond the painful reminder of the lack of Jewish control over the pace of their immigration to Palestine, it became evident that there was a type of evil which could not be dealt with by rational management. The result was a return to the old cultural patterns of dealing with evil through symbolic violence.

An interesting development was the expansion of the use of these patterns to struggle with a totally different evil—the "profiteers," as contemporaries used to call honest people who traded in land, because their dealings were at odds with the nationalist ideology, which considered the land to be national property. The idea of

---

[58] S. Frug, "Zemer le-Purim" [A Purim song], *Ha'aretz* 28.2.1934.

[59] Dizengoff's speech (English), TAMA, file 04–3222. The Hebrew version was quite similar (*Krovetz for Purim 1935*, I). Both versions were consecutively read in the opening ceremony.

[60] "Safsarim ve-rama'im be-masekhot" [Profiteers and cheaters in masquerades], *Doar-Hayom* 24.3.1935.

[61] Ben-Yishai, supra note 34.

a staged trial, which worked so well in 1934, recurred in 1935, when the carnival committee presented a satirical performance about "profiteering," embodied in a large monstrous crocodile which paraded in the procession and was captioned "slavery in freedom" (alluding to the notable essay by Ahad-Ha'am in which he criticized materialist western Jewry).[62] In preliminary discussions within the organizing committee, some members opposed the public execution of the crocodile, whereas others suggested burning Haman himself in the ceremony. Eventually the committee decided to drown the monster in the sea, with fireworks.[63] As always, putting profiteering on trial included a debasement of city life and a glorification of country life. The prosecutor and the choir demanded the expulsion of the crocodile in order to "purify our camp from this defilement." After hearing the testimonies of prominent Zionist leaders as well as a "simple farmer" and a representative of the JNF, the court came to the conclusion that the crocodile was a water animal and did not belong on land, and hence it was condemned to drowning.

The crocodile as a symbol of profiteering was much more ambivalent than the antisemitism dragon of the previous year. Land free-trading was troublesome to official Zionist ideology, which considered land to be a national property. That said, the "profiteering" was actually a crucial part of the construction industry, which was central to Tel Aviv's commerce and the *Yishuv* economy.[64] *Ha'aretz* reported that when the crocodile made the turn to Herzl Street during the procession, it veered a bit near its cafés, known as the venue for real-estate businesses, and caused the crowd to laugh. Whether the crowd really laughed or not, it is safe to say that the crowd knew to decode this symbol in its immediate sense and to connect it to a specific place, which was surely not abominable in their everyday life. As if to intentionally deepen this ambivalence, the full text of the street play "A Trial for the Crocodile" appeared in the municipal bulletin next to a huge commercial advertisement for "land for agriculture and construction"

---

[62] Thanks to Paula Hyman for this comment.
[63] The protocols of the committee meeting, 11.2.1935; 5.2.1935 — both in TAMA file 04-3221c.
[64] See: Metzer 1998: 219–220.

in Tel Aviv and the surrounding area, promising convenient prices, credit, and warranties.[65]

According to anthropologist Mary Douglas, a society makes use of concepts of *Purity and Danger* to interpret middle-areas of regular thought patterns, in which the borders between "in" and "out" are diffused.[66] In our case, the official ideology, disseminated mainly by the JNF, opposed private entrepreneurship in land-purchase, among other reasons, because it raised the prices of urban lands and was detrimental to the JNF's activity of land-purchase in cities—which was not coherent with its anti-urban propaganda.[67] The relationship between the city and the country struck a sensitive chord in the Zionist project, which on the one hand was deeply influenced by romanticist views that called for a "return to the soil," but on the other hand was in fact a project of far-reaching industrialization and widespread urbanization, relying mainly on private money, and creating a capitalist economy. As a cultural performance, "the profiteering crocodile" was an attempt to sharpen the signification of the community's borders and purify it from negative elements, while clearly exemplifying the ambivalence of the grey areas and articulating the very sensitivity of this nerve.

The "profiteering trial" could not have taken place in the conceptual frame of the pre-1933 period. Many floats preached in favor of agricultural village life over urban city life, but there were no linguistic and theatrical means by which to perform such a purification ceremony. The year 1933, first, enabled the onstage appearance of the ultimate evil as a prominent antagonist-protagonist in the drama of Jewish history, which brought back to consciousness the concepts of meta-historical good and evil, assuming that different forms of evil are different appearances of the same essence. Second, 1933 incorporated into the new Hebrew culture the social drama, which necessitates the figure of the scoundrel as a (negative) cultural hero. In the case of 1935, the prosecutor in the staged trial provided a genealogical hint: "For two years this crocodile has been threatening the country." In other words, the rise of Hitler in 1933 brought to Palestine "alien"

---

[65] *Krovetz for Purim 1935*, VII–XI.
[66] Douglas 1966; Douglas 1975: 47–59.
[67] Lavsky 1994.

elements, German-Jews with their private capital and lack of nationalist discipline. The fault of the profiteering was thus also to be placed with Hitler.

Two Cultural Performances, Two Myths

The reputation of the Tel Aviv municipality as a sovereign body, in charge of "the first Hebrew city," even if quite exaggerated in political and economic reality, was linked to the municipality's attempts to dull the historical hostility between the Jewish and Christian worlds by "civilizing" Jewish tradition via its selective interpretation in "rationalist" terms. Establishing a rationally-managed public sphere should have brought prosperity to the entire terrain and hence was an important ideological component in the Jewish demand to rule the country. However, the rise of a world leader who insisted on the unique role of the Jewish people in the drama of universal history transformed the Zionist patterns of thought by the painful smashing of the illusion of self-sovereignty. The events of 1933 made room for the ethnocentric approach, which suggested a different way to deal with world evil: public rituals of explicit symbolic violence as a means to achieve social cohesiveness, rather than rituals of rational politics and stable hierarchy. "Barbarian" rituals were now given a renewed place, alongside (but not instead of) rituals of rationality. The myth that every problem may be resolved by meticulous planning was supplanted by another myth.

Nevertheless, after World War II, things gradually returned to "normal," and in the *Adloyada* procession of 1955, Mordechai was again led on horseback by Haman. Quite clearly, as is the case with many other nationalist movements, the two approaches were, and still are, active in the construction of the Zionist civil sphere and identity as two juxtaposed myths: a myth of fraternity of nations and perfect rationality alongside a myth of an eternal struggle against meta-historical evil.

Chapter 6

"Our Only Romantic Festival":
Hebrew Queen Esther

The previous chapter dealt with the political performances of Mordechai, Haman, and the horse. The topic of this chapter is no less political, as it will analyze the performances of Esther, the main female protagonist of both the biblical story and the Tel Aviv carnival. The passing episode of Hebrew Queen Esther left a deep mark on Zionist and Jewish collective memory, as a unique combination of Jewish folklore, the European-Mediterranean carnivalesque tradition, and capitalist mass entertainment.[1] But as often happens with intersections of nationalism and gender, here the political and the personal were intermingled.[2]

Carnivalesque subversive traditions, including The East European tradition of *Purimspiel*, highlighted the war of the sexes as a guiding theme through the enactment of feminine roles by men's bodies masqueraded as women's, and displayed as ugly. This mocked not only the feminine inclination to decoration, but even sexual desire altogether. Until the industrial age, the more common Western carnivalesque ruler was usually a King, rather than a Queen. In some cases, there were separate parties for women who elected their own Queens (somewhat like the biblical Vashti). In Jewish folkloric traditions, especially in Eastern Europe, the "Purim Rabbi" or *Purimspielers* were always men as well—mostly yeshiva students.[3]

In bourgeois Tel Aviv, this kind of misogynistic tradition was barely present, and was replaced by the middle-class elevation of feminine beauty and heterosexual attraction. Unlike symbolic violence,

---

[1] Carmiel 1999: 9.

[2] On the different intersections of gender and nationalism see: Yuval-Davis 1993; Yuval-Davis 1997.

[3] Davis 1987: 105; Belkin 2001.

the carnivalesque motif of grotesque sexuality was totally rejected by the bourgeois ethos of respectability, as elucidated by Mosse.[4]

Nevertheless, in Mandatory Tel Aviv, the concept of respectability itself was contested with regard to public appearance of flesh-and-blood women. The public imagery of the industrial era entailed the relative disappearance of the masculine body from the public eye as an object of knowledge or desire. Meanwhile, with the waning of women's political activity in the public spheres of the rising middle class, their visual presence was increasing, "as though the real absence of women as actors in the bourgeois civil sphere was filled by compensatory fantasies—or constellations of fantasies—about femininity."[5]

The Zionist movement and bourgeois family values are no longer considered contradictory in scholarship. As recently discussed by Razi and others, the family was considered a significant socializing agent for nation-building. In fact, it was recently revealed, even the majority of anti-bourgeois pioneers got married and created monogamist families, in what historian Lilach Rosenberg-Freidman designates "conservative revolution."[6] Moreover, Zionism assumed masculine qualities of active political and cultural subjects, and women activists were less prominent in Jewish Nationalism, in Palestine and abroad, than in other modern Jewish political and social movements.[7] Despite the importance of the equalitarian ethos in pioneers' circles, women were underrepresented in politics, journalism, and many other realms of public life, whereas raising children was considered their main national role. At this point Zionist discourse corresponded with the bourgeois myths of the "house priestess."[8]

The Hebrew Queen Esther pageants were an overloaded intersection of gender, ethnicity, "family values," and nationalism, as

---

[4] Mosse 1985.

[5] Solomon-Godeau 1996: 117. For more about Woman-as-commodity see: Kuchta 1996; Roberts 1998; Tiersten 2001.

[6] Ze'ira 2002: 154–166, 265–272; Razi 2009; Razi 2010; Rosenberg-Freidman 2012a (quote from p. 121); Rosenberg-Freidman 2012b.

[7] Hyman 1995: 79–81.

[8] Bernstein 1992; Shilo 1996; Biale 1997: 176–203; Bernstein 1998a; Herzog 2002; Stoler-Liss 2003.

already shown by a number of scholars.[9] This chapter strives to demonstrate that the Zionist case was singled out from other bourgeois nationalisms not by the equalitarian pioneers' ethos, but by the biblical intertextuality. In particular, the biblical allusions frequently used in the public discourse about Hebrew Queen Esther were often understood as referring to an ancient Oriental past of the Jewish people, and hence reveal a complicated relationship between nationalism, Orientalism, and gender, and more particularly between nationalist, familial, and religious components of Jewish ethnic nationalism. Moreover, the biblical intertextuality was definitive for the local identity of the pageants in the face of the globalized beauty pageants.

Male Dominance? Masculine and Feminine Beauty

In 1926, Baruch Agadati announced a contest for

> Purim ball's Queen Esther—the prettiest and most typical Jewess in Tel Aviv, who that will qualify as biblical Esther. This Esther will be the Queen of the Purim ball and the Queen of the procession to be held in Tel Aviv's streets on the Purim festival.[10]

Usually, the Queen was elected in a special gala, held a month before Purim, by ticket-purchasers. At the carnival, the Queen-elect had several performative roles, the most important of which was the leading of the carnival street procession in an open car, accompanied by Agadati himself. The prize was not a sum of money, but a huge vase or another item of Oriental houseware.[11]

The pageants took place for four years, through 1929, and they were a huge success on both the local and the Jewish-international scale. Two or three years after the initiation of the pageant at Agadati's ball, almost every Purim ball across Palestine elected "the Ball's Girl," "Queen Esther" or an explicit "beauty Queen." Queens were elected by Jewish ethnic groups, regions, or youth clubs, and several of the

---

[9] Carmiel 1999: 116–155; Spiegel 2001: chapter 1 (thanks to Dr. Spiegel for sharing her work with me); Stern 2006.

[10] "Yafo ve-Tel-Aviv" [Jaffa and Tel Aviv], *Ha'aretz* 22.1.1926.

[11] Carmiel 1999: 116–156.

Chapter 6. "Our Only Romantic Festival": Hebrew Queen Esther

winners represented their group in larger balls or in the main carnival procession in Tel Aviv.[12] The custom was quickly popularized abroad as well, and many Jewish clubs elected their own Queen Esthers, inspired by Tel Aviv. Queen Esther pageants were so identified with Purim balls that in many places in the Jewish world Purim balls were called "Queen Esther Balls." In fact, this was the first cultural practice created in Tel Aviv that was disseminated throughout the Jewish world, positioning the young town as a prominent Jewish cultural center on a global scale.[13]

In 1930, as an outcome of a weighty political-cultural dispute, Agadati cancelled the pageant, and by 1933 it more or less disappeared from all Purim balls in Palestine (though the pageants continued to be held abroad). During this short lifetime, the pageants attracted great public attention from both supporters and opponents, and were the main grounds on which Agadati was defined as the "king" of Tel Aviv's entertainment culture.

The immediate inspiration were the beauty pageants of Atlantic City, which were initiated in 1921 as the "Miss America" contest and immediately gained currency all over the world—including the "first" and the "third" worlds.[14] As an icon, the Beauty Queen was active in the public culture of British Palestine, particularly in the context of Purim balls. A Purim ball in Tel Aviv featured Kriman Kallem from

---

[12] Such as: Tel Aviv's Yemenite Queen ("Hamalka hateimanit" [The Yemenite Queen], *Doar-Hayom* 21.3.1929); Queen Esther of Petah-Tiqwa ("Em hamoshavot holekhet be-iqvot Tel-Aviv" [The first colony follows Tel Aviv], *Doar-Hayom* 26.2.1928), of Safed ("Tzefat," *Ha'aretz* 2.4.1929), or of "Maccabi" (*Doar-Hayom* 11.3.1928). A promise was made that "all Purim queens that were elected this year all over the country" would attend a Jerusalemite Purim ball ("costumes ball," the posters collection, national library of Jerusalem, file V1969/3, and *Doar-Hayom* 29.3.1929).

[13] "Ester hamalka ha-ostralit" [Australian Queen Esther—in Melbourne], *Ha'aretz* 5.3.1931; "Kabalat panim le-ester hamalka mi-New York" [A reception to New Yorker queen Esther], The posters collection, national library of Jerusalem, file V1969/3; two Yiddish invitations to Purim ball in Madison Square Garden, New York, 1930, and Chicago, 1934 (photos collections, Beit Ariela, Tel Aviv, file 1460). For a detailed study of the significance of Queen Esther pageants for Jewish communities in Argentina up to the 1960s see: Brodsky 2004: chapter 3 (thanks to Dr. Brodsky for sharing her work with me).

[14] Bivans 1991: 8–12.

Turkey as the 1932 World Beauty Queen.[15] The Jewess Elisheva Simon, the 1929 "Miss Europe," attended the "Ophir" theatre Purim ball, and distributed the local pageant's prizes.[16] The presence of the Beauty Queen in public discourse was even more prominent in commercial language. The icon of the Beauty Queen was in frequent use to sell cigarettes, sewing machines, and other products.[17] In Jerusalem, "a Yemenite Queen" was driven in an open car to publicize the cosmopolite Purim balls of the "Bristol" café.[18]

Key cultural agents in the field, Agadati among them, refrained from declaring the pageant's winner the "Beauty Queen," and talked only about "Queen Esther." Nonetheless, the title "Beauty Queen" was habitually used in commercials and by the broader public, and the term was used commonly by its opponents, or when the speaker was "provincial" enough to make this "incorrect" use.[19] However, sometimes even the cultural elite slipped, such as when Mayor Dizengoff spoke during the festive "royal" reception in his office:

> Today you are the Queen of Tel Aviv, governing from the Yarkon to Jaffa's border. All this mass bows to your beauty and blesses you not only as Tel Aviv's Queen but also as the Queen of all Palestine. In European style—you are "Miss Palestine."[20]

"Miss Palestine" was the correct title only in "European style," while "for us" the correct title was "the Queen of Palestine." But the essential quality of the Queen, to be sure, was her beauty. Another feuilleton revealed to readers that the Mayor was to kiss the Queen on her cheek during this ceremony, and speculated about "how many residents

---

[15] "Tel-Aviv: Likrat Purim" [Tel Aviv: Towards Purim], *Ha'aretz* 9.3.1933.

[16] Advertisement to "Ophir" ball, *Doar-Hayom* 22.3.1929.

[17] Advertisement for cigarettes, *Doar-Hayom* 2.3.1931; Carmiel 1999, 148.

[18] "Hayom ha-rishon le-Purim" [The first day of Purim], *Doar-Hayom* 3.3.1931.

[19] Such as: "Yelidat yerushalayim: Malkat hayofi shel Tel-Aviv" [A Jerusalemite native: Tel Aviv's beauty Queen], *Doar-Hayom* 28.1.1929; "Bekhirat malkat hayofi" [Election of the beauty Queen], oriental pioneers organization in Jerusalem, 2.3.1929, and the posters collection, National Library of Jerusalem, file V1969/3; Carmiel 1999: 139.

[20] "Kabalat peney hamalka" [The reception to the Queen], *Doar-Hayom* 26.2.1929.

would like to have the Mayor's job at this moment?"[21] Funny or not, this joke was definitely an authentic expression of many men's fantasies. In other words, the pageant was based on the dominance of the male gaze.

These sexual fantasies had a wider context. The Purim balls, for example, were first and foremost a site for men and women to see and be seen—a one-time opportunity to wear fancy evening outfits, with only light "Purim holiday" decoration added, if any. Much effort and money were invested in costumes that would appear both original and attractive. Some balls were explicitly defined as "ball of fancy costume (no masks)."[22] Consistently with his carnivalesque cultural agenda, Agadati announced that no one would be allowed in to his balls without a face-mask, yet "many guests took off the masks right after entering the hall," and eventually, according to the reporter, "there were many fancy outfits, but only a few costumes with interest and content"—that is, "educational" costumes.[23] Another ball used rhyming phrases to promise that "your eyes will see things/ nice, pretty and fancy/ couples in the crowd/ guys and maidens will dance/ with or without costumes/ with buttoned outfits."[24] In due course, even Agadati renounced his agenda, and announced that "costumes *or* evening outfit is obligatory."[25]

Indeed, in photos from Purim balls, men were usually photographed wearing evening suits, and only occasionally did they sport a carnivalesque decoration such as a Tarbush, eye-mask, cloak, or Bukharian skullcap.[26] Uri Keisari described his preparations for the ball: "In my room, the abhorred smoking [sic; suit] is already winking, and the ironed cotton vest is already shining in its deceiving glow."[27]

---

[21] "Mezeg tov: Filitonim kalim" [A good character: Light feuilletons], *Ha'aretz* 6.3.1928.

[22] Advertisement, "Menorah" club ball, *Doar-Hayom* 6.3.1925.

[23] "Purim be-Tel-Aviv" [Purim in Tel Aviv], *Ha'aretz* 1.3.1926.

[24] Y.L. Mahalal'el, "Shir Mizmor le-neshef hamasekhot be-Purim tarpah" [A psalm to costumes ball of Purim 1925], an advertisement to "Eden" balls, *Ha'aretz* 10.3.1925.

[25] The posters collection, national library of Jerusalem, file V1969/4. Emphasis added.

[26] See for example: Carmiel 1999: 14, 19, 23–24, 123, 125, 126 and more.

[27] Uri Keisari, "Im ha-zerem …: Be-shulei megilat ester" (With the stream …: In the margins of the book of Esther), *Doar-Hayom* 8.3.1928.

Eventually, the balls visitors noticed "all around—frocks, smoking jackets, fancy outfits."[28]

Women tended to wear costumes more than men, especially during the years of the Hebrew Queen Esther pageants. However, as demonstrated by curator Batya Carmiel, many feminine costumes, Zionist-ideological costumes included, were based on Parisian evening dresses. Those were highly familiar to women in interwar Tel Aviv. Popular outfits included sailor costumes based on Coco Chanel's feminine sailor suit and Oriental-exotic costumes, which were popular in 1920s Europe.[29] Interwar Parisian feminine evening fashion was over-decorative, and these dresses were adorned with sequins, pearls, feathers, fabric flowers, lace decorations, and other such flourishes. Many women who could not afford evening wear bought or sewed for the ball a home-designed costume to resemble such an outfit. Indeed, many costumes were rented or inexpensively purchased from established theatres, which used the Purim season to clear out their storage wardrobes.[30] The decorative style of feminine evening wear in the interwar West somewhat blurred the distinction between evening clothes and costume.

Despite the difference in the functions of men's and women's evening wear, the transformation of every individual participant into a visual exhibit was evident for both genders—typical in interwar capitalist leisure cultures. This was quite natural for a festive event for young people pursuing sexual-romantic interests, as expressed in the following description of preparations for Purim balls:

> Against the mirrors/ girls stand/ the mirror is silent like an objective sphinx/ what is wrong/ with me, mirror/ tell me, don't hurt/ will I win/ the [male] neighbor's favor?[31]

---

[28] S. Samet, "Eikh "paramti" et haneshef herishon" (How I "purimized" the first ball), *Ha'aretz* 13.3.1933. About western men's evening cloth see: Marly 1985: 116–122; Byrde 1979: 84–85.

[29] Carmiel 1999: 27–36. Compare to contemporary typical Parisian evening clothes: Boucher 1987: 411–415. On the massive presence of Parisian fashion in Tel Aviv see: Raz 1996: 65–76.

[30] See: "Mezeg tov: Filitonim kalim" [A good character: Light feuilletons], *Ha'aretz* 6.3.1928.

[31] Agav, "Regaim: Al saf ha-Purim" [Moments: On the verge of Purim], *Ha'aretz* 15.3.1935. This was the pen-name of the poet Nathan Alterman.

Written by a man, this text reflects fantasy no less than reality. We can assume that, similarly, young men were also concerned about their appearance and their potential attractiveness to women. However, this likely symmetry was unexpressed in public discourse. Many ball advertisements depicted female bodies as part of their attractions, such as the rhymed advertisement for the *"hamataté"* theatre balls:

> From the palace of Ahasuerus/ we came here with headaches/ to demand gals/ the palace is in horrible condition/ there is no gal/ with good figure.

Since, unfortunately, the biblical "gals" — Vashti and Esther, and all the other maidens of Shushan — were too archaic, a different reference was needed for this masculine "we":

> Give! Let us have!/ A golden gal .../ something modern, impertinent!/ A girl that is engraved on the heart/ embellished, jazz-banded, fox-trotted/ that's exciting/ that's easy and pleasant/ that is findable in Tel Aviv!/ And that's why we're here/ looking in every jug/ unbelievable/ what a beauty, what a charm/ nothing like these in Shushan/ let us have them!/ Such as this one there in the side/ somewhat cross-eyed/ that's a nice thing/ or the swarthy/ what a gal!/ Or the blonde/ what a love!...[32]

The balls were often described as places where men may gaze their fill at pretty women. To guarantee that, some balls used the familiar technique of selling less expensive tickets to young women.[33] The display of female beauty was so important (for men) that some complained that it was marred by the costumes.[34]

---

[32] Anonymous, "Zeh efshar limtzo be-Tel-Aviv" [Findable in Tel Aviv], *Kalno'a* year 3, volume 4, 25.2.1934. From the archive of the Israeli center for the documentation of stage arts, file 62.3.7.

[33] "To a single male — 150 mil [1/1000 Palestine pound], to a single female — 100 mil" (A ball of the Haifa Hebrew Youth Organization, 1928, posters collection, national library of Jerusalem, file V1969/3).

[34] A report on "Betzalel" ball in Jerusalem ("Yerushalayim" [Jerusalem], *Ha'aretz* 12.3.1925).

Needless to say, the sexual tension at the balls remained mostly on the level of banal flirtations. Nevertheless, in addition to looking-without-touching, some describe real love-adventures of couples who first met at ball and left together. Some aimlessly called the mass balls "lust balls," or described the abandonment of the commandment "thou shall not covet."[35] Uri Keisari brought the story of Yosef Anski, a young man who was hanging out in the *"hamataté"* ball with a "terrific and friendly blonde, who wore minimal attire." After "they understood each other and went to the street" on their way to his place, it turned out that the blonde's purse has been stolen from her.[36] In the moralistic Tel Avivian tabloid *Iton Meyuhad*, the mass balls were depicted as places in which married men and women could search for prey and have adulterous adventures.[37]

Predictably, the masculine point of view produced misogynic jokes about the women's foppishness, squandering, and lust (while at the same time demanding that women dress up lavishly for these events).[38] One man spoke of giving all his clothes to his wife and her neighbors to use for the balls. Eventually, he was left without his pants and decided to wear only a sheet, so as to masquerade in the ball as Mahatma Gandhi.[39]

Almost all of the writers in the general Hebrew press (apart from women's newspapers) were men, and their point of view about the display of the female body was discursively dominant. They recognized that, in a parallel manner, women were likely to attend balls where handsome men were present, and hence, the writer Daniel Perski recommended that his male readers attend the "menorah" ball, organized by the discharged soldiers' club.[40] Moreover, in a few balls—not the central ones—the point of view was sometimes reversed and

---

[35] Halperin 1997: 266–270.

[36] Uri Keisari, "Keitzad hayim etzlenu: Mikrim bekhol yom vayom" [How do we live: Everyday occurrences], *Doar-Hayom* 27.3.1935.

[37] "A husband and wife cheat together on each other: A Purim adventure, whose happy end is grey and boring like life itself," *Iton Meyuhad* 27.3.1938.

[38] Compare: Hollander 1994.

[39] Baruch Li. [Liebarman], "Hamas sheli lenishfey Purim (viduy shel ba'al mishpaha)" [My tax to Purim balls (A true story of a family guy)], *Doar-Hayom* 22.3.1932.

[40] Daniel Perski, *Ha'aretz* 18.3.1932.

instead of a Queen, the ladies elected "Mr. Congeniality," or "the ball's sailor."[41] No doubt, men knew that they too were objectified by the female gaze and desire, and they dressed and behaved accordingly.

However, decoration was so identified with femininity in public culture that the city's preparations for the carnival were described like the preparations of a woman for a ball:

> Tel Aviv adorns herself
> her leaps in color.
> Her eyes in blue eye shadow.[42]

The banal metaphor of the city-as-woman was indeed highly developed in Mandate-era Tel Aviv. Although the heterosexual attraction was mutual, it turned out that only the female body was objectified, commercialized, and allegorized, while the male body tended to disappear from public discourse. The mutual sexual attraction was therefore politicized and masculinized. The concept of beauty was similarly politicized—and feminized. Let us examine popular understandings of feminine beauty, as were evident in the Queen Esther pageants.

Political Beauty

Until the 1990s, most Western beauty pageants presumed to offer objective, unified, and "natural" criteria for the concept of beauty, attempting to conceal its infinite diversity, suggestive nature, and socio-cultural, economic, and individual contexts.[43] Conversely, in our case, there was no attempt to depict beauty as a-political or "pure." Recall that in the first announcement quoted above, the criterion, besides beauty, was that the winner be "the typical Hebrew woman."[44] Interestingly, this was not an attempt to create definitive aesthetic criteria for Jewish/Hebrew beauty. In fact, the four elected queens

---

[41] Such as: the ball of "Palatin" hotel ("Tel-Aviv," *Doar-Hayom* 19.2.1931); *Doar-Hayom* 18.3.1932. See also: Abraham Shvadron, "Ke-ein krovetz la-carnival" [Alleged ode to the carnival], *Ha'aretz* 11.3.1931.

[42] Alterman, supra note 31.

[43] Ballerino-Cohen et al. 1996: 7.

[44] Supra note 10.

represented surprisingly diversified beauty types: a pale Russian in 1926, a Jerusalemite Sephardi, white-skinned with black hair and eyes, in 1927, a dark Yemenite in 1928, and an Aryan blonde in 1929. Of course, they all shared several conventionally defined features of beauty in that era, such as prominent cheekbones.[45] The "Jewish beauty" types thus represented the ethnic diversity of Jewish communities in Palestine, with no presumption of standardization and unification. In keeping with typical local pageants, Queen Esther should have represented the entire community with its diversities.[46] Hence, the contests were considered much more than entertainment. In such cases, it was not rare to find serious protests about biased procedures that affected the democratic nature of the elections.[47]

The pageants thus functioned as a factor of "glocalization." On one hand, the eminent western format, itself representing and realizing this globalization, "often functions as a badge of civilized, modern status."[48] On the other hand, it constructed particularistic identity against processes of globalization, and the unification of aesthetic standards.

Historically, it should be mentioned that beauty pageants themselves were developed from the carnivalesque custom of electing a "Queen" for grandiose events like balls, tournaments, and carnivals—such as the election of the "May Day Queen." In the spirit of carnivalesque tradition, Tel Aviv's Queen led the street procession in an open car or truckbed, cheered by the masses, who instead of applauding important guests such as Haim Weizmann or Winston Churchill applauded a young woman. In the "royal reception," the Queen appeared in the Mayor's office accompanied by her tough bodyguards, and received the city's "keys" for the festival days. This may be understood as a reversal only since the dichotomy of male/female was identified with the dichotomy of power/beauty, and due to the common discourse about a pretty woman being too immature

---

[45] See photos of four queens, seconds, and other candidates: Carmiel 1999: 117–132. For elaborate discussion see: Spiegel 2001: chapter 1.

[46] See: Lavenda 1988; Ballerino-Cohen et al. 1996: 3; Wu 1997; Pomfret 2004.

[47] "Misaviv limlakhot ha-Purim" [Around Purim queens], *Doar-Hayom* 6.3.1929.

[48] Borland 1996: 75.

to take the reins and her relative absence from the political arena.[49] Accordingly, Hebrew Queen Esther never really got a chance to be a "one-day Queen," and insult the community elders, leaders, and rabbis, as was customary with the Eastern European "Purim Rabbi." Generally, the Queen performed in complete silence and minimal physical movement on the "stage" of the balls and the street carnival. In none of her multiple performances during the carnival was the Queen requested to speak; she was expected only to display herself. In one known Purim song, the Queen allegedly sang:

> What can I do/ what can I do/ that I am so pretty/ that I am proficient/ at being exhibited?…[50]

Dubbed by males, this was all the Queen could ritually say.

As such, her leading the procession was an imagined cultural performance with the exact opposite effect of an upside-down carnivalesque space: a well-organized and culturally controlled space. If there was here any reversal-ritual, it was the inversion of the power structure of hierarchic representational relations. In modern political democratic nationalism, the representative usually masters the represented.[51] In this case, as a feminine symbol, commoditized and allegorized under the male gaze, the representative—the female body—was inferior to the represented—the community.

Orientalism/Ornamentalism: Gendered Ethnicity

The Queen thus represented the community as its "typical beauty." However, despite the clear capitalist–North-American origins of the pageants, and the evident lack of traditional customs in them, this beauty was historically grounded in Jewish traditions. Somewhat surprisingly, these traditions were not related to the feminine image of the new "halutza" [female pioneer] that emerged in Palestine and

---

[49] Banner 1983: 250–254; Ballerino-Cohen et al. 1996: 3; Carmiel 1999: 152–153.
[50] "Shirim le-Purim tartzag" [Songs for Purim 1933], in Alterman 1979: 216.
[51] Smith-Rosenberg 2000: 271–272; Habermas 1989: 18.

captured the Jewish imagination overseas.[52] Rather, in the spirit of the folkloristic tradition, they were those of the Orient and the feminized Oriental Jewry, which were long ago objectified and reified by Jewish-European artists, writers, and community leaders. Zionist Orientalism aimed at positioning the East as the "origin" of the true Hebrew culture, which was not degenerated in exile, and hence should be integrated into the new culture.[53]

Among Oriental Jewish communities, the Yemenites captured the *Yishuv*'s imagination as the most ancient Jewish branch, which retained the independent spirit of biblical times. Because they were the proletariat of Tel Aviv (and of the entire Jewish sector in Palestine), the Yemenites were considered to be "natural workers," "happy with their share."[54]

This Orientalism was evident at the street carnival, for which the Yemenite youth club prepared grandiose Orientalist floats and usually won prizes. Even the many critics of the carnival thought that these floats were the only ones that expressed a "real folk joy," based on the Yemenites' "primitive talents that are distinguished in simplicity and innocence."[55] Consider the following assessment:

> [The Yemenites' float] was marked by fresh folklore. In this regard we have a lot to learn from our Yemenite brethren. Creating new forms of folk culture is impossible without natural roots of tradition, of folkism that imbibes from many generations.[56]

Due to their alleged cultural stagnation, the Yemenite culture was considered a necessary component for a new authentic culture it was: stable and consistent, similar to the conceptualization of the Orient in European Orientalism as a cultural origin, while eliminating the actual Orient.[57]

---

[52] On Queen Esther as "Halutza" in Argentina, for example, see Brodsky 2012.
[53] Hirschfeld 2002: 1011–1024; Saposnik 2006.
[54] Druyan 1982: 134–138, 157–158; Manor 2004; Ofrat 2005: 20–26.
[55] Ramon 1935: 10–11.
[56] M. G. [Moshe Glikson], "Al haperek: Purim shel Tel-Aviv" [On the Agenda: Tel Aviv's Purim], *Ha'aretz* 28.3.1929. See: Stern 2006; Shoham 2006: 384–388.
[57] Said 1978.

Most visibly, the Queen's garments and jewelry were always "Oriental," although in reality they were manufactured by European-Jewish artists. The only exception was Tzipora Tzabari, of Yemenite origin, who indeed brought her own garments and jewelry from home.

The Oriental depiction of biblical Queen Esther was meant to identify the feminine with the Oriental, and the masculine with the Occidental. The gendered dichotomy was temporalized: women represented the primordial or atavistic past, which they were assigned to preserve, and men represented progress toward the future, which they were assigned to lead.[58] This reading may be supported by the understanding of Agadati as the "King," who remained steady as the sun, while the Queen was to be replaced every year by another, like the moon, thus contrasting mystique and elusive Oriental femininity with clear and stable western masculinity.

However, this interpretation does not reveal the entire story of Zionist Orientalism. In line with the folkloric discourse, the Queen's garment was based on the Yemenite bridal gown and its accessories.[59] The couple, Agadati and the annual Queen, appeared as a royal *family*, wearing wedding clothes and walking together. Exotic and oriental as the feminine figure was, it was also domesticated.

Zionist Orientalism was therefore quite similar to European Orientalism, except for one crucial factor: within the frame of Jewish ethnic nationalism, the Oriental origin was considered to be a true biological family of the modern people in the physical genealogical sense, and hence it held the power to generate new life for the emerging nation.[60] Rather than presenting the Other in its total Otherness—the display of tradition, the Oriental and feminine in the same concrete human body articulated *Ornamentalism*—a cultural agenda that is "...about the familiar and the domestic, as well as the different and the exotic: indeed, it was in large part about the domestication of the exotic."[61]

---

[58] McClintock 1996: 263–264; Wenke 2000.

[59] Compare Queen Esther's garments in Carmiel (1999: 118–126, 130, 151) with garments of Jewish brides in Yemen (Muchawsky-Schnapper 1994: 105; Muchawsky-Schnapper 2000: 92, 94).

[60] Falk 2006.

[61] Cannadine 2001: xix.

Oriental Jewish cultures were considered by bourgeois Zionism to be important components of the New Hebrew culture. However, the Queen represented not only the "Other" but also the "Self," and thus revealed a significant familial-bourgeois component in Jewish ethnic nationalism.

Biblical Polemics: Romantics and Prostitution

In addition to the Jewish-ethnic emphasis, public discourse in Jewish Palestine connected the commercial display of feminine beauty to biblical texts, and the debate about them was saturated with biblical language and allusions. However, the supporters and opponents of the pageants linked them to two different biblical cannons, which I will designate "the romantic" and "the patriarchal."

According to bible scholars, the Book of Esther belongs to a small cluster of biblical texts with a distinctive perspective regarding the relations between the sexes. Whereas patriarchalism rules the bible, in these texts the place of God is merely inferred, if it is revealed at all, and feminine activity may extend beyond motherhood and nurturing.[62] However, in the main canon of biblical literature, and especially the prophets, God is depicted as a redeeming patriarch who is paired with the woman/nation, commonly referred to as "Zion" in a feminine form, and demands her absolute loyalty in return. Together, the pair created a monogamist family in which any "flirtation" by Israel with other nations was judged as adultery.[63] These two discourses provided the polemic with different types of citations.

The Hebrew Queen Esther pageant was often understood as a performative interpretation of the Book of Esther. In particular it is the pageant episode, in which the most beautiful woman is selected as Queen of Persia [Esther 2:1–18], which may well be considered one of the first mythical beauty pageants in history.

To begin with, the dominance of the male gaze in Tel Aviv alluded to the Book of Esther. The satirist Yesha'ayahu Karniel offered

---

[62] See: Pardes 1992: 98–143; Brenner 1995; Lipton 1998. Thanks to Meira Poliack.

[63] On biblical nationalist-familial images see: Greenberg 1983: 298–306; Cohen 1996: 1–21; Pardes 2000. Thanks to Baruch Schwartz.

Chapter 6. "Our Only Romantic Festival": Hebrew Queen Esther

to rename Purim "the festival of Esther," since "this is our only romantic festival," and added:

> I would order the women to the "manicure" salon on Mammilla Street, to curl their hair and put on many sorts of perfumes, red pomades on their lips and their rose-colored-cheeks (like our lovely youngsters before going to the balls…), and like Esther before going to Ahasuerus' ball.

Here, too, the sexual tension was expressed through the male eye, which objectified the female body. To explain the romantic atmosphere of the festival, Karniel alluded again to the Book of Esther:

> This is a females' festival, of women-intrigues, a celebration of the exchange of a lady for a younger one, apparently with no horn on her forehead. This is, you see, a celebration of chamberlains, women-perfumes, and beauty secrets…[64]

The male gaze may further examine the female body, and, just like the old king Ahasuerus, watch all the beautiful women in the kingdom parading, in order for him to replace his contentious wife with her prettiest peer [Esther 1:19].

The biblical queen thus functioned as intertext for every other beauty queen. This was prominent, for example, in the reports on the "Miss Europe" pageant in 1929, and its winner, the Jewess Elisheva Simon, mentioned above. Simon, unlike the other contestants, "appeared with no makeup, not even face powder," just like Esther, who did not ask for anything from Hegai, the king's eunuch [Esther 2:15].[65] Interviewed by a Hebrew newspaper, she was asked about her Jewish origins, and replied: "True, but I don't want to outrage the world with that, since it can harm me"—again like Esther, who at the

---

[64] "Miba'ad la-masve (shiurim behistaklut)" [Beyond the veil (Lessons in looking)], *Doar-Hayom* 6.3.1925. See also: Daniel Perski, "Al regel ahat" [On one leg], *Ha'aretz* 10.3.1933.

[65] "Habekhirot lemalkat hayofi be-Paris" [Beauty pageant in Paris], *Doar-Hayom* 20.2.1929.

beginning of the story kept her national identity a secret, but revealed it when needed.[66]

The plot of the Book of Esther was another inter-textual point of reference. A French film, titled "Cinderella from Paris," was advertised as "a Purim film," since it was about a beautiful poor orphan girl who was invited to a ball, chosen to be its beauty queen, and would become rich, if only she would marry a rich elderly profligate.[67] The film was linked to Purim because of its similarity to the biblical plot, which was also about a young pretty orphan who marries a rich elderly profligate after winning a beauty contest.

Most of all, the queen herself was the mimetic representation of the biblical Esther, who was always considered a prototype of the beautiful Jewish woman, not only in the Book of Esther but in rabbinic literature as well. Some rabbinic opinions held that she was one of the four prettiest women in history (while others rabbis disagreed).[68] Among these beautiful women, Esther was exceptional in that she was the only one who used her physical appearance to struggle for her people. Among all biblical heroines, she stood out as the only one whose struggle had nothing to do with motherhood. In Tel Aviv's carnival, the performative imitation of the biblical Esther functioned as "the prettiest and most typical Jewess"—not only for interwar Palestine, but for Jewish beauty throughout thousands of years. Hence, it tied together the feminine physical appearances of Jewish past and present. Although a few other beauty pageants in the west were similarly inspired by the mythical beauty contest among the goddesses that triggered the Trojan War, such an intensive hermeneutical apparatus is unparalleled.[69]

Besides the *romantic discourse* in Mandatory Tel Aviv, there was a dominant *patriarchal discourse* that relied on other parts of the biblical canon. In the Jewish ethnic nationalism of the Yishuv, this perception was common among religious as well as nationalist spokesmen, for example in the matter of the exposure of feminine bodies

---

[66] "Leket: Re-ayon im miss eiropa" [An interview with Miss Europe], *Ha'aretz* 10.3.1929. On Esther's "outing" see: Berman 2001.

[67] "Yerushalayim: Seret hamat'im le-Purim" [Jerusalem: A Purim film], *Doar-Hayom* 10.3.1933.

[68] BT Megilah 15:1.

[69] Banner 1983: 253; Ballerino-Cohen et al. 1996: 3.

on the beach, as well as issues of derelict Jewish women, or prostitutes. In these debates, the feminine body was both objectified and nationalized.[70]

The debate about Hebrew Queen Esther bore similar discourses, with specific visual implications. Among the many opponents of the carnival, the pageants attracted harsh criticism. Interestingly, although these opponents were generally Orthodox rabbis and conservative spokesmen, their reasoning was almost solely nationalist, as their biblical intertextuality reveals.

An eminent spokesman of the protest against the pageants was the religious writer A.Z. Rabinowitch, who got a few public figures to sign a proclamation under the biblical title: "In the house of Israel I have seen indignity (Hosea 6)." According to this proclamation, the Purim carnival might have such results as described here:

> Hundreds and hundreds of decent girls and women will fall from their moral status.... While the civilized nations throw this bad custom over their backs, our provincials introduce it here, in the Orient, where strangers come to mock our downfall [see Lamentations 1:7], while keeping their own daughters dignified at home ... and they come to see the disgrace of our daughters and women....

After calling on everyone to avoid the balls, they appealed to the public:

> Celebrate the festivals with your families, don't bring your daughters and women to display themselves in front of strangers! Don't forget that publicity, noisemaking, and over-festivity defamed us among our enemies....
> Don't forget that we were the origin of universal morality![71]

Relying on a stiff division between public and private, the proclamation pointed out the foreigner's male gaze and its possible

---

[70] Helman 2003: 81–82; Bernstein 2008; Razi 2009.

[71] "Beveit yisrael ra'iti sha'aruriya (hoshe'a vav)" [In the house of Israel I have seen indignity (Hosea, Ch. 6)], a proclamation from 12.1.1931, posters collection, national library of Jerusalem, file V1836/e.

contaminating penetration into the collective body, whereas the male enemies themselves keep their women well-guarded in the private sphere. The source of national morality is thus the private sphere, automatically connected to "pure" women and femininity. Men alone were requested to guard their women, while women were not addressed in the proclamation. Elsewhere, Rabinowitch recalled the biblical verse in which Jacob's sons, Simon and Levi, replied to their father: "Should our sister be treated like a whore?" [Genesis 34:31]—justifying the mass killing of all of Nablus' men after Shechem "defiled" their sister, Dina.[72]

Rabinowitch and his colleagues empowered the one-sidedness of the male gaze in two senses: first, the only conceivable way for them to de-sexualize the public sphere was to hide the women, whose morality might be damaged, and thus naturalize the male gaze, whose morality was allegedly never in danger. Second, this gaze was further empowered by its projection to the point of view of an imagined Other, who desired "Our" sexual object, in a familiar pattern of xenophobia, which blames the Other for a stolen pleasure that was prohibited to "us."[73] Jewish men themselves were not explicitly accused of disrespectful gazing at attractive Jewish women. Instead, the guilt was suppressed and transferred to the Other, thus strengthening national identity through the perception of moral superiority. To be sure, other texts of the anti-Esther campaign explicitly targeted the institutionalization of the desirous Jewish-male gaze.

Given this context, it is hardly surprising that some Arab-Palestinian writers objected to the massive Arab attendance at Purim carnivals, for the exact same reasons of national indignity. Like Rabinowitch, the newspaper *Al-Jazeera* emphasized:

> The most irksome phenomenon [in the massive Arab attendance in Purim carnival] is the attendance of Muslim women, which considerably disgraces them.[74]

---

[72] Azar [A.Z. Rabinowitch], "Hirhurim" [Reflections], *Davar* 5.3.1929.

[73] Zizek 1990.

[74] Translated in: "Meha'itonut ha'arvit" [From the Arab press], *Ha'aretz* 2.3.1926.

Indeed, Arab-Muslim women attended the carnival in considerable numbers, and were quite visible in their "traditional" appearance—but Rabinowitch and his Jewish friends simply did not see them.[75]

Moreover, Western bourgeois values were linked here to what were perceived by Rabinowitch and many others as Muslim traditional values, "especially here, in the Orient." It was felt that Jews should have adopted local values when it came to the protection of women from strangers' penetrating gazes.

The desires and anxieties of men from both sides were reflected in each other's perceptions, while women remained in the middle, spoken about in third person and barely addressed directly. This discourse presented a tautology of woman and home, man and homeowner, mixing the meaning of "home" in its real sense, as the private sphere, with its metaphoric meaning as the national community.

It should be emphasized that the two biblical traditions invoked by both the supporters and opponents of Hebrew Queen Esther sought to objectify the female body under the dominant male gaze. Interestingly, for both sides the biblical tradition was mediated through the modern identification of beauty and femininity, whereas in the biblical literature itself men such as Joseph or Absalom could also be alluded to as beautiful.[76] The supporters thought that "beauty is power" and attempted to create a model of national beauty. In order to legitimize the male gaze on female bodies, they referred to the Book of Esther, perceived as a nice love-affair with nationalist implications. The opponents, on the other hand, employed the prophets' and Pentateuch's traditions that emphasized the similarity between Israel's unfaithfulness to God and adultery. Sexual gazes across national borders were considered a threat to national identity, and flesh-and-blood feminine visibility was defined as prostitution. Prostitution was thus used as much more than a metaphor, and emphasized the ethnic borders of the Nation, as guarded by decent women.

This hermeneutical debate deviated from the Hebrew Queen Esther polemics: in general, many intellectuals deeply disliked the choice of Esther and Purim as nationalist symbols, since they

---

[75] See photo: Carmiel 1999: 49; Mann 2006: 152–153.
[76] See: Synnot 1989: 617.

symbolized precisely the Diaspora mentality against which Zionism, allegedly, should have rebelled. Esther and Purim represented the "Jewish-exilic" struggle for survival by vulgar romantics, degenerate court intrigues, and probably worse—intermarriage, abandoning the Jewish woman to a lustful corrupted Gentile, and disregarding motherhood as her main duty.[77] It was a different Zionist ideology, bourgeois and urban, which symbolized the conquest of Palestine not by military heroism but by economic prosperity and consumption. At least symbolically, and in line with the thought of the bourgeois Zionist Theodor Herzl, intermarriage was not as abhorrent in Urban Zionism as is commonly presented in Jewish nationalist discourse.

However, the conservative campaign against Hebrew Queen Esther was successful, and the pageants were cancelled *de facto* in 1930. Perhaps as a substitute, in 1932 the municipality built "Esther's Palace," a huge, three-storied street theater, which was dominated by a 30-meter-high figure of Queen Esther on top of the third story. Orthodox rabbis and spokesmen were not as concerned about the obvious violation of the second commandment as they were about the appearance of flesh-and-blood women in the public sphere, and did not protest against this new figure—thus revealing the Victorian rather than rabbinic-Halakhic, origins of their anxieties.. This conservative discourse was perhaps religious in its language, but it was nationalist in content and bourgeois in its apprehensions.[78]

Feminist Struggles?

The impediments to breaking the links between the woman and domesticity were the probable background for the surprising silence of Zionist women's organizations with regard to Hebrew Queen Esther. In most places where beauty pageants were introduced during the 1920s, feminist organizations immediately protested against what they saw as the objectification of the female body and the fixation of

---

[77] For example: Uri Keisari, "Ester, Akhashverosh, Haman, Mordekhai et Kompani..." [Esther, Ahasuerus, Haman, Mordekhai, and co.], *Doar-Hayom*, 22.3.1932; idem, "Ester, Ester, mizgi lanu yayin" [Esther, Esther, pour us some wine], *Doar-Hayom*, 24.3.1935.

[78] See: Bernstein 2008: 241–269.

Chapter 6. "Our Only Romantic Festival": Hebrew Queen Esther

the dominance of the male gaze in the public sphere.[79] Indeed, many of the conservative critics of Hebrew Queen Esther raised quasi-feminist objections, claimed that, for example, "our historical women have never earned their reputation by their beauty"—disregarding several biblical heroines[80] and urged women's organizations to vocally object to the pageants, but the glove was not picked up. Indeed, only one of the fifteen signers of Rabinowitch's proclamations was a woman. One protest against Hebrew Queen Esther was signed by an "anonymous Yemenite woman," but the complete similarity between the wording of this petition and Rabinowitch's proclamation casts suspicion that this was a fiction. Yet, if Rabinowitch was the real author, the subterfuge indicates that he at least felt somewhat uncomfortable with the total absence of women's voices from the debate. If there were other women who indeed were uncomfortable with Hebrew Queen Esther, their perspective was not publicized.[81]

In this era, Zionist feminists were concerned with issues of suffrage, a right gained only in 1926, and with issues of labor, struggling to break out of women's total identification with the private sphere (but this was done, for the most part, without claiming that the home was not the foremost duty of a responsible woman).[82] Although the pageants could be seen as problematic from a feminist perspective, these organizations had no reason to cooperate with those who demanded that women be exclusively identified with domesticity.

This debate was circumscribed by the bourgeois discursive frame, which dictated the tangled intersections between Zionist nationalism and gender, for both the supporters and the opponents of Hebrew Queen Esther. Both sides separated the public from the private, identified women with the sphere of family, and were entangled with their expansion to the public sphere within the frame of ethnic nationalism. The major difference between them was their

---

[79] Ballerino-Cohen et al. 1996: 6–7.

[80] Y. Avizohar, "Yemey ha-Purim be-Tel-Aviv (mikhtav lama'arekhet)" [Purim days in Tel Aviv (a letter to the editors)], *Ha'aretz* 1.4.1929.

[81] "Bekhirot le-ester hamalka hateimanit" [Elections to Yemenite Queen Esther], *Davar* 25.3.1931, 3. Two historians in addition to me searched for such a response in archives, with no consequences. See: Helman 2006: note 71; and Stern 2006: 149.

[82] Fogiel-Bijaoui 1992; Razi 2009.

conceptualization of feminine visibility in interwar Western popular culture. The critics adhered to the Victorian identification of the woman with domesticity and motherhood, and objected to any feminine visibility in the public sphere. The pageants' fans claimed that "beauty is a decisive force in survival struggles," implicitly identifying this force with femininity.[83] As a perception of femininity, they preferred the new interwar model of "feminine mystique," within which sexual seductiveness was added to (but by no means replaced) domesticity.[84] While in interwar North America, the "feminine mystique" acquired dominance, its penetration into the *Yishuv* was much slower.

Gossip and Celebs

The tones in the debate between opponents and supporters of the Hebrew Queen Esther were particularly high with regard to the 1928 Queen, Tzipora Tzabari. Tzabari tried to leverage her fifteen minutes of glory into an international show-business career as an actress and dancer. She came from a south Tel Aviv slum and worked as a milk deliverer on the city's streets, a job she inherited from her father, who had become ill and died a few days before her Purim coronation. In contrast to the image of Yemenites as "happy with their share," she left her low-wage job after the carnival and travelled to Germany, the contemporaneous center of European cinema. Tzabari made it as far as Prague, where she took some courses in the theatrical arts. In the meantime, to make a living, she performed oriental dances in "dishonorable" cafés, worked in a circus, and may have even been photographed in a two-piece swim-suit—quite a daring act in the 1920s. As for what happened later, there are different versions. Some think that she "made it" in the German cinema scene, performed secondary roles as an "exotic girl" (including in one film in which she appeared with Marlene Dietrich), and returned to Palestine only a short while before World War II. On the basis of correspondence in the city's archive, it seems that after several months, she failed to gain recognition, and

---

[83] Yitzhak Lufban in: A. Borer, "Purim taratz" [Purim 1930], *Ketuvim 20–21*, 14.3.1930, 2.

[84] Banner 1983: 274–275.

Chapter 6. "Our Only Romantic Festival": Hebrew Queen Esther

traveled back to Tel Aviv. Her own retrospective memories are also not definitive.[85]

The sensational journey of "Miss Palestine" into the European show-biz world attracted huge interest in the Jewish media in Palestine and Central Europe. Contradictory rumors reached Palestine about her journey, but the polemics were not only about the facts. Since she was presented in Europe as "Miss Palestine," some men protested against the abuse of the nation's reputation, and considered it a "disgrace for the country and for us." Some of her critics employed a patronizing tone regarding the "poor Yemenite" who was stuck in a "cold and strange country." However, she also had some supporters, including Mayor Dizengoff, who gave her financial support and protected her reputation in the press and in private correspondence. In addition to their personal regard for her, Tzabari's supporters understood the potential contribution of this exceptional Cinderella story to prove the social mobility of the *Yishuv* and to dull domestic ethnic/socio-economic tensions in Palestine's Jewish society. The prevalence of the Cinderella theme in the popular press accompanied the growth of the beauty industry since the nineteenth century, because it proved that women's beauty could function as the means for social mobility.[86]

The loud tones of the Tzabari debate were derived from the visible public presence of a flesh-and-blood woman who deviated from being a mere representation. Within the context of capitalist mass entertainment, such a representative woman could be commercialized as a celebrity, that is, a specific person whose name and body belong not to herself but to the public (as was well-put by Marilyn Monroe).[87] In Zionist Tel Aviv's context, these were not only the names and bodies of actors and actresses (such as Hanna Robina), but also of great poets or thinkers such as Bialik or Ahad-Ha'Am, who were greatly honored

---

[85] See: "Tel-Aviv veyafo" [Tel Aviv and Jaffa], *Ha'aretz* 16.2.1928; A.N., "Ester hamalka motzi'ah monitin le-Tel-Aviv" [Queen Esther gives Tel Aviv a reputation], *Ha'aretz* 21.2.1929, 4; Carmiel 1999: 122 and note 22; Stern 2006: note 79; TAMA file 04-3452; and http://www.ynet.co.il/articles/0,7340, L-3315629,00.html.

[86] About the frequency of Cinderella stories in western popular media see: Banner 1983: 14–15. On Cinderella stories and social cohesion see: Pomfret 2004: 1454.

[87] Roach 2007: 1.

as embodiments of national culture. The city bestowed homes to these bodies on streets that were named after them in their lifetimes. Their birthdays were celebrated and their dates of death were commemorated.[88] On the one hand, these bodies were controlled by the public gaze, dominantly masculine in our case. But on the other hand, these people could still make use of their own names and bodies so as to move and speak "inappropriately" in public space.

Tzabari used her name and body to challenge the nationalist-bourgeois morality in the name of capitalist values of self-fulfillment. Through gossip, Tzipora Tzabari appeared in the public sphere not only as a representation of the national beauty, but also as a private body, a partial component of that nation which may be active and acquire different visibility in the public sphere. At the same time, as a celebrity, she used her body's cultural capital as the embodiment of national beauty for her personal benefit. Indeed, she was the exception, and her successor, Hanna Polani, for example, preferred to be photographed in a fashionable domestic silk dressing gown.[89] In most cases, as in other beauty contests globally, the contestants were back to their domestic roles and relative anonymity after the celebrations were over.

As "one of the few democratic fields of women's employment," mass entertainment offered new opportunities for women in the interwar West.[90] Even if opportunities did not abound in Palestine's show-business, this was a sphere in which the female body could at least de-mythologize Victorian domesticity. The emergence of gossip and celebrity culture contaminated the "pure" representation with real lives of real people, or even worse—of a real woman. This could happen only with the emergence of an urban-national public sphere in which capitalist mass entertainment was the major form of leisure, as was most prominently demonstrated by Hebrew Queen Esther pageants.

---

[88] On Bialik see: Hirschfeld 2002: 1025–1036; on Robina and other theatre actresses and actors: Shaked 1996. On cultural figures as "celebs" in the Jewish world see: Veidlinger 2009: 148–157.

[89] Carmiel 2004: 196.

[90] Banner 1983: 263.

Chapter 7
Another New Jew: Urban Zionist Ideology

The Purim carnival in Tel Aviv was the largest public event in British Palestine from the late Ottoman era until 1936. The tourist attraction of the carnival was found in its "combination of nationalist and entertaining aspects and the diversity of the celebrations, which appealed to various market segments."[1] Indeed, the carnival expressed a substantively unfamiliar Zionist ideology: pro-urban, bourgeois, and capitalist. Although this ideology did not advocate Puritanism and self-sacrifice but mere mundane joy, it did maintain that this happiness could be achieved within a national framework—and hence it was a nationalist ideology. This concluding chapter will stitch together the threads that were unraveled throughout the book, in order to explicate the ideology of Urban Zionism, using the Purim carnival as the canvas on which this ideology was depicted.

Urban Zionist Ideology

As an ideological stream, Urban Zionism is usually considered quite weak in Zionist politics and ideology, due to the difficulties in establishing a political base and gaining significant influence in the *Yishuv*'s institutions. Middle classes, or "civil circles," were commonly identified with the political party of "the general Zionists." However, as the party's name implies, its substantial ideological platform was to adhere to general Zionist goals "without external specific views" like socialism, religion, right-wing militarism, and other philosophies. These world views were perceived by general Zionists as obstacles to the Zionist project. They believed that Zionist institutions must find the golden way to resolve individual issues, rather than follow dogmatic thought systems. Hence, the general Zionists had difficulties

---

[1] Goldberg 2005: 109.

finding their voices in the Zionist discourse, in which problems on the agenda were discussed in the context of complex theoretical systems they had not taken part in developing.[2]

As was recently demonstrated by various scholars, the political weakness of the Zionist middle class traditionally portrayed by scholarship was the outcome of scholarly neglect of the ways in which the Jewish middle class took form in the British Mandate period.[3] Accordingly, the study of Zionist ideology, civic religion, and invented traditions ignored Urban Zionist ideology because its principles were never articulated by writers and thinkers, and were never deployed in the public sphere by a hierarchical political organization. The landmark study *Civil Religion in Israel* cited this reason to justify its neglect of the study of civil religion of the middle class.[4] Like most scholars of Zionist ideology, these authors understood "ideology" as an articulated and explicated system of principles. Such a system may, of course, clash with "reality" and show some flexibility, but analytically it is identified with a "consciousness" totally separated from "being."[5] Here I follow theoreticians who saw in ideology a comprehensive cultural system which was not necessarily explicit in texts.[6] Ideology refers here to ideas as praxis, and the study of ideology should thus focus on what ideas do in the public sphere. Anthropologically-oriented research can infer ideological maxims from implicit cultural practices.[7]

Many contemporaries identified Purim celebrations with "the civic bloc" (the unofficial name of the politically organized middle

---

[2] On general Zionists see: Shimoni 1995: 115–126 (quote from 117); Drory 1990: 11, 118–132.

[3] Shamir 2000; see also Shilo 1997; Ben-Porat 1999; Shamir 2002; Lavsky 2002; Shavit 2003; Troen 2003: 112–159; Karlinsky 2005.

[4] Liebman & Don-Yehiya 1983: 29.

[5] See: Swirsky 1979. His criticism is proven right by the definitions on which the study of Zionist ideology is based. See, for example: Shimoni 1995: 397 (note 1); Lissak 1999: 481.

[6] The literature on ideology is voluminous. For some organizing definitions see: Geertz 1973: 193–233; Larrain 1979: 13–16; Williams 1982: 26–30; Williams 1983: 153–157.

[7] Ricoeur 1991: 125–143. For a most notable example see: Geertz 1973: 412–453.

class), as evident in the following protest against the cancellation of the carnival in 1936: "Is the civic bloc so weak that it can't resist the destruction of the tradition of the first Hebrew city?"[8] This identification was quite inaccurate sociologically, but as I shall elaborate it was quite accurate ideologically. Tel Aviv's Purim celebrations epitomized the cultural grip of urban and capitalist culture in many social circles which did not necessarily belong to the urban bourgeoisie. To some extent, the implicitness of Urban Zionist ideology made it much harder to resist or control it, as is revealed in the Tel Aviv Purim celebrations.[9] This will be evident in the following ideological analysis.

In his thorough study of Zionist ideology, historian Gideon Shimoni defines two major conceptions, "functional" and "organic." The difference between these two conceptions is expressed in a broad-stroke manner in the concise formulation of Ahad-Ha'Am, who differentiated between those, like himself, who seek a solution for "the problem of Judaism," and others who are troubled by "the problem of the Jews," such as his bitter rival, Herzl.[10] The *functional conception* understood Jewish existence in exile as a crisis situation. In order to secure the very physical existence of the Jewish people, it was necessary to establish a state, and postpone the cultural debates, or better yet, not to deal with them at all.[11] The *organic conception*, contrastingly, maintained that the physical existence of the Jews is an old problem, and that establishing a state for its own sake as a Zionist goal is worth the bother only if it possesses unique Jewish qualities. For Ahad-Ha'Am, for example, these qualities were the special morality and cultural heritage of Judaism. For the Labor Movement-oriented thinkers, the state should be characterized by social justice, in keeping with socialist principles; or a return to the soil and earning a livelihood through physical labor, according to the more influential romanticist-*Narodnik* approaches (prominently represented by A.D. Gordon). Some religious-Zionist thinkers, in particular Rabbi Avraham Y. Kook (1865–1935), thought that the Jewish state should be "the foundation of God's

---

[8] Moshe Arkin, "Lama tashbitu et hasimkha? (mikhtav lama'arekhet)" [Why stop the joy? (editorial letter)], *Doar-Hayom* 26.2.1936.

[9] Helman 2006a.

[10] Shimoni 1995: 85–93, 104–107.

[11] Vital 1984: 256–266.

throne in the world," rather than a standard state, "which is no more than a large trust company."[12] The latter formula obviously disputed Herzl and the functional conception. Each Zionist ideological stream developed specific formulations of a cultural demand that somehow deviated from the narrow act of establishing a state. The major Zionist thinkers generally agreed that the political act is was necessary for the solution of "the Jewish problem," but insufficient in and of itself. The urge to create "new Jews," different from the old Jews not only in their location in political space and the right of citizenship but in the entirety of their lives, was therefore a powerful cultural force.[13]

It is commonly assumed that Herzl had no ideological successors. Scholars tend to think that with the ongoing colonization of Palestine and the building of Zionist institutions, the functional conception gradually lost power. According to this view, the functional conception continued to exist as a narrow political consensus regarding the need to establish a state and absorb Jewish refugees—but not as an ideological discourse.

The Purim celebrations analyzed in this book reveal not only the grip of Urban Zionist ideology but also its complexity. Functional Zionism was far from a simplistic political consensus about the need to resolve "the Jews' problem." It was a complex thought-system, which included a concrete understanding of the Jewish problem, concepts such as exile (*Galut*) and salvation (*Ge'ula*), the desired form of Jewish sovereignty, and "the new Jew." This thought system was based on a specific form of economic relations—capitalism; a specific form of space design—urbanization; the cultural engineering or public design of emotions; and a concrete understanding of the nature of the relations between past and present. This ideological system may be extracted from the practice of Zionist festive culture. Let us summarize it here, beginning with the problem of time, and follow it by discussing the construction of national space and the role of emotions in the new culture.

---

[12] Kook 1993: 160.

[13] For example: Even-Zohar 1981; Shapira 1997b; Eisenstadt 1998.

Time: Tradition and Alienation

As we have seen throughout this book, the uses of the concept of tradition in Urban Zionist culture were much more diverse than the acceptable image of the anti-traditional Zionist rebellion, which is frequently associated with the pioneering Zionist avant-garde. The myth of the rebellious pioneers has recently been challenged in several historical studies.[14] In chapter three above I have already described the complexity of the discourse on tradition, and I shall now point out the sharp difference between the complexes of urban circles and pioneers' circles with regard to the concept of *alienation*.

This difference is most evident in Gershon Hanoch's text, discussed above (pp. 85–87). Hanoch described the feeling expressed in the public and personal writings of many pioneers in rural settlements, who spoke and wrote about the burdensome emptiness of Sabbath days, festivals, and holidays, due to the absence of the old rituals that had been abandoned. Many pioneers felt that the new invented rituals were artificial.[15] On the other hand, they found it difficult to bear "365 days, 365 nights of the mundane [*Hulin*]," as it was well-put by poet Avraham Shlonsky (who was one of the Labor Movement cultural figures with a more religious—if by no means Orthodox—orientation).[16] David Maletz (1899–1981), at the time an influential writer among the settlers, argued that the feeling of alienation toward the new customs was not due to the fact that the actual practices were not attuned to the settlers' needs, but rather due to the fact that the new rituals were invented by the settlers, who found it difficult to revere their own handiwork. This is why the new rituals were seen as "fakes" which did not fit a secular and rational world.[17]

As we have seen, this dilemma existed in urban centers as well. Comparing the two venues, Hanoch argued that in rural settlements "it is still different; there, something is going and crystallizing, even though it happens with much agony and quivering." However, rather

---

[14] See: Kena'ani 1976; Shapira 1998; Ze'ira 2002.

[15] See, for example: Kena'ani 1976: 27–35, 47–55; Shapira 1998; Ze'ira 2002: 31–36, 57–61 and more.

[16] Quoted and translated in: Shapira 1998: 257.

[17] Ze'ira 2002: 85–88.

than explaining the new creation, Hanoch focused on the feeling of emptiness:

> There as well [in rural settlements], a day of Sabbath or holiday is the most difficult and laborious day for the public, and they still don't know what to do then ... the entire difficulty of the transformation into a different frame of life and "the broken will" is felt and depresses the spirit more than on any other day. And there, as well, some signs of reactionism are rising and sprouting: instead of the full confidence and courage with which we had left the family and the previous ties to tradition, and turned to the "new" there are now yearnings and actual attempts to renew family connections, occasionally accompanied by [renewing] well-known traditional customs....[18]

What was the difference between the rural settlements and the cities? According to Hanoch, in the rural settlements these questions were widely discussed and written about, whereas in the city

> the illness is not even felt. Here [rural] some lifeless life-orders are going and putting down their roots; here [urban] there is a mix of old and new drifting public "customs," without an attempt of improvement and even without criticism; here everything is accompanied by simplistic satisfaction; here our lives, internally and externally undisciplined in form and content, are provoking only the sound of theShofar's blasts, toward "overseas": "our masses," "our Hebrew city" — and that's enough for us....

As is clearly demonstrated in this book, as well as in other studies, this claim is mistaken if it was intended to target the urban organizers of the holiday events.[19] The urban entrepreneurs dedicated a great deal of thought, with the same depth as their rural colleagues, to the proper way to establish new traditions in the Jewish public sphere, with incessant self-criticism and attempts to make improvements. Unlike others in the Labor Movement, Hanoch did not denounce the

---

[18] G. Hanoch, "Sidrei-hayim (reshimot be-ikvot ha-Purim)" (Ways of life [Notes on Purim]), *Hapo'el Hatza'ir* 5.4.1929, 15–16. All ellipses are original.

[19] See in particular: Shavit & Sitton 2004: 29–37, 58–82; Helman 2008: 120.

very existence of the city, but because he did not, he found it necessary to give a proper account for the city dwellers' detachment from the old traditions, a problem that obsessively occupied the cultural entrepreneurs in rural settlement. His criticism was directed at the indifference, or ignorance, of the urban public towards the miseries of the rural settlers. The urbanites allegedly left the *"gemeinschaft,"* the original intimate community of Jewish exile, in favor of an alienated community based on the primacy of economic-utilitarian relationships. The urbanites did not talk about detachment and alienation, whereas the villagers, who established intimate communities of small groups, did not cease to talk about their share of loneliness and alienation in their new lives.[20] The wide and massive discourse produced in the Zionist "literary republic" about this alienation was vital to the constitution of Zionism as a revolutionary movement that generated a deep transformation in the lives of the Jews, from exilic traditional urbanites to New Hebrew secular peasants, as we have seen in the introduction to this book.[21]

Hanoch did not accept the relative ease with which the urbanites dealt with what he saw as the formative experience of immigration: alienation from old tradition, and at times from one's own family. Unlike their rural counterparts, urban cultural entrepreneurs gathered cultural practices from any possible cultural source, regardless of its historical origins. The act of inventing traditions without talking about detachment from the old tradition seemed to Hanoch to be educationally destructive. In fact, Hanoch admitted that in rural settlements there was a reactive tendency, a trend of return to the old tradition, and that some, God forbid, even renewed old family connections. Hanoch probably referred to the fact that observant people of the older generation joined some of the important centers of rural settlement in the Jezreel valley, such as Kefar-Yekhezkel, Nahalal, Ein-Kharod, or Balfuria. Those settlements had thus to provide religious services, such as kosher kitchens, Orthodox synagogues, or traditional burial

---

[20] Katriel 2011.

[21] See, in a nutshell: Raz-Karkotzkin 1993; Raz-Karkotzkin 1999; Eisenstadt 1998; Shapira 1997a, 1997b; Urian & Karsh 1999. For another, more balanced, approach, see: Saposnik 2008: 9–16.

rites.[22] Meanwhile, the new urban public culture was much more distant from the old tradition, but spoke about this distance much less.

As we have seen in chapter three, according to Hanoch's view a tradition could not be created intentionally. In internal debates in the Labor Movement, there were those, like the writer Yosef Haim Brenner (1881–1921), A.D. Gordon, and others, who objected to cultural entrepreneurship itself, and thought that the new culture should be created spontaneously, in intimate groups that would develop a close relationship with the soil and nature. Others who were less extreme saw cultural entrepreneurship as a necessary evil. In practice, cultural entrepreneurs from Labor Movement circles could not avoid inventing traditions.[23] Meanwhile, they saw that the Zionist urban culture was created in a way that seemed to their eyes spontaneous—and that posed a true logical discrepancy in the ideological doctrine. This discrepancy was projected by Hanoch back to the urban culture that was "artificial," without providing any argument as to what was so artificial about this culture, except for "they begin one song, and then stop it and move to another." Hanoch could not understand how a new culture could be built on a foundation other than explicit alienation from the old tradition, and yet be so different and remote from that tradition. This experience was the complete opposite of the dichotomist experience of the rural settlement, which spoke so much about alienation from tradition while its culture was surprisingly (and apprehensively) similar to the old tradition, and was much more threatened by a reactionary response. The ethos of rural settlement, which was influenced by Nietzsche in this matter, considered it impossible to create a meaningful culture without suffering, serious thought, and historical alienation.[24] In the eyes of the rural pioneers, this urban culture was unreflective, emotionally simplistic, and hence essentially flawed.

The urban understanding of the concept of tradition lacked this emphasis on alienation. The is spontaneity, which was mistakenly identified with lack of reflection, offered an instant dialogue with all available *traditions*, in the plural. Multiple and various cultural components could be modified and adopted, utilizing the most available

---

[22] See: Ze'ira 2002: 218–219.

[23] See: Brenner 1961: 66; Gordon 1957: 327–335. Also: Shavit 1989: 22; Shavit 1996: 341–343; Shavit 1998: 347–353; Ze'ira 2002: chapters 1–2.

[24] See: Tzur 2002; Ze'ira 2002: 107.

cultural materials at hand in an eclectic manner. Urban cultural entrepreneurs did not pay much attention to the origins of their cultural practices, or to the purist attempt to separate "Jewish" from "alien" origins. Rather, they identified Purim with the cosmopolite carnivalesque tradition. The new public culture was perceived as a multidimensional historical creation, continuous with many other historical phenomena, and hybrid: Jewish and Gentile, old and new, nationalist and cosmopolite, spontaneous and organized. Zionist Urbanites refrained from Jewish purism, from creating an imagined break-line with old tradition, and from affixing the great tradition as irrelevant.

Hanoch's tone of lamentation may be compared with the carefree tone of Agadati, who expressed surprisingly similar concerns regarding the difference between invented and great traditions:

> Regrettably, original Jewish customs take quite a small place among the new customs which are created in our land. And among the festive forms which include universal human foundation alongside national foundation, we transfer to the Land of Israel only the first [the universal], and somewhat neglect the second [the Jewish]. Our Purim should be not only a general human carnival but also a Jewish Purim.[25]

This opinion regarding the lack of traditional Jewish customs in Tel Aviv's Purim was expressed in variant forms and was quite common among Purim celebrators.[26] Agadati agreed with Hanoch that the invented tradition of Purim in Tel Aviv was dissimilar to traditional Purim celebrations. His own opinion was that Jewish customs should be re-appropriated (in reference to an attempt to renovate the custom of *Shalach-Monos* in the balls). However, the more important difference was that, for Agadati, this was just a question of quantity and balance between the different components which were to be adopted. There was an understanding that the dialogue with tradition could be dynamic and enable new interpretations—including totally new ones

---

[25] "Moré-derekh lenishfey hamasekhot hamasortiyim shel B. adagati" [A guide to Agadati's traditional Purim balls], 4, the archive of Israeli center of stage arts, file 62.3.7.

[26] Arieh-Sapir 2003: 115–118.

that had never previously been part of this tradition—without assuming that this tradition was, or should have been, thus abandoned.

This point was another Herzlian element in the urban culture of Tel Aviv. The creation of the Jewish public sphere liberated Jewish tradition from being a "problem" by widening its interpretive range and the ability to contain many "foreign" interpretations within the boundaries of Judaism. By employing the cultural apparatus of the invention of tradition, tradition was transformed from a problem into a useful instrument at the service of cultural entrepreneurship. The new Jew could therefore be "traditionist."[27]

Space: Capitalism and Urbanity

The gap between the rural image and the capitalist-urban reality of the Zionist project was too often explained as a glorious failure of the original platform of anti-urban Zionist ethos. It is too commonly assumed that capitalism as ideology had no real presence in Israeli public discourse before the 1970s. In fact, spokespersons for bourgeois Urban Zionism, among them Tel Aviv's Mayor Dizengoff, and a few additional industrialists and entrepreneurs, encouraged private entrepreneurship and objected to the nationalized economy that directed the actions of Zionist settlement institutions.[28] However, although they never achieved political dominance, and despite the pressure of Zionist propaganda which incessantly attacked private capital and city life, market forces had major influence on everyday life, and the bourgeois taste penetrated all social venues.[29] The bourgeois perception of the body as respectable, discussed in chapter four, or the bourgeois division of labor between the sexes, discussed in chapter six—were but two eminent examples of that.

Purim celebrations proved the strong connection between urbanism and Zionist ideology. Zionist doctrine depicted the alliance with mass entertainment at the carnival and particularly at the balls as a compromise with powerful forces, necessary to raise money and recruit public support. Yet, whatever the motives of the organizers, the cul-

---

[27] Yadgar 2011.

[28] Cohen 1977; Frenkel, Shenhav & Herzog 2000; Troen 2003: 89–100.

[29] See, for example: Helman 2003; Helman 2006a: 282–290; Helman 2010; Rosenberg-Freidman 2012b. On the puritan ethos see: Almog 2000: 209–225.

tural product of this process was a capitalist-nationalist culture, which assumed the correlation of national and personal happiness.

A notable capitalist aspect of the Urban Zionist ideology was the hedonist consideration of the "celebration of the economy" and the encouragement to consume "*Totzeret Ha'aretz*," that is, local-Jewish products.[30] Although the explicit goal of the latter was to support Jewish industry and agriculture, the actual result was indirect nationalist legitimization of "hedonist" consumer culture. True, no spokesperson defended the disproportionate increase of prices during the carnival; many people condemned the shameless display of this prosperity within the "the celebration of the economy"; and there were those who even condemned the very economic prosperity brought by the carnival as immodest and corrupt. In spite of it all, this prosperity, with its commercialized and hedonistic elements, was an important component of an ideology according to which Jews could live long and prosper in Palestine, apart from puritan asceticism.

When it came to urbanization, however, the *Yishuv*'s leaders could not just ignore the concentration of most of the Jewish population in the cities. Actually, it is most probable that the "disease of profiteering"— legitimate and legal real estate commerce by decent people who sought profit—would not have been thought of as such a problem if nationalist ideology had no interest in the cities. For the most part, this "disease" affected prices of urban lands, rather than rural lands, and swelled the expenses of Jewish National Fund, which actually invested a great deal in cities.[31]

For the classical Zionist doctrine which attempted to "reverse the pyramid," that is, to turn the Jewish city-dwellers into peasants, the city posed an ideological problem. It was mostly legitimized as an excuse: it was a market for agricultural production; a cultural-national center; or an attraction that would draw immigrants and money. But even among those who accepted the city because of its economic functions, urban culture (to be differentiated from national culture) was viewed as inauthentic due to its detachment from the soil. The urban project demanded constant justifications.[32]

---

[30] Shoham 2013c.
[31] Lavsky 1994.
[32] See, for example: Cohen 1977: 2–9; Graicer 1989.

In the Urban Zionist discourse described and analyzed throughout this book, the point of view was just the opposite. It was precisely in the city, and the city alone, where the new society or the new nation was created. Only the city established the presence of the mass society that can be justifiably called a "nation." The city created the only geographical location in which a new Jewish public sphere could have existed. If not for the city, the nation could be understood as an invention of groups of intellectuals or "literary republics," or, alternatively, of avant-garde groups—those who indeed imprinted the image of the pioneer on Zionist collective memory. The city was the geographical space in which the return to the homeland could have been experienced as a return not to an imagined utopian space, but to a real geographical place which contained the Jewish masses, a Jewish nation. It was the major Jewish public sphere, which at least symbolically, and in some cases practically, was indeed controlled by Jews.

This attention to the realistic geographical aspect of the place in which national identity was constructed—which in nationalist language is called "a homeland"—could not be articulated within narrow Zionist doctrine, in which the story of urbanization was usually told as a lamentation, embedded in a nostalgic narrative of deterioration, due to the "profiteering" of the land, "the living body of the homeland."[33] Nevertheless, the building of the city was emblematic to the building of the new Nation.

The "spatial turn" brought to Jewish life by Urban Zionism may be demonstrated through the narration of the story of Purim celebrations by the folklorist Yom-Tov Lewinsky:

> In Jaffa, like other cities with mixed populations, they were used to organize indoors Purim celebrations, in order not to irritate the Arab neighbors.[34]

This introduction to Lewinsky's narrative functions as an underpinning of the "outing" of Judaism brought by the first Hebrew city, which replaced the mixed cities in which Jewish culture allegedly existed only in closed spaces. In other words, Urban Zionism did

---

[33] According to the agitated anti-urban speech given by a figure in the film *This is the Land*. See: Shoham 2011b.
[34] Lewinsky 1955: 279.

not consider the transformation of Jewish life brought by Zionism in terms of "rebellion." Instead, it was understood as a *spatial* transformation from the semi-public spheres in which it existed in exile (again, according to this ideology, but not necessarily in historical reality), such as the synagogue, the houses of rich men (*G'virim*), and such locales—to the street, which, allegedly, "for the first time in two thousand years," was Jewish and was dominated by Jews. This digression of Jewish life from indoors to outdoors was reflected, among other ways, in the invention of traditions and in the creation of a new Jewish public culture and public sphere. It enabled the containment of wild interpretations of Jewish culture within the safe borders of Jewish identity, and made "Jewish tradition" much more flexible and diversified. The new Jew of Urban Zionism was first and foremost an outdoor Jew. This spatial transformation, characteristic of Urban Zionism, was much more important than the "secularization" of Jewish society, overstated in scholarship as the main transformation of the modern age and Zionism.[35]

Although urban space was not favored by the Zionist ethos, the rapid urban development of interwar Palestine forced itself on Zionist spatial imagery, since only urban mass society could indeed be convincingly designated by the pretentious term "nation."

"They Don't Want Anything but Happiness": Nationalist Fun

The creation of a Jewish public sphere assumed Zionist cultural dominance no less than its political dominance. The "Jewishness" of the public sphere through cultural media such as myths, symbols, and rituals was mediated by emotions, which were assumed to be controllable and manageable by cultural entrepreneurship. Various invented traditions made use of a variety of emotions. For example, the invented tradition of Tel-Hai made extensive use of emotions such as reverence and sadness.[36] Indeed, classical literature on nationalist invented traditions used to overemphasize such "religious"

---

[35] See supra note 21.

[36] Zerubavel 1995: 84–95.

emotions.[37] However, the emotion most frequently used in our case-study was that of happiness, much like in the case of the Zionist cult of the *Hora* dance with its alleged Hassidic origins, designed to help the pioneers mitigate their mundane troubles.[38] This emotion was characteristic of Urban Zionism.

As we have seen here, Purim was the main festival of the *Yishuv*, when everyone made a pilgrimage to Tel Aviv in order to take part in a cult of joy and fun. Happiness was thus at the core of urban-nationalist ideology, as opposed to the puritan ethos of restraint and reverence. The happiness was spoken about in two major ways, which I designate as "instrumental" and "normal."

The *instrumental discourse* spoke of happiness as a necessary rest from the hard work of nation-building, to allow for a return to that work immediately after the holiday. Dizengoff, for example, in his opening speech, explained that the festival would function as a "rest from our national work."[39] In this way, leisure was depicted as part of the collective effort and as a function of the world of work.[40]

In another vein, there were a number of spokespersons who emphasized happiness as a crucial component of the Zionist story of redemption from slavery to freedom, from exile to salvation. Happiness, in this *normality discourse*, was a fundamental component of a "normal" nation naturally residing in its own land. This was the reason, so it was claimed, that Jews in exile were deprived of joy. As implied by an ad for a ball, a "normal" nation has "negligence and fleet-footedness/ and happiness waving like a flag"; that is, the nation had to openly express this emotion in order to make a political-ideological statement.[41] Journalist Daniel Perski, for example, responded to the attacks on the "licentiousness" of Purim celebrations, and indicated, quite realistically, that in the carnival there was nothing of all these "merrymakings and parties and unruly behaviors." He added

---

[37] Mosse 1975; Hobsbawm & Ranger 1983; Ozouf 1988; Nora 1997; Ben-Amos 2000.

[38] See: Roginsky 2007.

[39] M. Dizengoff, "Birkat ha-hag" [The festival greeting], *Ha'aretz* 18.3.1935.

[40] See: Rojek 1985: chapter 4.

[41] Announcement of "Hamataté" [Broom] Purim ball, *Hapo'el Hatza'ir* 22.2.1934.

that "Since the commencement of Adar ... lamentations on Purim celebrations are increased"—alluding to Talmudic imperative "Since the commencement of Adar, joy is increased."[42] Perski confronted the joy's foes. He contended that "the simple and natural folk [...] are happy for the opportunity to have some fun in Purim joy." As a historical phenomenon embedded in Jewish tradition, it needed no further justification. Nevertheless, Perski noticed that for "cultured nations"

> The Gentiles have an important and big thing about it. In some towns in Belgium and in almost every city in Italy and other countries there is a continuous and attractive festivity with beautiful and weird matters, for three or four days each year. Entire books were customs to illustrate and elevate the festivity and mischievousness of a people, children and elderly, men and women. There, as well, there is a strong organization, already a month before. A detailed program is organized down to hundreds of details. There, as well, there is no break even in times of emergency and stress, including the Great War. Cancellation of the festival will not better our situation, but will spread melancholy and weakness.[43]

The normality of the "Gentiles" is evident not in the absence of political crises, but in the durability of their traditions in the face of these crises. The crises are not even the justification of joy, but an extreme case which exemplifies the power of "normality." Joy is more than a potential political tool for strengthening social cohesiveness during crises. This joy—perhaps, precisely in its most kitschy expressions—was exactly what the Jews lacked throughout long generations in exile, and still lacked in the new life in Palestine.

No wonder, then, that Purim, and not another Jewish festival, was chosen to depict this joy. Exilic Purim was perceived as a cultural practice that employed "intoxicating means whose function was to artificially create a mood of happiness" in the "darkness" of exile.[44] Purim was thus perceived as the most fun and the most cosmopolite

---

[42] BT Ta'anit 29:1.

[43] Daniel Perski, "Al regel ahat" [On one foot], *Ha'aretz* 10.3.1933.

[44] Dr. A. Tenenbaum, "Hirhurim le-Purim" [Reflections for Purim], *Doar-Hayom* 8.3.1936.

festival in the Jewish calendar. Its "fun" feature was strong enough to overcome the initial recoiling from the "exilic" character of its story, in which the Jews are rescued in quite an unheroic and non-macho manner. Purim's fun also overrode the uncivilized manner of traditional Purim practices. Moreover, this "artificial joy" fitted the artificial happiness at the core of capitalist entertainment culture, as the carnival critics have fully recognized.[45]

The integration of pre-modern Purim traditions into capitalist mass-entertainment required interpretation and adjustment. Many people disliked the positioning of Queen Esther as the "patron-saint" of the celebrations, and as we have seen above, Uri Keisari even implied that unlike Esther, Haman was a man of principle and knew to sacrifice himself—like national heroes such as Yosef Trumpeldor.[46] Despite the criticism, the main figure of the celebrations was a pretty blonde girl, who used her body to save her people. Within this interpretive framework, the first Hebrew city was associated with biblical Shushan, the decadent, hedonist, and multi-lingual city. These allusions celebrated Tel Aviv as a city of freedom and enjoyment.

Nevertheless, Tel Aviv's cosmopolitanism was a component of its nationalism. In a manner similar to Herzl's vision, the cosmopolitan city was exclusively populated by Jews, who at least ideologically acted in whatever way they chose and could be whatever they wanted to be. They could develop an eclectic culture which borrowed cultural practices and motifs from every possible source at hand. It was a cosmopolitan nationalism. The only way in which it was different from Herzl's vision was that from Herzl's perspective, the main source of influence was "respectable" central-European bourgeois *Kultur*, whereas Tel Aviv inclined toward "happy" North American capitalist mass-entertainment.

The "folk" rhetoric served the same purpose. The wild character of past Purim practices was understood as a historical necessity expressed by the "people" against the double oppression: the

---

[45] Hayim Shorer, "Ivelet-Purim" [Purim stupidity], *Hapo'el Hatza'ir* 8 (19), 14.3.1930, 2–3; idem "Hamasekha sheli" [My mask], *Hapo'el Hatza'ir* 22–23, 18.3.1932, 12; Avraham Shvadron, "Ke-ein krovetz lakarnival" [Sort of a *krovetz*—the carnival bulletin], *Ha'aretz* 11.3.1931.

[46] Uri Keisari, "Keitzad anu tolim ...: Ester, ester, mizgi li yayin!" [How we hang ...: Esther, Esther, pour me wine], *Doar-Hayom* 24.3.1935.

political-economic oppression by non-Jews, and the moralistic-religious pressure of rabbinical authorities. Since Urban Zionist ideology encouraged having fun and freedom with clean conscience, there was no need to subvert the new hierarchies. Here, again, free expression of Jewish personal and collective freedom was embedded in the functional conception, according to which "the problem of the Jews" took priority over "the problem of Judaism." According to Helman, Tel Aviv culture was characterized by "a unique combination of collectivism and individualism."[47] Capitalist prosperity was simultaneously individual and collective, and Urban Zionist ideology attempted to fit the prosperity of collective body into the prosperity of each individual body.

According to this ideology, even the social pressure of other Zionist ideologies, which demanded conducting some social or cultural program, would not cause the "people" to respond with an anarchic reaction. Everyday life in Tel Aviv offered enough personal freedom that the power of these demands was not excessive, and thus dissipated the potential need to rebel against them.[48]

Eventually, there was some consensus that Purim was "one of those holidays which would have no place among the Jews of Bucharest, Warsaw, or Berlin, and which would never be organized there for all the world's fortune, since they lack the sea of Jaffa, the sky of the land of Israel, and the sense of building the homeland."[49] The freedom of the new life in Palestine, expressed in urban festive culture, and the "outing" of Jewish culture outdoors, symbolized by sun and blue sky, did not contradict the sense of building the homeland, but were embedded in it.

Needless to say, the city was not really as hedonist as depicted in the celebrations. Moreover, it was doubtful what "fun" was actually experienced by the carnival's visitors.[50] It seems safe to assume that the assessments of the street carnival and the balls as kitschy and provincial had a point. However, this is precisely the nature of an ideology, according to which happiness is a social and even moral imperative

---

[47] Helman 2007: 240.
[48] Helman 2006a: 388–389.
[49] Editorial article, *Doar-Hayom* 26.2.1929.
[50] See supra, chapter two; Bolitho 1933: 106–107.

rather than a reflection of reality. The celebrations were an annual opportunity to culturally perform the nationalist-hedonist ideology. The freedom was imagined through the festival, and this was crucial for the ability to imagine the city as a "Jewish" space in which Jews could do whatever they wanted. Rather than reverent emotions, it was mainly happiness that could produce this perception of space.

That said, it should be recognized that Tel Aviv was, and still is, a celebrating city. In the interwar period, Purim functioned as paradigmatic for the multiple celebrations that took place in the city during the rest of the year. In other words, Purim celebrated the ability to celebrate and that ability's realization. When Alterman wanted to ridicule the multiplicity of celebrations in Tel Aviv, he wrote a satiric song in which he declared a new festival named *"haglayada"* [festival + Adloyada]—a special holiday in which, as an exception to the rule, there would be no celebrations.[51]

Urban Zionism's view of the Jewish past, described above, was also linked to the value of freedom. It embedded the personal freedom with interpretive freedom and the eclectic gathering of cultural practices from various traditions. Like the capitalist market, in which everything becomes a commodity, the "market of symbolic goods" of national ideology could use every cultural practice, without being punctilious about its sources and with a focus on the here-and-now symbolic needs of nationalist ideology.[52]

In that context, it is interesting to note that before the establishment of the State of Israel in 1948, the term "liberalism" was not to be found in ideological discourse. Personal freedom was almost undiscussed in the frequent ideological debates in the Zionist public sphere. Some argue that the term "liberalism" was identified with the Jewish-German reform movement, which was mainly anti-Zionist and was attacked by Zionists as assimilationist.[53] In a broader context, it may be added that personal freedom was implicit in the lack of actual sovereignty on the part of Zionist institutions. Ideological debates regarding liberalism commonly focus on tensions between the individual and the state, and negotiate the limits of the state's right to interfere in

---

[51] Alterman 1977: 47–51.

[52] Bourdieu 1993: 112–141. On the usability with which nationalist movements choose their cultural practices see: Smith 1986: 177–206.

[53] Shimoni 1995: 124–125.

concrete social affairs.⁵⁴ In the case of Zionist institutions in the pre-statehood *Yishuv*, authority was mainly acknowledged by the power of voluntary membership of individuals, and this pre-conditioned the (many) social affairs in which they could interfere.⁵⁵ The real political sovereignty was in the hands of the British government, which indeed enforced a liberal value system on many occasions. Among the Zionist institutions, the Tel Aviv municipality was an exception with regard to the origin of its power, which was not voluntary; such liberal debates were frequently to be found in its local affairs. On the explicit ideological level, the discussion of the relationship between personal freedom and the state was not a Zionist problem until 1948, when liberalism suddenly entered political debates.⁵⁶

Nevertheless, the portrayal here illuminates the concept of personal freedom as an essential aspect of Zionist public culture. Each year, on Purim, it celebrated the personal freedom that Jews could achieve in Tel Aviv via the Zionist vision. It was not a matter of explicit doctrine, but an implicit assumption that was performed in the celebrations.

Interestingly, opponents of Zionism detected this element and attacked it with a rhetoric similar to Zionist doctrine in its organic conception. When the German-Jewish philosopher Herman Cohen (1842–1918) was asked why, as a conscious Jew, he did not support Zionism, he was said to have responded: "these folks only want to be happy."⁵⁷ In other words, he considered Zionism an opportunist attempt to convert the elevated spiritual and moral universal destiny of Judaism into a childish and irresponsible aspiration for happiness. On that issue, Cohen was in line with most Zionist thinkers who espoused the organic conception, such as Ahad-Ha'Am, A.D. Gordon, and Rabbi Kook: establishing a state for the Jews for the purpose of mere personal or collective happiness was not worth it. In their view, the Jews were different from all other nations who had the right to a political life for its own sake. However, Herzl and Purim celebrators in Tel Aviv would disagree.

---

54 See, for example: Avineri & De-Shalit 1992; and the classics: Berlin 1958.
55 Horowitz and Lissak 1978: 120–122, 213–230; Migdal 2001: 3–15, 25–49.
56 Rozin 2005; Rozin 2007.
57 Katz 1977: 52. Katz himself cites this quotation to make the opposite point: that nationalism can by no means get along with the search for personal happiness.

The ideational and emotional complexity of the "nationalist fun" may be exemplified in the following description of a children's carnival. The writer, A.Z. Ben-Yishai, chose to describe his feelings after watching the wonderful costumes of the children and the excited parents:

> I turn my face aside from the crowd and accumulate satisfaction [*Nachat*], like Joseph when revealing himself to his brothers: tears rise up in my throat. The cry-baby inside me doesn't lower his head in a time of joy, on a day which is full of light and sun and somewhat smells of the future. In front of my eyes appear, in a large distance, beyond the "azure-blue" [*tkhelet*] sea, all these hundreds of thousands of the children of Israel who are captive within the Gentiles and have not the slightest taste of what its [Israel's] children taste here on festivals and holidays. I feel sorry for you, distant captive children![58]

The wonderful happiness which is the share of Tel Aviv's children is more than theirs alone. This is a happiness of Jews who are safe in their homeland and can experience something that exile Jews can never experience: freedom and public Jewishness. The opposition of exile and homeland is further sharpened "on festivals and holidays," in which the children of exile feel "captive" (this word recurs twice), since they lack a Jewish public culture—while Tel Aviv's children live in a world of "light," "sun," and "azure-blue."

However, the dichotomy between darkness and light, captivity and freedom, between miserable Jews who live among Gentiles and happy Jews who live with each other—was brought in the text just in order to be emotionally broken down. The writer's happiness provoked his tears, which reminded him of the tears of Joseph with his brothers—one of the most emotionally ambivalent scenes in biblical literature, strongly involving happiness and sadness. Since the rhetorical emphasis here was on the sorrow of children in exile, it turned out that the fundamental emotional effect of the celebration was not happiness but sadness. The celebration reminded him, first of all, of the deep emotional void of other people. In other words, Ben-Yishai chose to emphasize the empty half of the glass—the imagined point

---

[58] A.Z. Ben-Yishai, "Rega'im: Purim shel tinokot" [Moments: A children's Purim], *Ha'aretz* 6.3.1928; CZA, file KKL5/4917/1.

of view of the exilic Other. This boundary-crossing introduced gloom into the nationalist project, so that eventually the attempt to define the new homeland as a place of sheer happiness could not fully succeed.

It should be mentioned, in that context, that the cancellation of the carnival was publicly justified by "the difficult situation" of world Jewry.[59] Although it was only an excuse, as we have seen here—this excuse and its place in the public discourse about emotions reflected the collapse of the dichotomy which divided the world into cheerful and sad places.

As the main festival of Zionist urbanity, Purim in Tel Aviv was the time and place in which freedom, fun, and glee were celebrated and glorified—as a Zionist ideology. The Zionist festive culture of the British Mandate period commemorated the eleventh of Adar, the Tel-Hai day, as the heroic sacrifice for the Nation. On Tu B'shvat and on Shavu'ot (the first fruit festival) it celebrated the renewed bond to the soil; on Hanukkah and Lag Ba'omer—the new masculine heroism; on the twentieth of Tamuz, the day Herzl died (*Yahrtzeit*) —the striving for political independence; and on Purim—the freedom, fun, and glee that were embedded in the creation of a Jewish public sphere.[60] This public sphere was the urban sphere of Tel Aviv, but unlike the city's jubilees, Purim was not a festival of the city alone, but a festival celebrating the significance of the existence of the permissive Jewish city for the entire *Yishuv*.[61] The urban new Jew knew to have fun.

Conclusion: Polyphonic Ideology

The past decade has witnessed a massive wave of academic and non-academic studies dedicated to Tel Aviv as the core of the Zionist vision and reality, from various perspectives.[62] Today, the history of the Zionist

---

[59] "Bney Tel-Aviv asurim bahagiga: Rak hayeladim rasha'im lismoakh" [Celebration is forbidden on Tel Avivians: Only the children are alowd to be happy], *Doar-Hayom* 3.3.1936; quoted also in the protocol of the meeting of the city directorate, 3.2.1936, TAMA 04–3222.

[60] See: Liebman & Don-Yehiya 1983; Zerubavel 1995; Ben-Amos 2004.

[61] On Tel Aviv's jubilees see: Azaryahu 2009.

[62] To mention only those available in English: Schlor 1999; LeVine 2005; Mann 2006; Azaryahu 2007a; Azaryahu 2009 and the entire volume there; Troen & Azaryahu 2011.

project seems much more diverse and complex than in the traditional focus on the narrative produced by Labor Movement-oriented elites. However, the story of Urban Zionism is different than other "alternative" histories which tell the story of marginalized minorities. In a retrospective view of the history of Zionism over more than a century, Zionism now seems to be a massive industrialization and urbanization project, not only compared with rural pre-Zionist Palestine, but also as compared with the life conditions of the Jews who immigrated to Palestine from elsewhere—mostly from Eastern European and Muslim countries. Contemporary central Israel (between, say, Haifa, Ashdod, and Jerusalem) is an entire urban space in which there is a constant shortage of available land, and agriculture and natural landscapes are rapidly vanishing. Israel is a large metropolis, with Tel Aviv as its "downtown." Tel Aviv is for Israel what Manhattan is for New York City.

The massive scholarly and non-scholarly contemporary interest in Tel Aviv is thus more than a correction of the historiographical bias toward pioneers' Zionism. This is a shift in the interest in Zionist history from the way it was desired by many, as a transformation of middle class Jews into farmers and warriors—*to the way it actually happened, as an ongoing urbanization*. Retrospectively, we now understand Zionism as the diametrical opposite of the early premises of Zionist agriculturalist ideology. The fact that so many people continue to imagine Israel as a rural space says a lot about the relationship between space and imagination and the power of myths.

The marginalization of Urban Zionist ideology in scholarship was the result of an overemphasis on Zionist ideology in the narrow doctrinal sense. From this point of view, shared by both Zionist doctrines and the lion's share of scholarship on Zionism, city life was positioned as a conceptual problem, a weird phenomenon that demanded explanation—usually by its reduction to a mere interest or strain.[63]

Nevertheless, the cultural power of Urban Zionism, as revealed in Purim celebrations, also reveals the ideological tension between a concrete geographical space, which was (and still is) an urban space in a rapid industrialization process, and a utopian agricultural space characterized by a return to the soil. True, the anti-urban ethos did influence politicians, builders, and planners: new Jewish cities were

---

[63] These are two common explanations for ideology, rejected by Geertz (1973: 201–207).

not built in Palestine during the British Mandate, and national funds were mostly invested in purchasing agricultural lands.[64] That said, the analysis of Zionist cultural practices portrays Zionist ideology as much less coherent, and much more complex and polyphonic than it seems at the political-doctrinarian level.

Superficially, one could conclude that the urban culture of Tel Aviv functioned as a "counter-culture" to the dominant Zionist ideology, or, as it is often being referred to nowadays in Israel, "the bubble."[65] However, it was not that simple. Although Tel Aviv's municipality was mostly controlled by the "civic bloc," Purim celebrations were by no means a sectoral festival of the Zionist middle-class or bourgeoisie alone. In fact, the existence of class categories (separate from ethnic and religious lines) in *Yishuv* society is doubtful, and the different forms of Zionist ideology cannot be linked to different social groups.[66] Purim celebrations were organized and attended by major Zionist institutions and persons, included those who, on other occasions, struggled against the hedonist and cosmopolitan urban culture. Bialik, for example, criticized the hedonist form of Tel Aviv's Sabbath, when most Tel Avivians were mainly frequenting the sea and the promenade, or visiting cafés, watching sports events, or shopping; whereas he preferred to create a more intellectualist culture, for which he and colleagues established the "*Oneg Sabbath*" association in 1926.[67] Bialik himself was a permanent guest at the Purim balls.[68] The most extreme example was that of Ussishkin, the president of the JNF from 1923 to 1939, who was among the loudest warriors in favor of Zionist socialism and puritan life. He attended the balls of 1926 and 1928 as the senior representative of the Jewish National Fund, and indeed was personally attacked by A. Z. Rabinowitch for allowing the immodesty of Hebrew Queen Esther pageants.[69]

---

[64] Cohen Eric 1977; Efrat 1984: 1–18; Troen 2003: 112–140.

[65] This seems to be Helman's implicit opinion (for example: Helman 2007: 100–101, 126, 137 and more).

[66] Bernstein 1998b.

[67] Shavit & Bigger 2001: 312–316; Helman 2007: 91–99.

[68] "Purim Tel-Aviv," *Davar* 26.3.1926.

[69] *Davar* 7.3.1928; "Purim be-Tel-Aviv" [Purim in Tel Aviv], *Ha'aretz* 1.3.1926; Carmiel 1999: 123; Azar [Rabinowitch], "Hirhurim" [Reflections], *Davar* 5.3.1929.

In other words, this urban "sub-culture" was not merely a "subversive" substream that opposed mainstream Zionist ideology, but an integral part of it. True, this particular component was not coherent with the other components of Zionist ideology, but this tension does not negate their inner links. It portrays this ideology as a living world—and hence polyphonic—rather than a one-dimensional logical system. The polyphonic character of Zionist ideology was not a plurality of opinions regarding an agreed-upon goal, as it was notably portrayed by writer Amos Oz, who spoke about many "first names" within the common "surname" of Zionism.[70] Rather, it was an essential polyphony, an existential condition that constituted hybrid identity, which was not articulated in explicit ideology. On the other hand, this was a Zionist identity, which constituted a nationalist public sphere.

In my opinion, the polyphonic character of Zionist ideology can explain its impressive success in creating a Jewish public sphere with an extremely powerful ideological force. The secret of the success of Zionist ideology was not its ability to "take hold of the masses" or its "revolutionary mystery"—obscured and suggestive expressions, which are commonly brought to air without serious theoretical accounts of modern nationalism. This common rhetoric depicts the success of nationalist ideology as a circular success of the obscuring rhetoric: "How did nationalist ideology succeed? Well, by using obscurity, imagination, irrationality. So, what is that obscured imagination? Well, this is an obscured matter which works on the irrational parts of human beings, on their primeval instincts." This circular mode of speaking indeed obscures rather than explains.

The unusual success of Zionist ideology in mobilizing varied Jewish publics was a consequence of its ability to show some flexibility and to contain contradictory elements.[71] The ability to conceptualize these internal contradictions through cultural means acknowledged the dominance of Zionism in the Jewish public sphere. As long as ideology is studied as mere doctrine, it seems an unclear conglomerate of unreasonable contradictions, or worse, as a mass neurosis that provokes irrational instincts. However, when ideology is studied as

---

[70] Oz 1983: 128.
[71] Laclau 1977: 161.

a socio-cultural practice, it is understood as a diversified and vivacious life form, with unexpected powers of subsistence.

For parts of Zionist cultural elites, the city's "cultural diversity was presented as 'Babel' and as a threat to the Zionist aim of consolidating a monolithic national culture."[72] It is not surprising, therefore, that it was precisely the city that made the plurality and heterogeneity of the new society its prominent trademark. The ideology of Urban Zionism, as performed in the Tel Aviv Purim carnival, depicted the new Jew as free to design her or his own identity using the multitude of cultural, ideological, and political options available in the capitalist Jewish city.

---

[72] Helman 2008: 122.

REFERENCES

Archives:

Posters collection, national library of Jerusalem
TAMA—Tel Aviv Municipal Archive
CZA—Central Zionist Archive
Archive of Israeli center for the documentation of stage arts, Tel Aviv University
Spielberg archive—the archive of Jewish cinema

Newspapers, Journals, and Newsletters:

Doar-Hayom
Davar
Ha'aretz
Ha-heirut
Ha-olam
Hapo'el Hatza'ir
Iton Me'yuhad
Kalno'a
Karnenu
Kerovetz Le-Purim Tartzah (for Purim 1935)
Ketuvim
Palestine Post
Turim
Yediot Iriyat Tel-Aviv (Tel Aviv municipal newsletter)

Bibliography

Abrahams, Israel. 1912. *The Book of Delight and Other Papers*. Philadelphia: The Jewish Publications Society.
— — —. 1934. *Festival Studies: Being Thoughts on the Jewish Year*. London: Edward Goldston.
Abrahams, Roger D. 1982. "The Language of Festivals: Celebrating the Economy." In *Celebrations: Studies in Festivity and Ritual*, ed. Victor Turner, 161–77. Washington, D.C.: Smithsonian Institute, 1982.
Agnew, Jean-Christophe. 1986. *Worlds Apart: The Market and the Theatre in Anglo-American Thought 1550–1750*. New York: Cambridge University Press.
Alexander, Jeffrey C. 2004. "Cultural Pragmatics: Social Performance between Ritual and Strategy." *Sociological Theory* 22, 4: 527–573.
— — —. 2006. *The Civil Sphere*. New York: Oxford University Press.
Alexander, Jeffrey C., & Philip Smith. 1998. "Cultural Sociology or Sociology of Culture: Towards a Strong Program for Sociology's Second Wind." *Sociologie et Societes* 30 (1): 107–116.
Almagor, Dan. 1993. "Masa ha-Adloyada" [The Procession of Adloyada]. *Leshonenu La'am* 44 (2): 51–60.
Almog, Oz. 2000. *The Sabra: The Creation of the New Jew*, trans. Haim Watzman. Berkeley: University of California Press.
Alroey, Gur. 2003. "Gedud Ha'avoda shel ba'aley melakha: sipuro shel etos shenikhshal" [The Work Battalion of the Craftsmen: The Story of a Failed Ethos]. *Iyunim Bitkumat Israel* 13: 255–275.
— — —. 2004. *Immigrantim: ha-hagira hayehudit le-eretz yisrael be-reshit hame'a ha-esrim* [Immigrants: Jewish Immigration to Palestine in the early 1900s]. Jerusalem: Yad Ben-Zvi.
Alterman, Nathan. 1976. *Regaim: Sefer Rishon Tartzad-Tartzaz* [Moments: The First Book, 1934–1937]. Tel Aviv: Hakibutz Hame'uhad.
— — —. 1977. *Pizmonim ve-shirei zemer* [Songs], Vol. 1, ed. Menachem Durman. Tel Aviv: Hakibbutz Hameuchad.
— — —. 1979. *Pizmonim ve-shirei zemer* [Songs], Vol. 2, ed. Menachem Durman. Tel Aviv: Hakibbutz Hameuchad.

Anderson, Benedict. 1983. *Imagined Communities: Reflections on the Origins and Spread of Nationalism*. London and New York: Verso.

Arand, Aharon. 1999. "Se'udat hapurim shel rava verav Zeyra bir'i parshaney hatalmud" [Purim Meal of Rava and rav Zeyra, as Reflected in Talmud Commentators]. *Badad* 8: 65–75.

Arendt, Hannah. 1958. *The Human Condition*. Chicago: The University of Chicago Press.

Arieh-Sapir, Nili. 2003. "Karnaval be-Tel-Aviv: Hagigot Purim ba-ir ha-ivrit ha-rishona" [Carnival in Tel Aviv: The Purim Festival in the "First" Hebrew City]. *Mehkarey yerushalayim be-folklore* 22: 99–121.

Arieh-Sapir, Nili. 1997. *Sipurei tekasim ve-hagigot be-Tel Aviv ba-shanim 1909–1936* [Stories of Ceremonies and Celebrations in Tel Aviv, 1909–1936]. PhD diss., Hebrew University, Jerusalem.

Arikha, Yoseph. 1969. *Tel Aviv: Mikra'ah historit-sifrutit; perakim be-divre yeme ha-'ir me-reshitah ve-'ad yamenu.* [Tel Aviv: A Historical-Literary Reader], Tel Aviv: Tel Aviv municipality.

Avineri, Shlomo, & Avner De-Shalit (Eds.). 1992. *Communitarianism and Individualism*. Oxford: Oxford University Press.

Azaryahu, Maoz. 2007a. *Tel Aviv: Mythography of a City*. Syracuse: Syracuse University Press.

———. 2007b. "Tel Aviv: Bein merkaz le-periferiyah" [Tel Aviv: Between Center and Periphery]. In *Bein Sderot li-Sderot Rothschild: Yahasei merkaz u-periferiyaa ba-tarbut ha-yisre'elit* [Between Sederot and Rothschild Boulevard: Center and Periphery in Israeli Culture], 167–193. Tel Aviv: Resling.

———. 2009. "Tel-Aviv's Birthdays: Anniversary Celebrations of the First Hebrew City 1929–1959." *Israel Studies* 14, 3: 1–20.

Bakhtin, Mikhail. 1968. *Rabelais and his World*, trans. Helene Iswolsky. Cambridge: MIT Press.

———. 1981. *The Dialogic Imagination: Four Essays*, trans. Caryl Emerson and Michael Holquist. Austin: University of Texas Press.

———. 1984. *Problems of Dostoevsky's Poetics*, trans. Caryl Emerson. Minneapolis: University of Minnesota Press.

Ballerino-Cohen, Coleen, Richard Wilk & Beverly Stoeltje (Eds.). 1996. *Beauty Queens on the Global Stage: Gender, Contest and Power*. London and New-York: Routledge.

Ballerino-Cohen, Coleen. 1995. "Marketing Paradise, Making Nation." *Annals of Tourism Research* 22 (2): 404–21.

Banet-Weiser, Sarah. 1999. *The Most Beautiful Girl in the World: Beauty Pageants and National Identity.* Berkeley: University of California Press.

Banner, Lois W. 1983. *American Beauty.* New York: Knopf.

Barber, Richard W. 1991. *Pilgrimages.* Woolbridge: Boydell Press.

Bar-Gal, Yoram. 2003. *Propaganda and Jewish Education: The Jewish National Fund 1924–1947.* Rochester: the University of Rochester Press.

Bar-Ilan, Meir. 1987. "Rishumah shel i-yedi'at hakeri'a al hilkhot Megillah ve-Hallel" [The Consequences of Illiteracy on the Laws of Megillah and Hallel]. *Proceedings of the American Academy for Jewish Research* 54: 12–1.

Bar-Navi, Elli. 1986. "Ha-teritoriya shel ha-historiyon: Dialog im Emmanuel Le Roy Ladurie" [The Historian's Territory: A Dialogue with Emmanuel Le Roy Ladurie]. *Zemanim* 21: 58–69.

Bartal, Israel. 1998. "Cossack U-Bedu'i: Olam hadimuyim hale'umi hakhadash" [A Cossack and a Bedouin: The New Nationalist Images]. In *Ha-aliya hashniya: Mehkarim* [The Second Immigration: Studies], ed. Israel Bartal, 482–493. Jerusalem: Yad Ben-Zvi.

———. 2002. "Mavo: "Tarbut Israel o 'tarbuyot Israel'?" [Introduction: Israeli Culture or Israeli Cultures?]. In *Ha'agala ha-mele'a: Me'a ve-esrim shenot tarbut Israel* [The Full Carriage: A Hundred and Twenty Years of Israeli Culture], ed. Israel Bartal, 7–16. Jerusalem: Magnes.

Belkin, Ahuva. 1997. *Bein Shtey Arim: Hamahaze ha-ivri Simhat Purim* [A tale of two cities: The Hebrew play "Purim Joy"]. Lod: Haberman institute.

———. 2001. "The Scarf and the Toothache: Cross-Dressing in the Jewish Folk Theatre." In *Masquerade and Identities: Essays on Gender, Sexuality and Marginality,* ed. Efrat Tseëlon, 101–113. London and New York: Routledge.

———. 2002. *Ha-Purim-Spiel: Iyunim ba-te'atron ha-amami ha-yehudi* (The Purimspiel: Study of Jewish Folk Theatre). Jerusalem: Bialik Institute.

Ben-Amos, Avner. 2000. *Funerals, Politics, and Memory in Modern France, 1789–1996.* New York: Oxford University Press.

———. 2004. "Bama'agal ha-mezamer ve-hameraked: Tekasim patriyotiyim vahagogit ba-hevra ha-yisre'elit" [In the Dancing and Singing Circle: Patriotic Rites and Festivities in Israeli Society]. In *Patriotism: Ohavim otakh moledet* [We Love You, Homeland], ed. Avner Ben-Amos and Daniel Bar-Tal, 275–315. Tel Aviv: Dyunon.

Ben-Artzi, Yossi. 1996. "Between East and West: In Search of a "Local" Architecture in Palestine." In *The Mosaic of Israeli Geography*, ed. Yehuda Gradus and Gabriel Lipshitz, 441–449. Beer Sheva: Ben-Gurion University of the Negev Press.

Bendix, Regina. 1997. *In Search of Authenticity: The Formation of Folklore Studies*. Madison: The University of Wisconsin Press.

Ben-Israel, Hedva. 1996. "Heker ha-le'umiyut kefenomen histori" [The Study of Nationalism as a Historical Phenomenon]. In *Le-umiyut u-folitika yehudit: Perspektivot hadashot* [Jewish Nationalism and Politics: New Perspectives], ed. Judah Reinhartz, Gideon Shimoni and Yosef Salmon, 57–80. Jerusalem: Shazar center.

Bennett, Susan. 1997. *Theatre Audiences: A Theory of Production and Reception*. New-York: Routledge (2nd Edition).

Ben-Porat, Amir. 1999. *Heikhan hem ha-burganim ha-hem? Toldot ha-burganut ha-Yisre'elit* [Where are Those Bourgeois? The History of Israeli Bourgeoisie]. Jerusalem: Magnes.

Ben-Yishai, A. Z. 1936. *Tel-Aviv*. Jerusalem: Keren Hayesod.

Berger, John. 1980. *About Looking*. New York: Pantheon Books.

Berkowitz, Michael (Ed.). 2004. *Nationalism, Zionism and Ethnic Mobilization of the Jews in 1900 and Beyond*. Leiden: Brill.

–––. 1993. *Zionist Culture and West European Jewry before the First World War*. Cambridge: Cambridge University Press.

–––. 1997. "The Invention of a Secular Ritual: Western Jewry and Nationalized Tourism in Palestine, 1922–1933." In *The Seductiveness of Jewish Myth: Challenge or Response?*, ed. S. Daniel Breslauer, 73–95. Albany: State University of New York Press.

Berlin, Isaiah. 1958. *Two Concepts of Liberty*. London: Oxford University Press.

Berman, Joshua A. 2001. "'Hadassah bat Abihail': The Evolution from Object to Subject in the Character of Esther." *Journal of Biblical Literature* 120, 4: 647–669.

Berman, Lila Corwin. 2009. *Speaking of Jews: Rabbis, Intellectuals, and the Creation of an American Public Identity*. Berkeley: University of California Press.

Bernstein, Deborah (Ed.). 1992. *Pioneers and Homemakers: Jewish Women in Pre-State Israel*. New York: State University of New York Press.

–––. 1998a. "Daughters of the Nation: Between the Public and Private Spheres in Pre-state Israel." In *Jewish Women in Historical*

Perspective, ed. Judith R. Baskin, 287–311. Detroit: Wayne State University Press.

———. 1998b. "Strategies of Equalization, a Neglected Aspect of the Split Labor Market Theory: Jews and Arabs in the Split Labor Market of Mandatory Palestine." *Ethnic and Racial Studies* 21 (3): 449–475.

———. 2008. *Nashim bashulayim: Migdar u-leumiyut be-Tel-Aviv ha-mandatorit* [Women in the Margins: Gender and Nationalism in Mandate Tel Aviv]. Jerusalem: Yad Ben-Zvi.

Biale, David. 1994. "Confessions of a Historian of Jewish Culture." *Jewish Social Studies* 1 (1): 40–51.

———. 1997. *Eros and the Jews: From Biblical Israel to Contemporary America*. Berkeley: University of California Press.

———. 2002. "Preface," *Cultures of the Jews*, ed. David Biale, xvii-xxxiii. New York: Schoken.

Bialik, Hayim Nahman. 1960. *Kol Kitvey H.N. Bialik* [The Entire Writings of H.N. Bialik]. Tel Aviv: Dvir.

Bilu, Yoram. 2004. "The Sanctification of Space in Israel: Civil Religion and Folk Judaism." In *Jews in Israel: Contemporary Social and Cultural Patterns*, ed. Uzi Rebhun and Chaim I. Waxman, 371–393. Hanover: Brandeis University Press.

Bivans, Ann-Marie. 1991. *Miss America: In Pursuit of the Crown; The Complete Guide to Miss America Pageant*. New York: Master Media.

Bolitho, Hector. 1933. *Besides Galilee: A Diary in Palestine*. New York: D. Appleton-Century Company.

Bonnel, Victoria E. & Lynn Hunt (Eds.). 1999. *Beyond the Cultural Turn?* Berkeley: University of California Press.

Borland, Catherine. 1996. "The India Bonita of Monimbo: The Politics of Ethnic Identity in the New Nicaragua." In *Beauty Queens on the Global Stage: Gender, Contest and Power*, ed. Coleen Ballerino-Cohen, Richard Wilk and Beverly Stoeltje, 75–88. London and New York: Routledge.

Boucher, Francois. 1987. *20,000 Years of Fashion*. London and New York: Thames and Hudson.

Bourdieu, Pierre. 1993. *The Field of Cultural Production*, ed. Randal Johnson. New York: Columbia University Press.

Boyarin, Daniel. 1994. "Introduction: Purim and the Cultural Poetics of Judaism; Theorizing Diaspora." *Poetics Today* 15 (1): 1–8.

Boyer, Pascal. 1987. "The Stuff "Traditions" Are Made Of: On the Implicit Ontology of an Ethnographic Category." *The Philosophy Of Social Science* 17: 49–65.

―――. 1990. *Tradition as Truth and Communication: A Cognitive Description of Traditional Discourse*. Cambridge: Cambridge University Press.

Brenner, Athalya. 1995. "Looking at Esther through the looking Glass." In *The Feminist Companion to Esther, Judith and Susanna*, ed. Athalya Brenner, 73–85. Sheffield: Academic Press.

Brenner, Yosef Haim. 1961. *Kol kitve Y. H. Brener*, kerekh sheni [The Writings of Y.H. Brenner, volume 2]. Tel Aviv: Hakibutz hame'uḥad.

Brightman, Robert. 1995. "Forget Culture: Replacement, Transcendence, Relexification." *Cultural Anthropology* 10 (4): 509–546.

Brodsky, Adriana Mariel. 2004. *The Contours of Identity: Sephardic Jews and the Construction of Jewish Community in Argentina, 1880 to the Present*. PhD Diss., Duke University, Durham, NC.

―――. 2012. ""Miss Sefaradí," and "Queen Esther': Sephardim, Zionism, and Ethnic and National Identities in Argentina, 1933–1976." *Estudios Interdisciplinarios de América Latina y el Caribe* 23 (1): 35–60.

Brubaker, Roger. 1996. *Nationalism Reframed: Nationhood and the National Question in the New Europe*. Cambridge: Cambridge University Press.

Burke, Peter. 1987. *Popular Culture in Early Modern Europe*. London: Temple Smith.

―――. 1992. *History and Social Theory*. Cambridge: Polity Press.

Bursztyn, Yigal. 1990. *Panim Kisede-kerav: Ha-historiya hakolno'it shel hapanim hayisre'eliyot* [The Face as a Battlefield: The Cinematic History of Israeli Face]. Tel Aviv: Hakibutz Hame'uhad.

Byrde, Penelope. 1979. *The Male Image: Men's Fashion in Britain 1300–1970*. London: Batsford.

Cannadine, David. 2001. *Ornamentalism: How the British Saw Their Empire*. New York: Oxford University Press.

Carmi, Shulamit & Henry Rosenfeld. 1971. "Immigration, Urbanization and Crisis: The Process of Jewish Colonization in Palestine during the 1920s." *International Journal of Comparative Sociology* 12: 41–57.

Carmiel, Batya. 1999. *Tel Aviv be-tahposet va-keter: Hagigot Purim 1912–1935* [*Tel Aviv Crowned and Costumed: Purim Celebrations 1912–1935*]. Tel Aviv: Eretz-Israel Museum.

―――. 2004. *Korbman: Tzalam Tel-Avivi aher, 1919–1936* [Korbman: A Different Tel-Avivian Photographer, 1919–1936]. Tel Aviv: Eretz-Israel Museum.

Chartier, Roger. 1988. *Cultural History*, trans. Lydia G. Cochrane. Cambridge: Polity Press.

Chaterjee, Partha. 1993. *The Nation and its Fragments: Colonial and Postcolonial Histories*. Princeton: Princeton University Press.

Chaudhuri, Una (Ed.). 2007. *Animals and Performance*. Special issue of *The Drama Review* 51, 1.

— — —. 2009. "'Of All Nonsensical Things': Performance and Animal Life." *PMLA* 124, 2: 520–525.

Clutton-Brock, Juliet. 1992. *Horse Power: A History of the Horse and the Donkey in the Human Societies*. Cambridge: Harvard University Press.

Cohen, Eric. 1977. "The City in Zionist Ideology." *Jerusalem Quarterly* 4: 126–144.

— — —. 1992. "Pilgrimage and Tourism: Convergence and Divergence." In *Sacred Journeys: The Anthropology of Pilgrimage*, ed. Alan Morinis, 47–61. Connecticut and London: Greenwood.

Cohen, Gershon David. 1996. "The Song of Songs and the Jewish Religious Mentality." *The Samuel Friedland Lectures 1960–1966*, 1–21. New York: JTS.

Cohen, Uri S. 2003. "Hahaya Hatziyonit" [The Zionist Animal]. *Mehkarei Yerushalayim be-sifrut ivrit* 19: 167–217.

Cohen-Hattab, Kobi. 2006. *Latur et ha-aretz: Ha-tayarut be-Eretz Yisrael bi-tkufat ha-mandat ha-briti* [Exploring the Land: Tourism in Palestine during the British Mandate]. Jerusalem: Yad Ben-Zvi.

Cohn, Bernard S. [1987] 2000. *An Anthropologist among the Historians and Other Essays*. New Delhi: Oxford University Press.

DaMatta, Roberto. 1984. "Carnival in Multiple Planes." In *Rite, Drama, Festival, Spectacle: Rehearsals Toward A Theory of Cultural Performances*, ed. J. J. MacAloon, 208–240. Philadelphia: The Institute for the Studies of Human Issues.

Darnton, Robert. 1984. *The Great Cat Massacre and other Episodes in French Cultural History*. New York: Basic Books.

Davis, Natalie Zemon. 1978. "Women on Top: Symbolic Sexual Inversion and Political Disorder in Early Modern Europe." In *The Reversible World: Symbolic Inversion in Art and Society*, ed. Barbara A. Babcock, 147–190. Ithaca and London: Cornell University Press.

— — —. 1983. *The Return of Martin Guerre*. Cambridge: Harvard University Press.

— — —. 1987. *Society and Culture in Early Modern France*. Cambridge: Polity Press.

Derrida, Jacques. 2002. "The Animal That Therefore I Am (More to Follow)." *Critical Inquiry* 28: 369–418.
Dinur, Ben-Tzion (Ed.). 1955. *Toldot ha-Haganah, kerekh alef: Mehitgonenut le-hagana* [The History of Israeli Defense, volume 1: From Defending to Defense]. Tel Aviv: Ma'arakhot.
Doniach, Nakdimon S. 1933. *Purim, or the Feast of Esther*. Philadelphia: The Jewish Publication Society of America.
Dotan, Shmuel. 1999. "Me-hag ha-Hanukah le-'hag ha-hashmona'im': Tzmihato shel "hag le'umi" tziyoni" [From the Festival of Hanukah to "The Festival of the Hasmoneans": The Emergence of Hanukah as a Zionist Festival]. *Mehkarei Hag* 10: 29–53.
Douglas, Mary. 1966. *Purity and Danger: An Analysis of Concepts of Pollution and Taboo*. New York: Praeger.
―――. 1975. *Implicit Meanings: Essays in Anthropology*. London: Routledge & Kegan Paul.
―――. 1982. *Natural Symbols: Explorations in Cosmology*. New York: Pantheon.
Drory, Yigal. 1987. "Hit'argenut hama'amd he-beinoni be-eretz Israel: Nisyonot le-hit'argenut politit bishnot he-esrim" [The Organization of the Middle Class in Palestine: Attempts of Political Organizations in the 1920s]. *Katedra* 44: 116–125.
―――. 1990. *Ben yamin li-semol: "ha-ḥugim ha-ezraḥiyim" bi-shenot ha-esrim* [Between Right and Left: "Civil Circles" in the 1920s and 1930s]. Tel Aviv: Mif'alim universitaiyim.
Druyan, Nitza. 1982. *Lelo Marvad Kesamim: Yehudei Teyman be-eretz yisrael 1883–1914* [No Magic Carpet: Yemenite Jews in Palestine 1882–1914]. Jerusalem: Yad Ben-Zvi.
Druyanov, Alter (Ed.). 1936. *Sefer Tel Aviv* [The Book of Tel Aviv]. Tel Aviv: Tel Aviv Municipality.
Dunning, Eric. 1999. *Sport Matters: Sociological Studies of Sport, Violence, and Civilization*. London and New York: Routledge.
Durkheim, Emile. 1915. *The Elementary Forms of the Religious Life*. London: Allen & Unwin.
―――. 2008 [1912]. *The Elementary Forms of Religious Life*, trans. Carol Cosman. Oxford and New York: Oxford University Press.
Efrat, Elisha. 1984. *Urbanization in Israel*. London: Croom Helm.
Eidar, Dror. 2003. *Alterman–Baudelaire, Paris–Tel Aviv: Urbaniyut u-mitos be-shirei "pirhei ha-ra" ve-"kokhavim ba-hutz"* [Urbanism and Myth in the Poetry of Nathan Alterman and Charles Baudelaire]. Jerusalem: Carmel.

Eilberg-Schwartz, Howard (Ed.). 1992. *People of the Body: Jews and Judaism from an Embodied Perspective*. Albany: SUNY.

Eisenstadt, Shmuel Noah. 1983. *Tradition, Change and Modernity*. New York: John Wiley and Sons.

— — —. 1998. "Did Zionism Bring the Jews back to History?" *Jewish Studies* 38: 9–29.

Eliade, Mircea. 1954. *The Myth of the Eternal Return, or Cosmos and History*, trans. Willard R. Trask. Princeton: Princeton University Press.

Elias, Norbert & Eric Dunning. 1986. *Quest for Excitement: Sport and Leisure in the Civilizing Process*. Oxford: Basil Blackwell.

Elias, Norbert. 1978. *The Civilizing Process: The History of Manners*, trans. Edmund Jephcott. Oxford: Blackwell Publishers.

Eliav, Mordechai. 1974. "Me'ora'ot yafo be-Purim tarsakh" [The Riots in Jaffa on Purim 1908]. *Hatziyonut* 3: 152–197.

Eshel, Ruth. 1991. *Lirkod im ha-halom: Reshit ha-mahol ha-omanuti be-Erets-Yisra'el, 1920–1964* [Dancing with the Dream: The Beginnings of Artistic Dancing in Palestine, 1920–1964]. Tel Aviv: Sifriyat po'alim.

Even-Zohar, Itamar. 1981. "The Emergence of a Native Hebrew Culture in Palestine, 1882–1948." *Studies in Zionism* 4: 167–184

Falk, Raphael. 2006. "Zionism, Race, and Eugenics." In *Jewish Tradition and the Challenge of Darwinism*, ed. Geoffrey Cantor and Marc Swetlitz, 137–162. Chicago: University of Chicago Press.

Feldstein, Ariel L. 2009. *Halutz, Avoda, Matzlema: Ha-kolno'a besherut ha-idiologiya ha-tziyonit 1917–1939* [Pioneer, Toil, Camera: Cinema in Service of the Zionist Ideology 1917–1939]. Tel Aviv: Am Oved.

Fireberg, Hayim. 2003a. "Hagralat hamigrashim shel Akhuzat-Bayit: Hivatzruta shel mitologiya ironit" [The Land Lottery of Akhuzat Bayit: The Creation of Urban Mythology]. *Israel* 4: 87–103.

— — —. 2003b. *Tel-Aviv: Temurot, retzef ve-ribuy panim shel hevra ve-tarbut ironiyim bitkufat ma'avak, 1936–1948* [Tel Aviv: Transformations, Continuum and Multiplicity of Urban Culture and Society in Time of Struggle, 1936–1948]. PhD diss., Tel Aviv University.

Fisch, Harold. 1994. "Reading and Carnival: On the Semiotics of Purim." *Poetics Today* 15, 1: 55–74.

Fisher, Yona (Ed.). 1984. *Tel Aviv: 75 shanah shel omanut* [Tel Aviv: 75 Years of Art]. Tel Aviv: Masada.

Fogiel-Bijaoui, Sylvie. 1992. "On the Way to Equality? The Struggle for Women's Suffrage in the Jewish Yishuv, 1917–1926." In *Pioneers and Homemakers: Jewish Women in Pre-State Israel*, ed. Debora Bernstien, 211–233. New York: State University of New York Press.

Frazer, James George. 1994. *The Golden Bough*, ed. Robert Frazer. Oxford: Oxford University Press.

Frenkel, Michal, Yehuda Shenhav & Hanna Herzog. 2000. "The Ideological Wellspring of Zionist Capitalism: The Impact of Private Capital and Industry on the Shaping of the Dominant Zionist Ideology." In *The New Israel: Peacemaking and Liberalization*, eds. Gershon Shafir and Yoav Peled, 43–69. Boulder: Westview.

Gadamer, Hans-George. 2002. *Truth and Method*, trans. J. Weinsheimer and D.G. Marshal. New York: Continuum (2nd ed.).

Gaster, Theodor Hertzl. 1953. *Festivals of the Jewish Year*. New-York: William Sloane.

– – –. 1969. *Myth, Legend and Custom in the Old Testament*. New-York: Harper and Row.

Geertz, Clifford. 1973. *Interpretation of Cultures: Selected Essays*. New York: Basic Books.

– – –. 1990. "History and Anthropology." *New Literary History* 21 (2): 321–335.

Gellner, Ernst. 1983. *Nations and Nationalism*. Ithaca: Cornell University Press.

Genihovsky Dov. 1994. "Lekorot "Hag Haperahim" birushalayim ve-Tel-Aviv" [The History of "The Flower Festival" in Jerusalem and Tel Aviv]. *Ariel* 100–101: 72–81.

Gertz, A. (Ed.). 1947. *Statistical Handbook of Jewish Palestine*. Jerusalem: Jewish Agency.

Giladi, Dan. 1973. *Ha-Yishuv bi-tekufat ha-'aliyah ha-revi'it (1924–1929): Behinah kalkalit u-folitit* [The Yishuv during the Fourth Immigration (1924–1929): A Political Economic Study]. Tel Aviv: Am oved.

Ginzburg, Carlo. 1992. *The Cheese and the Worms: The Cosmos of a Sixteenth-Century Miller*, trans. John and Anne Tedeschi. Baltimore: Johns Hopkins University Press.

Goldberg, Yossi. 2005. "Hitpathut tashtit ha-tayarut be-Tel Aviv bi-tkufat ha-shilton ha-briti (1917–1948)" [The Development of the Tourism Infrastructure in Mandatory Tel Aviv]. M.A. thesis, Bar-Ilan University, Ramat Gan.

Goldstein, Jacob & Yaacov Shavit. 1981. "Yosef Trumpeldor kidmut mofet ve-haviku'akh al "shayakhuto" hatnu'atit" [Josef Trumpeldor as a Role Model and the Debate regarding his Political "Affiliation"]. *Kivunim* 12: 9–21.

Goodman, Philip. 1949. *Purim Anthology*. Philadelphia: The Jewish Publications Society.

———. 1950. "The Purim Association of the City of New York (1862–1902)." *Publications of the American Jewish Historical Society* 40 (1–4): 135–172.

Gordon, Aharon David. 1957. *Ha-uma veha-Avoda* [The Nation and the Labor]. Tel Aviv: Haifa council of workers and Zionist library.

Gorski, Philip. 2000. "The Mosaic Moment: An Early Modernist Critique of Modernist Theories of Nationalism." *American Journal of Sociology* 105 (5): 1428–1468.

Govrin, Nurit. 1985. *"Me'ora Brenner": Hama'avak al hofesh habituy* ["The Brenner Controversy": The Struggle for the Freedom of Speech]. Jerusalem: Yad ben-Zvi.

Graicer, Iris. 1989. "Social Architecture in Palestine: Conceptions in Working-Class Housing, 1920–1938." In *The Land That Became Israel: Studies in Historical Geography*, ed. Ruth Kark, 287–307. New Haven: Yale University Press.

Greenberg, Moshe. 1996. *Ezekiel 1–20: A New Translation with Introduction and Commentary*. Garden City, NY: Doubleday.

Gross, Nahum. 2000. *Lo al ha-ruah levadah: Iyunim bahistoryah hakalkalit shel Erets-Yisra'el ba-et ha-hadashah* [Not Merely on the Spirit: Studies in the Economic History of Modern Palestine]. Jerusalem: Magnes.

Gross, Nathan & Yaakov Gross. 1991. *Ha-seret ha-ivri: Perakim betoldot ha-re'ino'a ve-hakolno'a be-Israel, 1896–1991* [The Hebrew Cinema: The History of Israeli Cinema, 1896–1991]. Jerusalem: self-published.

Gunn, Simon. 2001. "The Spatial Turn: Changing Histories of Space and Place." In *Identities in Space: Contested Terrains in the Western City since 1850*, ed. Simon Gunn and Robert J. Morris, 1–18. Aldershot and Burlington: Ashgate.

Habermas, Jürgen. 1989. *The Structural Transformation of the Public Sphere: An Inquiry into a Category of Bourgeois Society*, trans. Thomas Burger with Frederick Lawrence. Cambridge: MIT Press.

Halachmi, Yosef. 1995. *Vihi Mah: Perakim bedivrey yemey haseret ha'ivri* [No Matter What: Chapters in the History of Hebrew Cinema]. Jerusalem: Spielberg archive.

Halamish, Aviva. 2006. *Be-meruts kaful neged ha-zeman: Mediniyut ha-'aliyah ha-Tsiyonit bi-shenot ha-sheloshim* [Running against Time: Zionist Immigration Policy in the 1930s]. Jerusalem: Yad Ben-Zvi.

Hall, Colin Michael. 1995. *Hallmark Tourist Events: Impacts, Managements and Planning*. London: Belhaven.
Hall, Stuart. 1980. "Cultural Studies: Two Paradigms." *Media, Culture and Society* 2: 57–72.
Halperin, Hagit (Ed.). 1997. *Me-agvaniya ad Simfoniya: Hashira hakala shel Avraham Shlonsky u-farodiyot al Yetzirato* [From Tomato to Symphony: Song-writing of Abraham Shlonsky and Parodies on his Work]. Tel Aviv: Sifriyat Po'alim.
Halperin, Liora. 2011. *Babel in Zion: The Politics of Language Diversity in Jewish Palestine 1920–1948*. Ph.D Diss., UCLA.
Handelman, Don. 1990. *Models and Mirrors: Towards an Anthropology of Public Events*. Cambridge: Cambridge University Press.
Handler, Richard. 1988. *Nationalism and the Politics of Culture in Quebec*. Madison: The University of Wisconsin Press.
Hanegbi, Zohar. 1998. "Minhagey ha-Purim bahalakha u-va-omanut" [Purim Customs in Halakha and Art]. In *Minhagey Yisrael* [The Customs of Israel], Volume 6, ed. Daniel Sperber, 192–206. Jerusalem: Rabbi Kook Institution.
Har'el, Yaron. 2004. "Likhvod ha-umah ve-likhvod elohey yisrael: Hashpa'at hareformot ha-othmaniot al bitul minhag haka'at Haman ve-Amalek" [To Honor the Nation and God: The Influence of Ottoman Reforms on the Cancellation of the Beating of Haman and Amalek." *Ladinar* 3: 9–30.
Harari, Yehudit. 1947. *Bein Hakeramim* [Between the Vineyards], volume II. Tel Aviv: Dvir.
Haris, Monford. 1977. "Purim: The Celebration of Dis-Order." *Judaism* 26: 161–170.
Harshav, Benjamin. 1993. *Language in Time of Revolution*. Berkeley: University of California Press.
Hayman, David. 1983. "Toward A Mechanics of Mode: Beyond Bakhtin." *Novel* 16 (2): 101–120.
Hazan, Meir. 2002. "Reshit ha-metinut be-mifleget Hapo'el Hatza'ir bashanim 1905–1917" [The Beginnings of the Moderateness Policy in Hapo'el Hatza'ir Party in the Years 1905–1917]. *Iyunim Bitkumat Israel* 12: 239–269.
Hazony, Yoram. 1995. *The Dawn*. Jerusalem: Shalem.
Heelas, Paul. 1996. "Introduction: Detraditionalization and its Rivals." In *Detraditionalization*, ed. P. Heelas, P. Morris and S. Lash, 1–20. Cambridge: Blackwell Publishers.

Helman, Anat. 1999. "East or West: Tel Aviv in the 1920s and 1930s." *Studies in Contemporary Jewry* XV: 68–79.
— — —. 2003. "European Jews in the Levant Heat: Climate and Culture in 1920s and 1930s Tel Aviv." *Journal of Israeli History* 22 (1): 71–90.
— — —. 2006a. "Two Urban Celebrations in Jewish Palestine." *Journal of Urban History* 32 (3): 380–403.
— — —. 2006b. "Hues of Adjustment: "Landsmanshaftn" in Inter-war New York and Tel-Aviv." *Jewish History* 20 (1): 41–67.
— — —. 2007. *Or ve-yam hikifuha: Tarbut Tel Avivit bi-tkufat ha-mandat* [Surrounded by Light and Sea: Tel Avivian Culture during the Mandate]. Haifa: Haifa University Press.
— — —. 2008. "Was There Anything Particularly Jewish about "the First Hebrew City'?" In *The Art of Being Jewish in Modern Times*, ed. Barbara Kirshenblatt-Gimblett and Jonathan Karp, 116–127. Philadelphia: University of Pennsylvania Press.
— — —. 2010. *Young Tel Aviv: A Tale of Two Cities*, trans. Haim Watzman. Waltham: Brandeis University Press.
Herzfeld, Michael. 1982. *Ours Once More: Folklore, Ideology, and the Making of Modern Greek*. Austin: University of Texas Press.
Herzl, Theodor. 1987. *Old-New Land (Altneuland)*, trans. Lotta Levinson. New York: Markus Wiener Publishing and the Herzl Press.
— — —. 1998. *Inyan Hayehudim: Sifrey yoman 1895–1904* [Jewish Affairs: Diary 1895–1904], Volume 1, trans. Yosef Vancrat. Jerusalem: Bialik institution and Zionist Library.
Herzog, Hanna. 2002. "Redefining Political Spaces: A Gender Perspective on the "Yishuv" Historiography." *Journal of Israeli History* 21 (1–2): 1–25.
Hirsch, Dafna. 2008. "'Interpreters of Occident to the Awakening Orient': The Jewish Public Health Nurse in Mandate Palestine." *Comparative Studies in Society and History* 50 (1): 227–255.
Hirschfeld, Ariel. 2002. "Locus and Language: Hebrew Culture in Israel, 1890–1990." In *Cultures of the Jews*, ed. David Biale, 1011–1160. New York: Schoken.
Hoberman, J. 1991. *Bridge of Light: Yiddish Film between Two Worlds*. New York: The Museum of Modern Art.
Hobsbawm, Erik & Terence Ranger (Eds.). 1983. *The Invention of Tradition*. Cambridge: Cambridge University Press.
Hobsbawm, Erik J. 1992. *Nations and Nationalism since 1780: Programme, Myth, Reality*. New York: Cambridge University Press.

Hollander, Anne. 1994. *Sex and Suits*. New York: Knopf.
Horowitz, Dan & Moshe Lissak. 1978. *Origins of the Israeli Polity: Palestine under the Mandate*. Chicago: University of Chicago Press.
Horowitz, Elliot. 1994. "The Rite to be Reckless: On the Perpetration and Interpretation of Purim Violence." *Poetics Today* 15 (1): 9–54.
———. 2006. *Reckless Rites: Purim and the Legacy of Jewish Violence*. Princeton and Oxford: Princeton University Press.
Hunt, Lynn (Ed.). 1989. *The New Cultural History*. Berkeley: University of California Press.
Hyman, Paula E. 1995. *Gender and Assimilation in Modern Jewish History: The Roles and Representation of Women*. Seattle: University of Washington Press.
Joselit, Jenna Weissman. 1994. *The Wonders of America: Reinventing Jewish Culture 1880–1950*. New York: Hill and Wang.
Kahn, Dorothy Ruth. 1936. *Spring Up, O Well*. London: Jonathan Cape.
Kapakh, Yosef. 1961. *Halikhot Teiman: Khayey Hayehudim Be-tzan'a Uvnoteiha* [Yemenite Ways: Jewish Life in Greater Tzan'a]. Jerusalem: Yad Ben-Zvi & Kiryat Sefer.
Kaplan, Marion A. 1991. *The Making of Jewish Middle Class: Women, Family, and Identity in Imperial Germany*. Oxford: Oxford University Press.
Kark, Ruth. 1980. "Ha-kehila ha-yehudit be-yafo be-sof tekufat ha-shilton ha-otomani" [The Jewish Community in Jaffa in the End of Ottoman Period]. *Katedra* 16: 13–24.
———. 1990. *Jaffa: A City in Evolution, 1799–1917*, trans. Gila Brand. Jerusalem: Yad Ben-Zvi.
Karlinsky, Nahum. 2005. *California Dreaming: Ideology, Society, and Technology in the Citrus Industry of Palestine, 1890–1939*, trans. Naftali Greenwood. Albany: State University of New York Press.
Katriel, Tamar. 2011. "Precursors to Postmodern Spirituality in Israeli Cultural Ethos." In *Kabbalah and Contemporary Spiritual Revival*, ed. Boaz Huss, 311–328. Beer-Sheva: Ben-Gurion University of the Negev Press.
Katz, Jacob. 1977. "Zionism and Jewish Identity." *Commentary* 63 (5): 48–52.
———. 1979. *Le'umiyut yehudit: Masot u-mehkarim* [Jewish Nationalism: Essays and Studies]. Jerusalem: Zionist Publication.
Katz, Yossi. 1986. "Ideology and Urban Development: Zionism and the Origins of Tel-Aviv, 1906–1914." *Journal of Historical Geography* 12, 4: 402–424.

Kaynar, Gad. 1998. "National Theatre as Colonized Theatre: The Paradox of Habima." *Theatre Journal* 50, 1: 1–20.

Kellerman, Aharon. 1993. *Society and Settlement: Jewish Land of Israel in the Twentieth Century*. Albany: State University of New York Press.

Kena'ani, David. 1976. *Ha-Aliyah ha-sheniyah ha-'ovedet ve-yaḥasah la-dat vela-masoret* [The Pioneering Second Immigration and Its Relation to Religion and Tradition]. Tel Aviv: Sifriyat po'alim.

Kertzer, David. 1988. *Ritual, Politics and Power*. New-Haven: Yale University Press.

Khalidi, Walid. 1984. *Before their Diaspora: A Photographic History of the Palestinians, 1876–1948*. Washington, D.C.: Institute for Palestine Studies.

Kieval, Hillel J. 1999. "Antisemitism and the City: A Beginner's Guide." In *People of the City: Jews and the Urban Challenge*, ed. Ezra Mendelson, 3–18. Studies in Contemporary Jewry 15. New York: Oxford University Press.

Kirshenblatt-Gimblett, Barbara, & Brooks McNamara. 1985. "Processional Performance: An Introduction." *Drama Review* 29 (3): 2–5.

Kirshenblatt-Gimblett, Barbara. 2005. "The Corporeal Turn." *Jewish Quarterly Review* 95 (3): 447–461.

Kook, Abraham Isaac. 1993. *Orot: Yisra'el u-tehiyato* [Lights: The Revival of Israel]. Jerusalem: Rabbi Kook Institution.

Koselleck, Reinhart. 2002. *The Practice of Conceptual History: Timing History, Spacing Concepts*, trans. Todd Samuel Presner. Stanford: Stanford University Press.

Kristeva, Julia. 1980. *Desire in Language: A Semiotic Approach to Literature and Art*, trans. Thomas Gora, Alice Jardine and Leon S. Roudiez. New York: Columbia University Press.

———. 1986. *The Kristeva Reader*, ed. Toril Moi. New York: Columbia University Press.

Kuchta, David. 1996. "The Making of the Self-Made Man: Class, Clothing and English Masculinity, 1688–1832." In *The Sex of Things: Gender and Consumption in Historical Perspective*, ed. Victoria de Grazia with Ellen Furlough, 54–78. Berkeley: University of California Press.

Laclau, Ernesto. 1977. *Politics and Ideology in Marxist Theory*. London: New Left Books.

Larrain, Jorge. 1979. *The Concept of Ideology*. London: Hutchinson.

Lavenda, Robert H. 1988. "Minnesota Queen Pageants: Play, Fun and Dead Seriousness in a Festive Mode." *Journal of American Folklore* 101: 168–75.

Lavsky, Hagit. 1994. *Keren Kayemt Le-Yisrael: Halakha U-ma'ase Bitkufat Hamandat Habriti* [Jewish National Fund: Theory and Praxis in British Mandate Period]. Jerusalem: The Institution for the Study of JNF history.

———. 2002. "Tarbut kalkalit ve-kalkalat ha-tarbut ba-" medina sheba-derekh"" [Economic Culture and the Culture of Politics in the "State in Becoming"]. In *Ha'agala ha-mele'a: Me'a ve-esrim shenot tarbut Israel* [The Full Carriage: A Hundred and Twenty Years of Israeli Culture], ed. Israel Bartal, 3–23. Jerusalem: Magnes.

Le-Roy Ladurie, Emmanuel. 1978. *Montaillou: The Promised Land of Error*, trans. Barbara Bray. New York: G. Braziller.

Le-Roy Ladurie, Emmanuel. 1979. *Carnival in Roman*, trans. Mary Feeney. New York: George Braziller.

Lev Tov, Boaz. 2007. *Biluyim be-mahaloket: Defusey biluy vetarbut populariyim shel yehudim be-eretz Israel beshanim 1882–1914 kimshakfim tmurot hevratiyot* [Controversial Recreation: Patterns of Leisure and Popular Culture of Jews in Palestine Between 1882–1914, as Reflecting Social Transformations]. PhD diss., Tel Aviv.

LeVine, Mark. 2005. *Overthrowing Geography: Jaffa, Tel-Aviv, and the Struggle for Palestine 1880–1948*. Berkeley: University of California Press.

Lewinsky, Yom Tov (Ed.). 1947. *Keitzad hiku et Haman bi-tefutzot Israel: Yalkut folklori le-Purim* [How was Haman Bitten in Jewish Diasporas: A Folkloric Anthology for Purim]. Tel Aviv: Yeda-Am.

——— (Ed.). 1955. *Sefer ha-mo'adim* (The Book of festivals), Vol. 6, *Purim, Lag ba-Omer, Tu be-Av*. Tel Aviv: Dvir.

——— (Ed.). 1970. *Entziklopediya shel havay u-masoret bayahadut* [An Encyclopedia of Jewish Life and Traditions]. Tel Aviv: Dvir.

Liebman, Charles & Eliezer Don-Yehiya. 1983. *Civil Religion in Israel: Judaism and Political Culture in the Jewish State*. Berkeley: University of California Press.

Likhovsky, Asaf. 2010. "Post-Post-Zionist Historiography." *Israel Studies* 15 (2): 1–23.

Linder, Amnon. 1983. *Hayehudim Vehayahadut Bekhukey hakeisarut Haromit* [Jews and Judaism in Roman Law]. Jerusalem: Israeli National Academy.

Linnekin, Jocelyn S. 1983. "Defining Tradition: Variations on the Hawaiian Identity." *American Ethnologist* 10 (2): 241–252.

Lipton, Diana. 1998. "The Woman's Lot in Esther." In *Bodies, Lives, Voices: Gender in Theology*, ed. Kathleen O'Grady, Ann L. Gilroy & Janette Gray, 133–151. Sheffield: Academic Press.

Lissak, Moshe. 1999. "Hahazara la-historiya: Memad hazman bitfisot ideologiyot batarbuyot hapolitiyot bayishuv u-vimdinat Israel" [Back to History: The Time Dimension in Ideological Perceptions of Political Cultures in the Yishuv and in the State of Israel]. In *ha-Tsiyonut veha-hazarah le-historyah: Ha'arakha nehadash* [Zionism and the Return to History: A Re-evaluation], ed. Shmuel N. Eisenstadt and Moshe Lissak, 480–494. Jerusalem: Yad Ben-Zvi.

Lynd, Robert S. & Helen Merrell Lynd. [1929] 1956. *Middletown: A Study in American Culture*. New-York: Harcourt, Brace & World.

MacCannell, Dean. 1975. *The Tourist: A New Theory of the Leisure Class*. New York: Schocken.

Mandel, Neville J. 1976. *Arabs and Zionism before World War I*. Berkeley: University of California Press.

Mann, Barbara E. 2006. *A Place in History: Modernism, Tel-Aviv, and the Creation of the Jewish Urban Space*. Stanford: Stanford University Press.

— — —. 2010. 'Tel Aviv after 100: Notes toward a New Cultural History.' *Jewish Social Studies* 16 (2): 93–110.

Manor, Dalia. 2004. "Orientalism and Jewish National Art: The Case of Bezalel." In *Orientalism and the Jews*, ed. Ivan Davidson Kalmar and Derek J. Penslar, 142–161. Waltham: Brandeis University Press.

Manor, Giora (Ed.). 1986. *Agadati: Haluts ha-mahol he-hadash be-Erets Yisra'el* [Agadati: The Pioneer of the New Dance in Palestine]. Tel Aviv: Sifriyat po'alim.

Mantgen, Gerd. 1994. "Hivatzruta shel habduta shel alilat hadam" [The Creation of the Blood Libel]. *Tzion* 59 (2–3): 343–349.

Marcus, Ivan. 1996. *Rituals of Childhood: Jewish Acculturation in Medieval Europe*. New Haven: Yale University Press.

Marly, Diana de. 1985. *Fashion for Men: An Illustrated History*. New York: Holmes & Meier.

McClintock, Ann. 1996. "'No Longer in a Future Heaven': Nationalism, Gender, and Race." In *Becoming National: A Reader*, ed. Geoff Eley and Ronald Grigor Suny, 260–284. New York: Oxford University Press.

McGuigan, Jim. 2011. "The Cultural Public Sphere: A Critical Measure of Public Culture?" *Festivals and the Cultural Public Sphere*, ed. Liana Giorgi, Monica Sassatelli and Gerard Delanty, 79–91. London & New York: Routledge.

Metzer, Jacob. 1998. *The Divided Economy of Mandatory Palestine*. Cambridge: Cambridge University Press.

Michels, Tony. 2005. *A Fire in Their Hearts: Yiddish Socialists in New-York*. Cambridge: Harvard University.

Migdal, Joel Shmuel. 2001. *Through The Lens of Israel: Explorations in State and Society*. Albany: State University of New-York.

Moore, Alexander. 1980. "Walt Disney World: Bounded Ritual Space and the Playful Pilgrim Center." *Anthropological Quarterly* 53 (4): 207–218.

Moore, Sally F. & Barbara G. Myerhoff. 1977. "Secular Ritual: Forms and Meanings." In *Secular Ritual*, ed. Sally F. Moore and Barbara G. Myerhoff, 3–24. Amsterdam: Van Gorcam.

Morinis, Alan (Ed.). 1992. *Sacred Journeys: The Anthropology of Pilgrimage*. Connecticut and London: Greenwood.

Mosse, George L. 1975. *The Nationalization of the Masses: Political Symbolism and the Mass Movements in Germany from the Napoleonic Wars Through the Third Reich*. New York: H. Fertig.

– – –. 1985. *Nationalism and Sexuality: Middle-Class Morality and Sexual Norms in Modern Europe*. New York: H. Fertig.

Moykher-Sforim, Mendele. 1991. *The Three Great Classic Writers of Modern Yiddish Literature*, ed. Marvin Zuckerman, Gerald Stillman, and Marion Herbst. Vol. 1, *Selected Works of Mendele Moykher-Sforim*, Malibu: Pangloss Press.

Muchawsky-Schnapper, Esther. 1994. *The Jews of Yemen: Highlights of the Israel Museum Collection*. Jerusalem: The Israel Museum.

– – –. 2000. *The Yemenites: Two Thousand Years of Jewish Culture*. Jerusalem: The Israel Museum.

Muir, Edward. 1997. *Ritual in Early Modern Europe*. Cambridge: Cambridge University Press.

Naor, Mordechai. 2003. "Mis-hakey Rehovot: 1908–1914" [Rehovot Games, 1908–1914]. In *Tarbut ha-guf veha-sport be-Israel be-me'a ha-esrim* [Body and Sports Culture in 20th Century Israel], ed. Haim Kaufman and Hagay Harif, 81–88. Jerusalem: Yad ben-Zvi and the Wingate institute.

Neumann, Boaz. 2009. *Teshukat Hahalutzim* [The Passion of the Pioneers]. Tel Aviv: Am-Oved and Sapir Academic College.

Nitzan-Shiftan, Alona. 1996. "Contested Zionism—alternative Modernism: Erich Mendelsohn and the Tel Aviv Chug in Mandate Palestine." *Architectural History* 39: 147–180.

Nora, Pierre (Ed.). 1997. *Realms of Memory, Volume II: Tradition*, trans. Arthur Goldhammer. New York: Columbia University Press.

Ofrat, Gideon. 2005. *Bikurey Omanut: Al omanim yisre'elim* [Art Visits: On Israeli Artists]. Jerusalem: Zionist Library.

Oinas, Felix J. (Ed.). 1978. *Folklore, Nationalism and Politics*. Columbus: Slavica.

Okin, Susan Moller. 1999. *Is Multiculturalism Bad for Women?* Princeton: Princeton University Press.

Oz, Amos. 1983. *In the Land of Israel*, trans. Maurie Goldberg-Bartura. San Diego: Harcourt Brace Jovanovich.

Ozouf, Mona. 1988. *Festivals and the French Revolution*, trans. Alan Sheridan. Cambridge: Harvard University Press.

Pardes, Ilana. 1992. *Countertraditions in the Bible: A Feminist Approach*. Cambridge: Harvard University Press.

———. 2000. *The Biography of Ancient Israel: National Narratives in the Bible*. Berkeley: University of California Press.

Pecora, Vincent P. (Ed.). 2001. *Nations and Identities: Classic Readings*. Oxford: Blackwell.

Penslar, Derek Jonathan. 1991. *Zionism and Technocracy: The Engineering of Jewish Settlement in Palestine, 1870–1918*. Bloomington: Indiana University Press.

———. 2003. "Transmitting Jewish Culture: Radio in Israel." *Jewish Social Studies* 10 (1): 1–29.

———. 2007. *Israel in History: The Jewish State in Comparative Perspective*. New York: Routledge.

Perski, Daniel. 1944. *Zemanim Tovim* [Happy Days]. New York: Pardes.

Piekarz, Mendel. 1990. *Hasidut Polin: Megamot Ra'ayoniyot bein shtey hamilhamot ivegzeirot tash-tashah* [Poland Hassidism: Philosophical Trends in Interwar Era and during the Holocaust]. Jerusalem: Bialik Institution.

Pleck, Elizabeth H. 2000. *Celebrating the Family: Ethnicity, Consumer Culture, and Family Rituals*. Cambridge: Harvard University Press.

Polish, Daniel F. 1999. "Aspects of Esther: A Phenomenological Exploration of the Megillah of Esther and the Origins of Purim." *Journal for the Study of the Old Testament* 85: 85–106.

Pomfret, David M. 2004. "'A Muse for the Masses': Gender, Age and Nation in France, fin-de-siècle." *American Historical Review* 109 (5): 1439–1474.
Povinelli, Elizabeth A. 1999. "Settler Modernity and the Quest for an Indigenous Tradition." *Public Culture* 11 (1): 19–48.
Pulzer, Peter G.Z. 1964. *The Rise of Political Anti-Semitism in Germany and Austria*. New York: Wiley.
Rafeld, Meir. 1998. "Ad-delo-yada: Hashikhrut be-Purim; mekorot, parshanut venohagim" [Beyond Cognition: The Drunkenness in Purim; Sources, Interpretations and Customs]. In *Minhagey Yisrael* [The Customs of Israel], Volume 6, ed. Daniel Sperber, 207–226. Jerusalem: Rabbi Kook Institution.
Ram, Hanna. 1996. *Ha-Yishuv ha-Yehudi be-Yafo ba-et ha-ḥadashah: Miḳehilah Sefaradit lemerkaz Tsiyoni* [Jewish Jaffa in Modern Era: From Sephardic Community to Zionist Center]. Jerusalem: Carmel.
Ramon, Ya'akov. 1935. *Yahadut Teyman be-Tel-Aviv* [Yemenite Jewry in Tel Aviv]. Jerusalem: Zuckerman.
Ratzhabi, Yehuda. 1988. *Be-ma'agalot Teiman* [In Yemenite Circles]. Tel Aviv: self-published.
Raz, Ayala. 1996. *Halifot Ha-itim: Me'a shenot ofna be-eretz Israel* [The Time's Suits: Hundred Years of Fashion in Palestine]. Tel Aviv: Yediot Aharonot.
———. 1998. "Fashion in Eretz-Israel: What We Were Wearing in the Early Days of this Century." *Ariel* 107–108: 160–182.
Razi, Tammy. 2009. *Yaldei hahefker: He-khatzer ha'ahorit shel Tel-Aviv ha-mandatorit* [Forsaken Children: The Backyard of Mandate Tel Aviv]. Tel Aviv: Am-Oved.
———. 2010. "The Family Is Worthy of Being Rebuilt: Perceptions of the Jewish Family in Mandate Palestine, 1918–1948." *Journal of Family History* 35 (4): 395–415.
Raz-Karkotzkin, Amnon. 1993. "Galut betokh ribonut: Levikoret "shlilat hagalut" batarbut hatziyonit" [An Exile within Sovereignty: Critique of "Exile Negation" in Zionist Culture]. *Te'orya uvikoret* 4: 23–55.
———. 1999. "Ha-shiva el ha-historiya shel hage'ula, o: Mahi hahistoriya" she-eleyha mitbatza'at ha-shiva, babituy "ha-shiva el hahistoriya'?" [The Return to the History of Redemption, or: What Is the "History" to which There is a Return?]. In *ha-Tsiyonut veha-ḥazarah le-hisṭoryah: Ha'arakha ne-hadash* [Zionism and the

Return to History: A Re-evaluation], ed. Shmuel N. Eisenstadt and Moshe Lissak, 249–276. Jerusalem: Yad Ben-Zvi.
Read, Alan (Ed.). 2000. *On Animals*. Special issue of *Performance Research* 5, 2.
Reader, Ian. 1993. "Introduction." *Pilgrimage in Popular Culture*, ed. Ian Reader and Tony Walter, 1–25. London: Macmillan.
Redfield, Robert & Milton Singer. 1969. "The Cultural Role of Cities." In *Classic Essays on the Culture of Cities*, ed. Richard Sennett, 206–232. New York: Meredith.
Redfield, Robert. 1960. *Peasant Society and Culture*. London: The University of Chicago.
Ricoeur, Paul. 1967. *The Symbolism of Evil*, trans. Emerson Buchanan. New-York: Harper & Row.
— — —. 1991. *From Text to Action: Essays in Hermeneutics II*, trans. Kathleen Blamey and John B. Thompson. Evanston: Northwestern University Press.
Roach, Joseph. 2007. *It*. Ann Arbor: University of Michigan Press.
Roberts, Mary Louise. 1998. "Gender, Consumption, and Commodity Culture." *American Historical Review* 103: 817–844.
Roginsky, Dina. 2007. "Folklore, Folklorism, and Synchronization: Preserved-created Folklore in Israel." *Journal of Folklore Research* 44 (1): 41–66.
Rojek, Chris. 1985. *Capitalism and Leisure Theory*. London and New-York: Tavistock.
Rosenberg-Friedman, Lilach. 2012a. "Traditional Revolution: The Issue of Marriage on Religious Kibbutzim, 1929–1948; A Comparative View." *Journal of Israeli History* 31 (1): 109–128
— — —. 2012b. "Wedding Ceremony, Religion, and Tradition: The Shertok Family Debate, 1922." *Israel Studies Review* 27 (1): 98–124.
Roshwald, Aviel. 2004. "Jewish Identity and the Paradox of Nationalism." In *Nationalism, Zionism and Ethnic Mobilization of the Jews in 1900 and Beyond*, ed. Michael Berkowitz, 11–24. Leiden and Boston: Brill.
— — —. 2006. *The Endurance of Nationalism: Ancient Roots and Modern Dilemmas*. Cambridge: Cambridge University Press.
Rosman, Moshe. 2007. *How Jewish Is Jewish History?* Oxford and Portland: The Littman Library of Jewish Civilization.
Rotbard, Sharon. 2005. *Ir levanah, ir shehorah* [White City, Black City]. Tel Aviv: Babel Press.
Roth, Cecil. 1933. "The Feast of Purim and the Origins of the Blood Accusation." *Speculum* IV: 520–526.

———. 1959. *The Jews in the Renaissance*. New-York: Harper & Row.

Rozin, Orit. 2005. "The Austerity Policy and the Rule of Law: Relations between Government and Public in Fledgling Israel." *Journal of Modern Jewish Studies* 4 (3): 273–290.

———. 2007. "Forming a Collective Identity: The Debate Over the Proposed Constitution, 1948–1950." *Journal of Israeli History* 26 (2): 251–271

———. 2011. *The Rise of the Individual in 1950s Israel*. Hanover: Brandeis University Pres.

Sagi, Avi. 2007. *Lihyot Yehudy: Y. H Brenner ke-ekzistentzialist yehudi* [Being a Jew: Y.H. Brenner as a Jewish Existentialist]. Ramat-Gan: Bar-Ilan University Press.

———. 2008. *Tradition vs. Traditionalism: Contemporary Perspectives in Jewish Thought*, trans. Batya Stein. Amsterdam and New York: Rodopi.

Said, Edward W. 1978. *Orientalism*. New York: Vintage.

Saposnik, Arieh Bruce. 2006. "Europe and Its Orients in Zionist Culture before the First World War." *Historical Journal* 49 (4): 1105–1123.

———. 2008. *Becoming Hebrew: The Creation of a Jewish National Culture in Ottoman Palestine*. Oxford: Oxford University Press.

Sassatelli, Monica. 2011. "Urban Festivals and the Cultural Public Sphere: Cosmopolitanism between Ethics and Aesthetics." In *Festivals and the Cultural Public Sphere*, ed. Liana Giorgi, Monica Sassatelli and Gerard Delanty, 12–28. London and New York: Routledge.

Sassatelli, Roberta. 2007. *Consumer Culture: History, Theory and Politics*. London: Sage.

Schechner, Richard. 1985. *Between Theatre and Anthropology*. Philadelphia: University of Pennsylvania Press.

Schlor, Joachim. 1999. *Tel-Aviv: From Dream to City*, trans. Helen Atkins. London: Reaktion Books.

Schrire, Dani. 2011. *Isuf shivrey hagola: heker hafolklor be-yisrael bishnot ha-arba'im vehahamishim bemabat bikorti* [Collecting the Pieces of Exile: A Critical View of Folklore Research in Israel in the 1940s-1950s.] PhD Diss., Hebrew University of Jerusalem.

Segal, Er'el. 1999. "Hamashma'ut shel harkavat Mordechai al hasus" [The Meaning of the Bringing of Mordechai on Horseback]. *Megadim* 30: 115–116.

Sewell, William H., Jr. 1999. "The Concept (s) of Culture." In *Beyond the Cultural Turn?*, ed. Victoria E. Bonnel and Lynn Hunt, 35–61. Berkeley: University of California Press.

Shaked, Gershon. 1996. "Israeli Actors as a Reflection of their Generation." In *Theater in Israel*, ed. Linda Ben-Zvi, 85–100. Ann Arbor: University of Michigan Press.

Shamir, Ronen. 2000. "Burganut yehudit be-palestina ha-kolonialit: Kavey mit'ar le-seder yom mehkari" [Jewish Bourgeoisie in Colonial Palestine: A Preliminary Research Agenda]. *Sotzyologiya Yisre'elit* 3 (1): 133–148.

———. 2002. "The Comrades Law of Hebrew Workers in Palestine: A Study in Socialist Justice." *Law and History Review* 20 (2): 279–306.

Shapira, Anita. 1988. *Hahalikha al Kav Ha-ofek* [Walking on the Horizon]. Tel Aviv: Am Oved.

———. 1992. *Land and Power: The Zionist Resort to Force, 1881–1948*, trans. William Templer. New York: Oxford University Press.

———. 1995. "Zionism and Anti-Semitism." *Modern Judaism* 15 (3): 215–232.

———. 1996. "Kuvlanato shel shternhal" [Shternhel's Complaint]. *Iyunim Bitkumat Israel* 6: 553–567.

———. 1997a. *Yehudim Hadashim Yehudim Yeshanim* [New Jews Old Jews]. Tel Aviv: Am Oved.

———. 1997b. "The Origins of the Myth of the "New Jew': The Zionist Variety." *Studies in Contemporary Jewry* XIII: 253–268.

———. 1998. "The Religious Motifs of the Labor Movement." In *Zionism and Religion*, ed. Shmuel Almog, Judah Reinharz, and Anita Shapira, 251–272. Hanover: University Press of New England.

Shapira, Yosef. 1968. *Ha-Po'el ha-tsa'ir: Ha-ra'yon veha-ma'aseh* [Hapo'el Hatza'ir: Ideas and Praxis]. Tel Aviv: Ayanot.

Shapiro, Yonathan. 1976. *The Formative Years of the Israeli Labour Party: The Organization of Power, 1919–1930*. London: Sage Publications.

Shavit, Jacob & Shoshana Sitton. 2004. *Staging and Stagers in Modern Jewish Palestine: The Creation of Festive Lore in a New Culture, 1882–1948*, trans. Chaya Naor. Detroit: Wayne State University.

Shavit, Jacob. 1989. "Ma'amada shel hatarbut be-tahalikh yetzirata shel hevra le'umit be-eretz Israel: Emdot yesod u-musgey yesod" [The Status of Culture in the Process of the Creation of National Society in Palestine: Basic Approaches and Concepts]. In *Toldot ha-Yishuv ha-yehudy be-eretz Israel me-az ha'aliya ha-rishona* [The History of the Jewish Settlement in Palestine since the First Immigration], volume 4, ed. Moshe Lissak and Gabriel Cohen, 9–29. Jerusalem: National Academy of Sciences.

———. 1996. "Haroved Hatarbuti hahaser U-miluyo: Bein "tarbut amamit rishmit" le-"tarbut amamit lo rishmit" batarbut ha-ivrit ha-le'umit be-eretz yirsael" [The Missing Cultural Layer and Its Completing: Between "Formal Folk Culture" and "Informal Folk Culture" in the National Hebrew Culture in Palestine]. In *Hatarbut Ha'amamit* [Popular Culture], ed. B.Z. Keidar, 327–345. Jerusalem: Shazar center.

———. 1998. "Tarbut u-matzav kulturi: Kavey yesod lehitpat'hut hatarbut ha-ivrit bitkufat ha'aliya hashniya" [Culture and Cultural State: Basic Lines in the Development of Hebrew Culture in the Period of the Second Immigration]. In *Ha'aliya Hashniya: Mehkarim* [The Second Immigration: Studies], ed. Israel Bartal, 343–366. Jerusalem: Yad Ben-Zvi.

———. 2003. "Madu'a lo havshu be-Tel-Aviv kippa aduma? Beyn idi'alism le-re'alism be-farshanut shel toldot hayishuv; Tel-Aviv ke-mashal" [Why Didn't They Wear a Red Headcover in Tel Aviv? Between Idealism and Realism in Interpretations of the History of the Yishuv; Tel Aviv as a Fable]. In *Kalkala ve-hevra bimey hamandat, 1918–1948* [Economy and Society in Mandate Period], ed. Avi Bareli and Nahum Karlinsky, 59–78. Beer-Sheva: Ben-Gurion University.

Shavit, Yaacov & Gideon Bigger. 2001. *Ha-historiyah shel Tel Aviv: Mi-shekhunot le-ir (1909–1936)* [The History of Tel Aviv: From Neighborhoods to City]. Tel Aviv: Ramot.

———. 2007. *Ha-historiyah shel Tel Aviv: Me-ir medina le-ir bamedina (1936–1952)* [The History of Tel Aviv: From a State-city to a City within a State]. Tel Aviv: Ramot.

Shavit, Zohar. 1986. *Poetics of Children's Literature*. Athens: University of Georgia Press.

Shenhav, Yehuda. 2004. *Ha-Yehudim ha-Arvim: Le'umiyut, dat, ve-etniyut* [The Arab-Jews: Nationality, Religion, Ethnicity]. Tel Aviv: Am oved.

Shenker, Yael. 2005. *Al sipa shel eretz hadasha: "Tarbut yisre'elit" o ribuy tarbuyot* [On the Verge of a New Land: "Israeli Culture" or Multiple Cultures]. Jerusalem: The Center for the Instruction of Judaic Studies, Hebrew University.

Sheva, Shlomo. 1977. *Ho Ir, Ho Em* [O City, O Mother]. Tel Aviv: Israel-American publishing company.

Shilo, Margalit. 1989. "Mi-yafo lirushalayim: Yahasa shel hahistadrut hatziyonit lirushalayim bitkufat ha'aliya hashniya" [From Jaffa to Jerusalem: The Attitude of Zionist Organization to Jerusalem during the Period of the Second Immigration]. In *Yerushalayim batoda'a uva-asiya ha-tziyonit* [Jerusalem in Zionist Consciousness and Actions], ed. Hagit Lavsky, 91–106. Jerusalem: Shazar Center.

———. 1996. "The Transformation of the Role of Women in the First Aliah, 1882–1903." *Jewish Social Studies* 2 (2): 64–86.

———. 1997. "Mabat hadash al ha'aliya hashniya (tarsad-tar'ad, 1904–1914)" [A New View of the Second Immigration, 1904–1914]. *Kivunim* 11–12: 117–140.

Shils, Edward. 1981. *Tradition.* Chicago: The University of Chicago Press.

Shimoni, Gideon. 1995. *The Zionist Ideology.* Hanover: University Press of New England.

Shmueli, Ephraim. 1990. *Seven Jewish Cultures: A Reinterpretation of Jewish History and Thought.* Cambridge: Cambridge University Press.

Shnitzer, Meir. 1994. *Ha-kolno'a ha-yisre'eli: Uvdot, alilot, bama'im, ve-gam bikorot* [Israeli Cinema: Facts, Plots, Directors, Critiques]. Jerusalem: Israeli cinematic archives & Kineret.

Shoham, Hizky. 2006. *Hagigot Purim be-Tel Aviv, 1908–1936: Iyun mehudash be-mashma'utam shel smalim, masoret u-sferah tziburit be-tarbut amamit tziyonit* [Purim Celebrations in Tel Aviv, 1908–1936: A Reexamination of the Meaning of Symbols, Tradition, and the Public Sphere in Zionist Popular Culture]. Ph.D. diss., Bar-Ilan University.

———. 2008. "Eikh nir'ah yehudi? Kri'ah mehudeshet ba-mahazeh ha-geto he-hadash" [What Does a Jew Look Like? A New Reading of the Play *The New Ghetto*]. In *Herzl az ve-hayom: Yehudi yashan—adam hadash?* [Herzl Then and Now: An Old Jew or a New Person?], ed. Avi Sagi and Yedidya Stern, 285–323. Jerusalem: Keter.

Shoham, Hizky. 2011a. "Rethinking Tradition: From Ontological Reality to Assigned Temporal Meaning." *European Journal of Sociology* 52 (2): 313–340.

———. 2011b. "Of Other Cinematic Spaces: Urban Zionism in Early Hebrew Cinema." *Israel Studies Review* 26 (2): 109–131.

———. 2012. "Tel-Aviv's Foundation Myth: A Constructive Perspective." In *Tel-Aviv, the First Century: Visions, Designs, Actualities*, ed. Maoz Azaryahu and S. Ilan Troen, 34–59. Bloomington: Indiana University Press.

———. 2013a. "From "Great History" to "Small History': The Genesis of the Zionist Periodization." *Israel Studies* 18 (1): 31–55.

———. 2013b. *Mordechai rokhev al sus: Hagigot Purim be-Tel-Aviv (1908–1936) u-vniyata shel uma hadasha* [Mordechai Is Riding a Horse: Purim Celebrations in Tel Aviv (1908–1936) in the Building of a New Nation]. Ramat-Gan: Bar-Ilan University Press.

———. 2013c. "'Buy Local" or "Buy Jewish'? Separatist Consumption in Interwar Palestine." *International Journal of Middle East Studies* 45 (3): 469–489.

Shprut, Ezra. 1990. "Hagogit Purim be-Tel-Aviv veha-agadah al Baruch Agadati" [Purim Celebrations in Tel Aviv and the Tale about Baruch Agadati]. *Mehkarei Hag* 2: 106–114.

Shternshis, Anna. 2006. *Soviet and Kosher: Jewish Popular culture in the Soviet Union, 1923–1939*. Bloomington: Indiana University Press.

Simmel, George. 1997. *Simmel on Culture*, ed. David Frisby and Mike Featherstone. London: Sage.

Singer, Milton. 1972. *When a Great Tradition Modernizes: An Anthropological Approach to Indian Civilization*. New York, Washington and London: Praeger Publishers.

Smith, Anthony David. 1971. *Theories of Nationalism*. London: Duckworth.

———. 1986. *The Ethnic Origins of Nations*. Oxford: Blackwell.

———. 1991. "The Nation: Invented, Imagined, Reconstructed." *Millennium: Journal of International Studies* 20 (3): 353–368.

———. 2000. *The Nation in History: Historiographical Debates about Ethnicity and Nationalism*. Hanover: University Press of New England.

Smith-Rosenberg, Carroll. 2000. "Political Camp and the Ambiguous Engendering of the American Republic." In *Gendered Nations: Nationalisms and Gender Order in the Long Nineteenth Century*, ed. Ida Blom, Karen Hagemann and Catherine Hall, 271–292. Oxford and New York: Berg.

Solomon-Godeau, Abigail. 1996. "The Other Side of Venus: The Visual Economy of Feminine Display." In *The Sex of Things: Gender and Consumption in Historical Perspective*, ed. Victoria de Grazia with Ellen Furlough, 113–150. Berkeley: University of California Press.

Sperber, Daniel. 2002. *Keitzad Makim et Haman* [How is Haman Being Beaten]. Ramat-Gan: Bar-Ilan University.

Spiegel, Boaz. 2004. "Hayayin u-se'udat ha-Purim: hebetim hilkhatiyim vesifrutiyim besugiyat habavli, Megillah zayin beit" [The Wine and Purim Meal: Halakhic and Literary Aspects in the Discussion of Babylonian Talmud, Megillah 7:2]. *Badad* 15: 43–63.

Spiegel, Nina. 2001. *Jewish Cultural Celebrations and Competitions in Mandatory Palestine, 1920–1947: Body, Beauty and the Search for Authenticity*. PhD Diss., Stanford University, California.

Stallybrass, Peter & Allon White. 1986. *The Politics and Poetics of Transgression*. Ithaca: Cornell University.

Stanton, Andrea L. 2013. *"This Is Jerusalem Calling": State Radio in Mandate Palestine*. Austin: University of Texas Press.

Stern, Bat-Sheva Margalit. 2006. "Who's the Fairest of them all? Women, Womanhood, and Ethnicity in Zionist Eretz Israel." *Nashim* 11: 142–163.

Sternhell, Ze'ev. 1998. *The Founding Myths of Israel: Nationalism, Socialism, and the Making of the Jewish State*, trans. David Maisel. Princeton: Princeton University Press.

Stoler-Liss, Sachlav. 2003. "'Mothers Birth the Nation': The Social Construction of Zionist Motherhood in Wartime in Israeli Parents' Manuals." *Nashim* 6: 104–118.

Susman, Warren I. [1973] 1984. *Culture as History: The Transformation of American Society in the Twentieth Century*. New-York: Pantheon Books.

Swirsky, Shlomo. 1979. "He'arot la-sotziyologiya ha-historit shel tkufat hayishuv" [Comments on Historical Sociology of the Yishuv period]. *Mahbarot le-mehkar ule-vikoret* 2: 5–41.

Synnot, Anthony. 1989. "Truth and Goodness, Mirrors and Masks: Part 1." *British Journal of Sociology* 40 (4): 607–636.

Tavori, Yosef. 1990. "Le-ofiyo Shel Yom ha-Purim" [The Character of Purim Day]. *Mehkarey Hag* 2: 17–30.

Taylor, Charles. 1999. "Two Theories of Modernity." *Public Culture* 11 (1): 153–174.

Thompson, John B. 1996. "Tradition and Self in a Mediated World." In *Detraditionalization*, ed. P. Heelas, P. Morris and S. Lash, 89–108. Cambridge: Blackwell.

Thornton, T. C. G. 1986. "The Crucifixion of Haman and the Scandal of the Cross." *Journal of Theological Studies*, 37 (2): 419–426.

Tidhar, David. 1959. *Entziklopedia Le-khalutzey Hayishuv U-vonav: Demuyot U-temunot* [Encyclopedia for the Yishuv's Pioneers and Builders: Figures and Images], *volume 10*. Tel Aviv: self-published.

Tiersten, Lisa. 2001. *Marianne in the Market: Envisioning Consumer Society in Fin-de-Siècle France*. Berkeley: University of California Press.

Troen, Ilan S. 1999. "Frontier Myths and their Application in America and Israel: A Transnational Perspective." *Journal of American History* 86 (3): 1209–1230.

———. 2003. *Imagining Zion: Dreams, Designs and Realities in a Century of Jewish Settlement*. New Haven: Yale University Press.

Troen, Ilan S. & Maoz Azaryahu (Eds.). 2011. *Tel-Aviv, the First Century: Visions, Designs, Actualities*. Bloomington: Indiana University Press.

Tryster, Hillel. 1995. *Israel before Israel: Silent Cinema in the Holy Land*. Jerusalem: Steven Spielberg Jewish Film Archive.

Tuan, Yi-Fu. 1977. *Space and Place: The Perspective of Existence*. Minneapolis: Minneapolis University.

———. 1978. "The City: Its Distance from Nature." *The Geographical Review* 68 (1): 1–12.

Turner, Victor W. 1969. *Ritual Process: Structure and Anti-Structure*. London: Routledge & Kegan Paul, 1969.

———. 1974. *Dramas, Fields and Metaphors: Symbolic Action in Human Society*. Ithaca: Cornell University.

———. 1982a. "Introduction," *Celebrations: Studies in Festivity and Ritual*, ed. Victor Turner, 11–29. Washington, D.C.: Smithsonian Institute Press.

———. 1982b. *From Ritual to Theatre: The Human Seriousness of Play*. New York: PAJ.

———. 1987. *The Anthropology of Performance*. New York: PAJ.

Turner, Victor & Edith Turner. 1978. *Image and Pilgrimage in Christian Culture: Anthropological Perspective*. Oxford: Blackwell.

Tzahor, Ze'ev. 1998. "Tzemihat ha-zramim ha-politiyim ve-irguney ha-po'alim" [The Emergence of Political Currents and the Workers' Organizations]. In *Ha'aliya Hashniya: Mehkarim* [The Second Immigration: Studies], ed. Israel Bartal, 215–234. Jerusalem: Yad Ben-Zvi.

Tzur, Muki. 2002. "Nietzsche Vereshit Hatenu'a Hakibbutzit: Reshamim Ishiyim" [Nietzsche and the Beginning of the Kibbutz Movement: Personal Impressions]. In *Nietzsche Batarbut Ha'ivrit* [Nietzsche in Hebrew Culture], ed. Jacob Golomb, 219–228. Jerusalem: Magnes.

Urian, Dan & Efraim Karsh (Eds.). 1999. *Search of Identity: Jewish Aspects of Israeli Culture*. London and Portland: Frank Cass.

Urian, Dan. 1996. *Demut Ha'arvi bate'atron ha-yisre'eli* [Representations of the Arab in Israeli Theater]. Tel Aviv: Or-Am.

Veidlinger, Jeffrey. 2009. *Jewish Public Culture in the Late Russian Empire*. Bloomington: Indiana University Press.

Vital, David. 1984. *Hamahapekha Hatziyonit: Shenot ha'itzuv* [The Zionist Revolution: The Formative Years], trans. Baruch Moran. Tel Aviv: Am Oved.

Wahrman, Dror. 2004. *The Making of the Modern Self: Identity and Culture in Eighteenth-Century England*. New Haven: Yale University Press.

Welter, Volker M. 2009. "The 1925 Master Plan for Tel-Aviv by Patrick Geddes." *Israel Studies* 14 (3): 94–119.

Wenk, Silke. 2000. "Gendered Representations of the Nation's Past and Future." In *Gendered Nations: Nationalisms and Gender Order in the Long Nineteenth Century*, ed. Ida Blom, Karen Hagemann & Catherine Hall, 63–77. Oxford and New York: Berg.

Werses, Shmuel S. 1986. "An-ski's "Tsvishn Tsvey Veltn (Der Dybbuk)'/'Beyn Shney Olamot (Hadybbuk)'/'Between Two Worlds (The Dybbuk)': A Textual History." In *Studies in Yiddish Literature and Folklore*, 99–185. Jerusalem: Hebrew University.

Williams, Raymond. 1982. *Culture*. Chicago: The University of Chicago Press.

———. 1983. *Keywords: A Vocabulary of Culture and Society*. New-York: Oxford University Press.

Wilson, William A. 1976. *Folklore and Nationalism in Modern Finland*. Bloomington: University of Indiana Press.

Wistrich, Robert S. 1989. *The Jews of Vienna in the Age of Franz Joseph*. Oxford: Oxford University Press.

Wu, Judy Tzu-Chun. 1997. "'Loveliest Daughter of our Ancient Cathay!': Representations of Ethnic and Gender Identity in the Miss Chinatown U.S.A Beauty Pageant." *Journal of Social History* 31 (1): 5–31.

Yadgar, Yaacov. 2011. *Secularism and Religion in Jewish-Israeli Politics: Traditionists and Modernity*. New York: Routledge.

Yassif, Eli. 2002. "The "Other" Israel: Folk Cultures in the Modern State of Israel." In *Cultures of the Jews*, ed. David Biale, 1062–1096. New York: Schoken.

Yekuti'eli-Cohen, Edna. 1990. *Tel Aviv ke-makom ba-sipurim, Tarsat—Tartzat* [Tel Aviv as a Place in Stories, 1909–1939]. Israel: Ministry of Education.

Yuval-Davis, Nira. 1993. "Gender and Nation." *Ethnic and Racial Studies* 16 (4): 621–632.

― ― ―. 1997. *Gender and Nation*. London: Sage.

Zakim, Eric. 2006. *To Build and Be Built: Landscape, Literature and the Construction of Zionist Identity*. Philadelphia: Penn University Press.

Ze'evi, Rehav'am (Ed.). 1988. *Ir Be-moda'ot: Yafo ve-Tel-Aviv 1900–1935* [A City by Announcements: Jaffa and Tel Aviv 1900–1935]. Tel Aviv: Eretz-Israel museum.

Ze'ira, Moty. 2002. *Keru'im Anakhnu* [Split We Are]. Jerusalem: Yad Ben-Zvi.

Zerubavel, Eviatar. 2003. *Time Maps: Collective Memory and the Social Shape of the Past*. Chicago: University of Chicago.

Zerubavel, Yael. 1995. *Recovered Roots: Collective Memory and the Making of Israeli National Tradition*. Chicago: The University of Chicago Press.

Zer-Zion, Shelly. 2005. "'The Dybbuk" reconsidered: the emergence of a modern Jewish symbol between East and West." *Leipziger Beiträge zur jüdischen Geschichte und Kultur* 3: 175–197.

Zimmerman, Moshe. 2001a. *Tel-Aviv me-olam lo haytah keṭanah* [Tel Aviv Was Never Small]. Tel Aviv: Miśrad ha-biṭaḥon.

― ― ―. 2001b. *Simaney Kolno'a: Toldot hakolno'a ha-yisre'eli bein hashanim 1896–1948* [Signs of Cinema: The History of Israeli Cinema 1896–1948]. Tel Aviv: Dyunon.

Zipperstein, Steven J. 1985. *The Jews of Odessa: A Cultural History 1794–1881*. Stanford: Stanford University Press.

Zizek, Slavoj. 1990. "Eastern Europe's Republics of Gilead." *New Left Review* 183 (1): 50–62.

Index

Aberman, Yemima 115
Abrahamov, N. 58n72
Abrahams, Israel xxiin50, 21n71, 54, 93, 93n13
Adloyada 1, 28, 30n104, 33, 43, 54, 74n42, 79, 94n16, 96n22, 97, 99, 101–102, 118, 131n53, 132n54, 133n56, 137, 180
Agadati, Baruch 12–15, 20–22, 33, 35, 40, 46, 55, 66, 71–72, 108–109, 140–143, 151, 171
Agnew, Jean-Christophe xviin27
Ahad Ha'am (Ha-Am) 36, 135, 161, 165, 181
Aldema, Avraham (Eisenstein) 7–8, 10, 94
Alexander, Jeffrey C. xvii, xviiin33, 26, 112,
Almagor, Dan 99, 100n33
Almog, Oz xxn44, 21n71, 172n29
Alroey, Gur xivn16, xvin24, xxn43
Alterman, Nathan (Agav) 55–57, 59, 79, 103, 123, 124n29, 144n31, 147n42, 149n50, 180
Amalek 122, 131n52
Anderson, Benedict xvn20, xviin31
Anski, Yosef 146
Arab revolt 33–35, 103, 128
Arand, Aharon 100n36
Arendt, Hannah xviin30
Ariav, H. 30n104
Arieh-Sapir, Nili 8n26, 35n125, 73n36, 83n57, 171n26
Arikha, Yoseph 119n18
Arkin, Moshe 165n8

Arlosoroff, Haim 29
Asaf, Simcha 72n34, 82n53
Avineri, Shlomo 181n54
Avizohar, Y. 76n45, 159n80
Axelrod, Natan 98n27
Azaryahu, Maoz xviii, 25n87, 35n123, 39n9, 57n69, 74n40, 119n18, 183n61–62
Bakhtin, Mikhail 91, 95, 98n26, 102, 110, 113
Ballerino-Cohen, Coleen 147n43, 148n46, 149n49, 154n69, 159n79
Banner, Lois W. 149n49, 154n69, 160n84, 161n86, 162n90
Barber, Richard W. 50n44
Bar-Gal, Yoram 9n33, 17n56
Bartal, Israel 64n3, 121, 121n25
Barzilay, Yehoshua 9n30
Baudelaire, Charles 60n80
Beauty Queen 55, 140–142, 153–154
Bedouins 28, 44, 121
Beitar (movement) 15, 29
Belkin, Ahuva xxiin49–50, 45n31, 92n9, 92n11, 114n5, 138n3
Ben-Amos, Avner 176n37, 183n60
Ben-Artzi, Yossi xxn44
Bendix, Regina xxiiin59, 82n54
Ben-Gurion, David xiv
Ben-Israel, Hedva xvin26
Benjamin, Walter 60n80
Bennett, Susan 6n21
Ben-Porat, Amir xvn23, 164n3
Ben-Ya'akov, Y. 24n81, 69n21
Ben-Yehuda, Eliezer, xxii, 27, 95,
Ben-Yishai, A.Z. (Azov) 97n23, 118n15, 125, 134,182

Berger, John 119n17
Berkowitch, Y.D. 99
Berkowitz, Michael xxn44, 39n10, 64n3
Berlin, Isaiah 181n54
Berman, Joshua A. xxn42, 154n66
Bernstein, Deborah xxn43, 139n8, 155n70, 158n78, 185n66
Biale, David xxn41, 90n3, 139n8
Bialik, Haim N. 29, 35, 69, 74–76, 82–83, 132, 161, 162n88, 185
Bigger, Gideon xivn13, 10n35, 41, 185n67
Bilu, Yoram xxn44
Bivans, Ann-Marie 141n14
Bolitho, Hector 60n79, 179n50
Bonnel, Victoria E. xviin27
Book of Esther xxii, 6, 26–27, 57, 80–81, 95, 106, 111, 114–115, 117, 122, 133, 143, 152–154, 157
Borland, Catherine 148n48
Boucher, Francois 144n29
Bourdieu, Pierre 2n4, 13, 22, 180n52
Bourgeois, bourgeoisie xi, xvii, xxiv, 3, 7, 83n58, 90–99, 104–111, 129, 138–140, 152, 157–159, 162–165, 172, 178, 185
Boyarin, Daniel 90n4
Boyer, Pascal 65n6
Brenner, Athalya 152n62
Brenner, Yosef Haim 170
Brightman, Robert xviin27
British (mandate, rule) ix-x, xiii, xvii, 10, 37, 66, 93, 164, 183, 185
British (police) 23, 29, 121
Brodsky, Adriana Mariel 36n127, 141n13, 150n52
Brubaker, Roger xvn20, 63n1
Burke, Peter xviiin35, 82n54, 91n8, 92n12
Bursztyn, Yigal 98n28
Byrde, Penelope 144n28
Cannadine, David 151n61
Capitalism xviii, xxiv, 16, 22, 38, 166, 172–175
Carmi, Shulamit xvin24
Carmiel, Batya 11n37, 13n42, 14n44–45, 20n70, 22n74, 26n90, 27n92, 27n95, 29n99, 29n102, 31n108, 32n110, 44n25, 68n20, 94n16, 94n18, 118n15–16, 129n47, 127n37, 132n54, 138n1, 140n9, 140n11, 142n17, 142n19, 143n26, 144, 144n29, 148n45, 149n49, 151n59, 157n75, 161n85, 162n89, 185n69
Celebrity 13, 161–162
Chanel, Coco 144
Chartier, Roger xviin27, xviiin35, 91n8
Chaterjee, Partha xvn20
Chaudhuri, Una 119n17
Chavas, Bracha 72
Churgal, Zalman 103n46
Cinema (cinemataic) 12, 28n97, 34, 39, 58n73, 99, 102, 104, 160
Civil religion xxi, 61–62, 164
Civilizing process 51, 92, 104–105, 107
Clutton-Brock, Juliet 120n23
Cohen, Eric xiiin12, 38n1, 172n28, 173n32, 185n64
Cohen, Gershon David 152n63
Cohen, Herman 181
Cohen, Rosa 30
Cohen, Uri S. 120n22, 130n51
Cohen-Hattab, Kobi 39n8, 42n24
Cohn, Bernard S. xviii
Collective memory 31, 118, 138, 174
Communitas xixn38, 38, 59–61,
DaMatta, Roberto 91n8, 99n29
Darnton, Robert xviiin35
Davis, Natalie Zemon xviiin36, 91n8, 138n3
Democratic 95–96, 148–149, 162
Derrida, Jacques 119n17
De-Shalit, Avner 181n54
Dickens, Charles 17, 60n80
Dietrich, Marlene 160
Dinur, Ben-Tzion 5n15
Disney, Walt 14
Dizengoff, Meir xvi, 8, 25n84, 30, 32–33, 35, 43, 46, 52, 53n54, 58, 78n48, 94, 99n32, 114n6, 118, 131–132, 133n55, 134, 142, 161, 172, 176
Doniach, Nakdimon S. 27n94, 82n53, 97n23

Index

Don-Yehiya, Eliezer xn2, xxn43, 164n4, 183n60
Dotan, Shmuel xxiin52
Douglas, Mary xixn37, 88n65, 136
Drory, Yigal xvn22, xvin24, 164n2
Druyan, Nitza 150n54
Druyanov, Alter 5n15, 41
Dunning, Eric 121n24
Durkheim, Emile xix, 38n5, 61–62
Efrat, Elisha xiin7, 39n8, 185n64
Eidar, Dror 57n69, 60n81, 119n18
Eilberg-Schwartz, Howard 90n2
Eisenstadt, Shmuel Noah xiiin11, xxiin51, 64n3–4, 130n49, 166n13, 169n21
Eisenstein, Avraham see Aldema, Avraham
Eliade, Mircea 119n19
Elias, Norbert xviin30, xviiin35, 121n24
Eliav, Mordechai 5n15
Engels, Friedrich 60n80
Escapism 16, 22, 81
Eshel, Ruth 12n39
Even-Zohar, Itamar xxn43, 166n13
Exile xxiii–xxiv, 17–18, 36, 39, 54, 110, 126, 150, 165–166, 169, 175–177, 182
Falk, Raphael 151n60
Fireberg, Haim 74n40, 119n18
Feldstein, Ariel L. 99n30
Feminism, feminist 158–160
Festive culture xxi, 12, 25, 34, 166, 179, 183
Fireworks 6, 135
Fisch, Harold 92, 92n10
Fisher, Yona 28n97, 58n73,
Fogiel-Bijaoui, Sylvie 159n82
Folklore, folklorism xxii–xxiii, 6, 66, 82, 85, 87, 90–93, 124–126, 138, 150, 174
Folkloric discourse 82, 87–88, 95–104, 107–108, 110–111, 151
Frazer, James George 92n9, 100n35
Frenkel, Michal xvin25, 172n28
Friedman, A.D. 104n49
Frug, S. 134n58
Gadamer, Hans-George 65n6
Gal, Noam 119n17
Gandhi, Mahatma 146

Gaster, Theodor Hertzl 35n125, 92n10, 100n35, 114n5,
Geertz, Clifford xvn19, xviiin35, 164n6–7, 184n63
Gefen 94n15
Gellner, Ernst xii, xiin8, xiii–xiv, xvi, xx, 63
General Zionists 163–164
Genihovsky, Dov 10n36
Gershenson, Olga 99n31
Gertz, A. xivn13, 41
Giladi, Dan xvn23
Ginzburg, Carlo xviii36
Glikson, Moshe 54n59, 105n51, 127, 150n56
Goldberg, Yossi 39n8, 40n11, 43n24, 107n61, 163n1
Goldstein, Jacob xn2
Goodman, Philip 3n6, 82n53, 114n5, 131n52
Gordon, A.D. 165, 170, 181
Gorski, Philip 63n1
Govrin, Nurit 4n10
Graicer, Iris 173n32
Greenberg, Moshe 152n63
Gross, Nahum 5n13
Gross, Nathan 12n39
Gross, Yaakov 12n39
Guttman, Nahum 26
Habermas, Jurgen xvii, xviin28, 149n51
Halachmi, Hayim 98n27
Halachni, Yosef 98n28
Halamish, Aviva xvn18
Halevi, Moshe 31, 32n110–111, 33n113, 132
Hall, Colin Michael 40n11
Hall, Stuart xviin27
Halperin, Hagit 56n66, 102n41, 146n35
Halperin, Liora xxin45, 59n75
Hame'iri, Avigdor 53, 97n25, 130
Handelman, Don xixn37, 30n105
Handler, Richard xxiiin59
Hanegbi, Zohar xxiin49, 92n10, 114n5
Hanoch, Gershon 31n108, 60n78, 85–86, 167–171
Hanukkah 183

Har'el, Yaron xxiin50, 92n11, 103n48
Harari, Yehudit 94n18
Haris, Monford xxiin49, 92n10
Harshav, Benjamin xxn43
Hayman, David 91n8
Hazan, Meir 5n15
Hazony, Yoram 117n12
Hebrew city, first 25, 39, 58–59, 73, 76, 104, 110, 120, 133, 137, 165, 168, 174, 178
Hebrew Queen Esther (pageant) xxiv, 13–14, 20–22, 35, 58, 67, 76, 84, 97, 138, 140–162, 185
Heelas, Paul 64n4
Hegay ben Hegay 96n22
Heiman, A.M. 7n23
Helman, Anat xvi24, xvii, xviiin32, xxn44, xxi, 15n46, 21, 22n74, 35n125, 54, 69n21, 83n55, 91n6, 93, 111, 155n70, 159n81, 165n9, 168n19, 172n29, 179, 185n65, 185n67, 187n72
Heme'iri, Avigdor 97
Herzfeld, Michael xxiin59
Herzl, Theodor 125, 128–130, 158, 165–166, 172, 178, 181, 183
Herzog, Hanna xvin25, 139n8, 172n28
Hillels, Shlomo 55n62
Hirsch, Dafna xxin46, 91n6
Hirschfeld, Ariel 150n53, 162n88
Hitler, Adolf 131–134, 136–137
Hobbes, Thomas 119
Hobsbawm, Erik J. xiiin9, 1n1, 65, 74n41, 176n37
Hollander, Anne 146n38
Hora (dance) 85, 176
Horowitz, Dan xivn15, 181n55
Horowitz, Elliot xxiin50, 92, 92n10, 114n5, 131n52
Hoz, Dov 103n47
Hunt, Lynn xviin27
Hyman, Paula 83n58, 135n62, 139n7
Ideology xi–xii, xiv–xvi, xx, xxiv, 2, 10, 12, 21–22, 52, 54, 57–59, 61–62, 89, 91, 93, 95–96, 134–136, 158, 163–166, 172–187
Industrialization xii–xii, 10, 136, 184
Intellectuals xxii, 3, 24, 70, 74, 86, 91, 114, 157, 174

Intertext, Intertextuality 140, 153, 155
Jazz 13–14, 80, 145
JNF (Jewish National Fund) xxii, 2, 7–10, 12, 15, 17–25, 29, 35–36, 40, 48, 50, 53, 67, 69, 72n34, 77, 97n23, 114–115, 129, 135–136, 185
Joselit, Jenna Weissman xixn40, xxiin50, 3n7
Kahn, Dorothy Ruth 39n9
Kallem, Kriman 141
Kamini, A. 24n81, 69n21
Kapakh, Yosef 114n5
Kaplan, Marion A. 83n58
Kark, Ruth xiin7, 6n19
Karlinsky, Nahum xvn23, 164n3
Karni, Yehuda 124
Karniel, Yesha'ayahu 46–48, 48n36, 49, 57, 153
Karsh, Efraim 169n21
Katriel, Tamar 169n20
Katz, Jacob 64n3, 181n57
Katz, Yossi xiin7, xvin24, 9n30, 120n21
Katzenelson, Berel xiv
Katzenelson, Yitzhak 6
Kaynar, Gad xxiin55
Keisari, Uri ix–xii, 53n52, 58, 71n31, 72n34, 80–81, 117n12, 143, 146, 158n77, 178
Kellerman, Aharon xiin7, 6n19
Kena'ani, David 167n14–15
Kertzer, David 112n2
Khalidi, Walid 36n129
Kideckel, David 1n1
Kieval, Hillel J. xiiin10
Kirshenblatt-Gimblett, Barbara 1n1, 51n49, 90n2
Kook, Avraham Y. 165, 166n12, 181
Koselleck, Reinhart 89n66
Kristeva, Julia 90, 90n1, 91n7
Kuchta, David 139n5
Laclau, Ernesto 186n71
Lag Ba'omer 183
Larrain, Jorge xvn19
Lavenda, Robert H. 148n46
Lavonsky, S. 101n39
Lavsky, Hagit 18, 18n58, 136n67, 164n3, 173n31

Leisure xxi, xxiv, 3–7, 34–35, 38–40, 54, 144, 162, 176
Leon, Nissim xviiin34
Le-Roy Ladurie, Emmanuel xviii, 91n8, 92n9
Lev Tov, Boaz, 4n9, 4n12, 5, 5n18, 6n19
Levant Fair 40, 130
LeVine, Mark xviiin32, 10n35, 119n18, 183n62
Lewinsky, (Levinsky) Yom-Tov xxiii, 5n15, 8n26, 58n72, 72n33, 82n53, 97n25, 100n33, 114n5, 118n15, 131n52, 174
Liebman, Charles xn2, xvn23, xxn43, 164n4, 183n60
Linder, Amnon 114n5
Lipton, Diana 152n62
Lissak, Moshe xivn15, 164n5, 181n5,
Lubarsky, Avraham Shaul 101n39
Lubin, Arye 32n110
Lufban, Yitzhak (A. Borer) 95–96, 160n83
Lynd, Helen Merrel 3n8
Lynd, Robert 3n8
Maccabia 40
MacCannell, Dean 38n1, 48n36, 49n41,
Mahalal'el, Y.L. 143n24
Maimonides 9n32
Maletz, David 167
Mandel, Neville J. 5n15
Mann, Barbara E. xviii, xxn43, 39n9, 48n36, 119n18–19, 157n75, 183n62,
Manor, Dalia 8n25, 150n54
Manor, Giora 12n39
Mantgen, Gerd 92n10, 114n5
Marcus, Ivan xxn41
Marly, Deana de 144n28
Marx, Karl 132
McGuigan, Jim xixn37, 1n2
McNamara, Brooks 1n1, 51n49
Metzer, Jacob xiin7, 135n64
Michels, Tony 3n8
Micro-history xviiin36, 2
Migdal, Joel Shmuel 181n55
Milo, Roni 118
Modernist (discourse) 82, 84–88, 126

Modernity 62–64, 82, 87, 88, 92
Modernization 63, 120
Monroe, Marilyn 161
Moore, Alexander 38n6
Moore, Sally F. 1n1, 38n6, 62n84
Morinis, Alan 38n1, 38n3, 39n7, 49n40, 50n47, 57n70
Mosse, George L. xviin30, 91, 139, 176n37
Moykher-Sforim, Mendele 48
Muchawsky-Schnapper, Esther 151n59
Muir, Edward 91n8
Myerhoff, Barbara G. 1n1, 38n6, 62n84
Naor, Mordechai 4n9
Nationalism xv, 1, 16, 22, 39, 138–140, 149, 178, 181n57
   Arab 128
   bourgeois 140
   comparative xii, 124
   cosmopolitan 178
   ethnic 130, 140, 151–152, 154, 159
   European 91
   Jewish xxii, 89, 91, 139, 152, 154
   modern xii-xiii, xvii, 1, 63–64, 149, 186
   polycentric 125–126, 129–130
   Zionist 159
Nationalist x-xvi, 28, 37, 51, 57, 76, 95, 127–129, 153n63, 154–157, 162, 171, 174–175, 182–186
   bloodshed 5
   culture xx, 16, 173
   discourse 16, 158
   ideology xi, 2, 21–22, 54, 59, 134, 163, 173, 176, 180
   movement xiii-xiv, xxiii, 63, 89, 91, 124–125, 137, 180n52
Neumann, Boaz 90n2, 111
Nietzsche, Friedrich 170
Nitzan-Shiftan, Alona xxn44
Nodorolsky, Reuven 97n24
Nora, Pierre 176n37
Nordau, Max 19
Ofrat, Gideon 150n54
Ofri, Avshalom 101n37, 101n39
Oinas, Felix, J. xxiiin58
Operman, Yeshayahu 103–104

Oriental, Orientalism 5, 8, 27–28, 114, 120–121, 128, 140, 142n19, 144, 149–152, 160
Orthodox (y) 44, 84, 98, 104, 155, 158, 167, 169
Ottoman 3–5, 7, 11, 66, 163,
Oz, Amos 186
Ozouf, Mona 176n37
Pardes, Ilana 154n62–63
Passover 33, 50n46
Pecora, Vincent P. 63n1
Penslar, Derek Jonathan xxn44, xxiiin60, 63n2, 120n20
Peretz, Y. L. 6
Perski, Daniel 73n36, 102, 131n52, 146, 153n64, 176–177
Peshkov, Gershon 133n55
Piekarz, Mendel 131n52
Pilgrimage ix, xxiv, 31, 37–61, 176
Pleck, Elisabeth xixn40
Polani, Hanna 162
Poliack, Meira 152n62
Polish, Daniel xxiin49, 100n35
Pomfret, David M. 148n46, 161n86
Public sphere xv, xvii–xix, xxiv, 7, 10, 23, 36–37, 59–62, 75, 83, 87, 107, 110, 123, 125, 128, 130, 137, 139, 156, 158–164, 168, 172–175, 180, 183, 186
Pulzer, Peter G. Z. xiiin10
Purimspiel 6, 18, 92, 126, 138
Rabin, Yitzhak 30
Rabinowitch, A.Z. (Azar) 16, 84, 155–157, 159, 185
Rabinowitz, Yaakov xxii, xiin52, 9
Radio 26, 67, 80
Rafeld, Meir 100n36
Ram, Hanna 4n9, 6n19
Ramon, Ya'akov 150n55
Ranger, Terence 1n1, 74n41, 176n37
Ratzhabi, Yehuda 103n48, 114n5
Raz, Ayala xxn44, 144n29
Razi, Tammi xvn18, xxn43, 17n54, 60n81, 83n58, 139, 139n6, 155n70, 159n82
Raz-Karkotzkin, Amnon xxiiin53, 64n3, 169n21
Read, Alan 119n17

Reader, Ian 38n1
Redfield, Robert 65, 70, 70n26, 72
Ricoeur, Paul xvn19, 122, 164n7
Roach, Joseph 161n87
Roberts, Mary Louise 139n5
Robina, Hanna 161, 162n88
Roginsky, Dina xxiiin56, 91n5
Rojek, Chris 4n9, 176n40,
Rosenberg-Freidman, Lilach 139, 139n6, 172n29
Rosenblit, F. 19n62
Rosenfeld, Henri xvin24
Roshwald, Aviel xxiiin60, 63n2
Rosman, Moshe xxn41–42
Rotbard, Sharon 10n35
Roth, Cecil 114n5
Rozin, Orit xxn43, 181n56
Sagi, Avi 65n6, 84n62
Said, Edward W. 150n57
Samet, S. 94n18, 144n28
Saposnik, Arieh Bruce xxiiin60, 7n22, 8n28, 63n2, 150n53, 169n21
Sassatelli, Monica xixn38, xxin47
Sassatelli, Roberta 54n61
Schechner, Richard xviiin33, 17n53
Schlor, Joachim 183n62
Schnorr 9, 18
Schrire, Dani xxiiin54, xxiiin58
Schwartz, Baruch 152n62
Segal, Er'el 117n12
Shaked, Gershon 162n88
Shaked, Yosef 111n68
Shalach Monos 8–9, 18–19, 72, 81, 95, 171
Shamir, Ronen xvn23, 164n3
Shapira, Anita xiiin11, xivn14, xxiin51, 5n15, 64n3, 84n62, 129, 130n49, 166n13, 167n14, 169n21
Shapira, Avraham 30, 118
Shapira, Yoseph 4n10
Shapiro, Yonathan xivn15
Shvadron, Avraham 178n45
Shavit, Yaakov xn2, xivn13, xvin24, xxn44, xxin48, xxiii, 4n10, 8n28, 9n33, 10n35, 35n125, 41, 125n33, 164n3, 168n19, 170n23, 185n67
Shavit, Zohar 115n8
Shavu'ot 183

Index

Shenhav, Yehuda xvin25, 18n58, 172n28
Shilo, Margalit 9n30, 139n8, 164n3
Shils, Edward 64n4
Shimoni, Gideon xvin26, 164n2, 164n5, 165, 180n53
Shlonsky, Avraham 56n66, 85, 102n41, 126, 131–133, 167
Shmueli, Ephraim xxn41
Shnitzer, Meir 12n39
Sholem Aleichem 6
Shorer, Hayim 16n52, 178n45
Shprut, Ezra 33n116, 35n124
Shternshis, Anna xxn42, 3n8
Silman, Kadish Y. 118
Simmel, Georges xix, 55n63, 60n80, 109
Simon, Elisheva 142, 153
Singer, Milton 70, 70n26, 72, 112
Sitton, Shoshana xxn48, xxiiin53, 8n28, 9n33, 35n125, 125n33, 168n19
Smith, Anthony xiin6, xvi, 63n1, 124, 125n32, 180n52
Smith, Philip xviin27,
Smith-Rosenberg, Carrol 149n51
Social Contract 119
Socialism, socialist xii-xvi, 6, 29, 163, 165, 185
Socialist Zionism xvi, 29
Solomon-Godeau, Abigail 139n5
Sperber, Daniel 114n5
Spiegel, Boaz 100n34, 100n36
Spiegel, Nina 97n23, 140n9, 148n45
Stallybrass, Peter 91n8
Stanton, Andrea L. 26n91
Stern, Bat-Sheva Margalit 97n23, 140n9, 150n56, 159n81, 161n85
Sternhel, Ze'ev Sternhel xivn14
Stoeltje, Beverly 147n43, 148n46, 149n49, 154n69, 159n79
Stoler-Liss, Sachlav 139n8
Sukenik, Hasya (Feinsod) 42
Susman, Warren 1n3
Swirsky, Shlomo xvn21, 164n5
Synagogue 26, 102–103, 114, 133, 169, 175
Synnot, Anthony 157n76
Tavori, Yosef 100n36

Taylor, Charles 64n4
Teneboym, A. 117n12
Tenenbaum, Avraham 101n39
Theatre 6, 11n38, 14–15, 28, 31, 39, 51, 66–68, 71, 101–102, 112–113, 129, 142–145, 162n88
Theme park 13, 38
Thornton, T.C.G. 114n5
Tidhar, David 73n36
Tiersten, Lisa 139n5
Toennies, Ferdinand 60n80
Totzeret ha'aretz 20, 21n71, 53, 173
Traditionalism 64, 65n6
Troen, Ilan S. xiin7, xvin24–25, xxn46, 56n65, 164n3, 172n28, 183n62, 185n64
Trumpeldor, Yosef ix-xi, 178
Tryster, Hillel 98n28
Tu B'shvat 183
Tuan, Yi-Fu 119n19
Turkish (rule, police, currency) 4n13, 5
Turner Edith 1978 38n2
Turner, Victor W. xviiin33, xixn38, 4n9, 6, 6n21, 38, 46n32, 47, 51, 51n48, 61, 112
Tzabari, Tzipora 97, 151, 160–162
Tzahor, Ze'ev 4n10
Tzur, Miki 170n24
Urbanization xii-xiii, 3, 10, 70, 136, 166, 173–174, 184
Urian, Dan 129n45, 169n21
Ussishkin, Menahem 9n40, 185
Utopia, utopian 91, 109, 128–129, 174, 184
Veidlinger, Jeffrey xxn42, 3n8, 162n88
Vilna'i, Ze'ev 58n72
Vital, David 125n33, 165n11
Wahrman, Dror 119n17
Wassermann, Henry 132
Werses, Shmuel xxiiin55
White, Allon 91n8
Wilk, Richard 147n43, 148n46, 149n49, 154n69, 159n79
Williams, Raymond xvn19, xviin27, xviin30, 164n6
Wilson, William A. xxiiin59
Wistrich, Robert xiiin10

World War I xxiv, 3, 7, 10–11, 66, 72
World War II 131, 137, 160
World Zionist Organization 125
Wu, Judy Tzu-Chen 148n46
Yadgar, Yaacov 172n27
Yassif, Eli xxn44
Yekuti'eli-Cohen, Edna 34n122
Yemeni, A. 53n56
Yemeni, H.S. 127n38
Yemenite 5, 15, 27, 97, 114n6, 141n12, 142, 148, 150–151, 159–161
Yuris, A.S. 30n103
Yuval-Davis, Nira 138n2

Zak, David Zvi 97n24
Zakim, Eric xvn17, xxn43
Ze'evi, Rehav'am 6n20, 14n45, 22n74, 66n11, 67n12, 94n15, 94n18, 132n54
Ze'ira, Moti 84n62, 139n6, 167n14–15, 167n17, 169n22, 170n23–24
Zerubavel, Evitar xixn39
Zerubavel, Yael xn2, xiiin11, xxn43, 175n36, 183n60
Zer-Zion, Shelly xxiiin55
Zimmerman, Moshe 34
Zipperstein, Steven 119n19
Zizek, Slavoj 156n73

CPSIA information can be obtained at www.ICGtesting.com
Printed in the USA
LVOW10*2103170314

377802LV00003B/44/P

9 781618 113511